P9-DZY-250

THE NEGRO GENIUS

Photograph by A. N. Scurlock

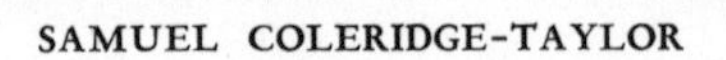

SAMUEL COLERIDGE-TAYLOR

THE NEGRO GENIUS

A NEW APPRAISAL OF THE ACHIEVEMENT OF THE AMERICAN NEGRO IN LITERATURE AND THE FINE ARTS

BY

BENJAMIN BRAWLEY

ILLUSTRATED

BIBLO and TANNEN
NEW YORK
1969

Reprinted by
BIBLO and TANNEN
BOOKSELLERS and PUBLISHERS, Inc.
63 Fourth Avenue New York, N.Y. 10003

Library of Congress Catalog Card Number: 66-17517

Printed in U.S.A. by
NOBLE OFFSET PRINTERS, INC.
NEW YORK 3, N. Y.

TO MY WIFE

HILDA PROWD BRAWLEY

CO-WORKER ON LIFE'S PILGRIMAGE

PREFACE

SOME years ago I published a little book, *The Negro in Literature and Art*. This went through several editions but is now out of print. In the meantime the general subject with which it dealt has advanced so rapidly that no mere revision could longer suffice. What seemed to be needed was a new work altogether, one with a complete reorganization of the material, more comprehensive treatment, and especially with more attention to living or recent figures. It is this place that *The Negro Genius* endeavors to fill.

One thing the book does not attempt is a review of all the novels of Negro life that have been written within the last two decades by persons not identified with the race. Some of these must necessarily be touched on incidentally, but most of them were written simply to exploit certain phases of the subject, and it is understood that all are beyond the province of the present work.

I wish to thank the individuals and publishing firms that have graciously co-operated—especially the Harmon Foundation, New York; Mr. William Stanley Braithwaite, Dr. Leslie Pinckney Hill, Mr. J. Harvey L. Baxter, Mrs. Georgia Douglas Johnson, Mrs. Effie

Lee Newsome, and Miss Mae Cowdery for permission to use the quotations from their poems; Dodd, Mead and Company for the quotations from Paul Laurence Dunbar; Harcourt, Brace and Company for the quotations from Claude McKay and Sterling Brown; The Viking Press for those from James Weldon Johnson; Harper and Brothers for those from Countee Cullen; and Alfred A. Knopf, Inc., for that from Langston Hughes.

BENJAMIN BRAWLEY

Washington, D. C.,
January 1, 1937.

CONTENTS

ILLUSTRATIONS

INTRODUCTION: THE NEGRO GENIUS

About the Negro in the United States two things are observable. One is that distinction so far won by members of the race has been most frequently in the arts. The other is that, aside from enforced labor, any influence exerted on civilization has been mainly in the field of æsthetics. As to the first point, we might refer to a long line of beautiful singers, to the sensuous poetry of Dunbar, the picturesque style of DuBois, the mysticism of the paintings of Tanner, and to the striving of many younger artists. Even Booker T. Washington, most practical of men, is largely remembered for his anecdote and vivid illustration. The influence on the country's life will be referred to more than once as we proceed.

If one has taken note of the homes of Negro peasants in the South, he must have observed that the instinct for beauty insists upon an outlet. If no better picture is available, there will be a flaming advertisement on the walls. Few homes have not at least a rosebush in the garden or a geranium on the windowsill. Conversely, those things that are most picturesque make to the Negro the readiest appeal. *Faust* has been popular with those who would never think of going to another play of its class. The applause leaves one in no doubt as to the reason for Goethe's popularity. It is the suggestiveness of the love scenes, the red costume of Mephistopheles, the electrical effects, and the rain of fire that give the thrill desired. *Faust* is a good show as well as a good play.

In some of our communities Negroes are often known to "get happy" in church. It is never a sermon on the theory of the Atonement that awakens such ecstasy. Instead, this accompanies a vivid description of the beauties of heaven—the walls of jasper, the angels with palms in their hands, and, best of all, the feast of milk and honey. It is the sensuous appeal that is most effective. The untutored Negro is thrilled not so much by the moral as by the artistic and pictorial elements of religion.

Just why this should be so is a question for the anthropologist. At present we are concerned simply with the fact. Behind any achievement of the race is temperament, and that of the Negro has been shown to be pre-eminently imaginative and sensuous. It is subjective too, so that in general Negro authors and composers have been better in poetry and music than in the novel and the drama. The temper seeks an outlet in vivid, striking expression. Naturally this would be seen first of all in the folklore.

In the life and history of the Negro has developed an unusual store of customs, superstitions, and tales.

Frederick Douglass and William Wells Brown called attention to this, but Charles W. Chesnutt was the first writer of the race to give it sustained literary treatment. Its chief monument so far has been in the Uncle Remus tales of Joel Chandler Harris. One must be careful of course not to claim too much for the Negro. The study of sources and analogues is far from being as simple as some might suppose. It takes one far afield, not only to Africa but even to India and the Continent of Europe.

Important as is Negro folklore, however, the folk-music is even more so. In recent years this has been claimed for other countries or nations; but, just as in the folklore there is distinctive imagination, so in the music there is a quality peculiarly the Negro's own. One has to consider both the "spirituals" and the secular songs.

Unlike the English and Scottish popular ballads, the spirituals depend for their merit more upon their tunes than their words. They are also more affected by nature. A meteoric shower, a thunder-storm, or the dampness of a furrow was sufficient to give birth to a hymn; and there was the freest possible use of figures of speech. As in the ballads, the sentiment becomes universal, and there is a tendency toward what has been called incremental repetition; thus, after a number of old people had been crooning "I'm a-Rollin' " before a fire, someone would begin a stanza, "O brothers, won't you help me?" Then would follow, "O sisters, won't you help me?" Obviously such a process could be prolonged indefinitely. One soon observes different stages in the development of this music. The first gives that which is simple and elemental, taking one to the African wilderness, as in "See Fo' an' Twenty Elders on Deir Knees." The second stage exhibits the great class of Afro-American melodies, like "Steal Away" and "I've been a-listenin' all de night long." The third shows a blending of Negro music and that of the adopted country, as in "Bright Sparkles in the Churchyard." Those melodies that are most original are generally sorrowful in tone, growing out of the Negro's trials in slavery, like "Nobody Knows de Trouble I See" and "Sometimes I Feel Like a Motherless Child." In some, however, there is a note of triumph, as in "Oh, Give Way, Jordan" and "I'm Gwine to Jine de Great 'Sociation." No one is able to tell just how many of these melodies are in existence, for, though there have been many collections, there is not yet one that is definitive.

Just as the spirituals reflect the higher life of the Negro—that of prayer and hope and yearning, with some influence from the evangelical hymns—so do the secular songs reflect his lower life—that of the railroad camp, the turpentine camp, and the chain-gang. Only within recent years have these received scholarly study. To some extent they were submerged by minstrelsy, and the influence of the churches was naturally against them. In 1911, however, Howard W. Odum began to publish articles on "Folk-Songs and Folk-Poetry as found in the Secular Songs of Southern Negroes," and he and Guy B. Johnson have since produced *The Negro and his Songs* and *Negro Workaday Songs*. Other writers have followed and Professor Johnson has also published *John Henry*, about the "big steel-drivin' man" who died with a hammer in his hand. The ballads that have grown up about this heroic figure are typical of the songs at their best. It appears that John Henry had a contest with a steel-driving machine in which he was victorious at the cost of his life. "There is pretty good evidence that the ballad is based on an incident which occurred about 1871 during the building of the Big Bend Tunnel on the C. & O. Railroad in West Virginia."

> John Henry said to his captain,
> "Well, a man ain't nothing but a man,
> But before I'll be beaten by your old steam drill,
> I'll die with my hammer in my han',
> Lawd, I'll die with my hammer in my han'."

There are numerous other work songs, songs about women, and "blues," these last being "the sorrowful songs of the workaday Negro." There is also much "bad man stuff," one of the best known songs being about Stacker Lee (more commonly, Stagolee), who could shoot the buttons off a man's coat but whose reputation paled somewhat when he met John Henry.

Stagolee was a bully man an' everybody knowed
When dey seed Stagolee comin' to give Stagolee de road.
Oh, dat man, bad man, Stagolee done come.

This reference to the spirituals and even to songs of a different temper calls up something far deeper than sensuous beauty. No people can rise to the heights of art until it has passed through suffering. The Russians are a case in point; they have endured much and their literature is one of power. The same future beckons to the Negro. There is something elemental about the race—something that finds its origin in the forest and the sighing of the nightwind. There is something grim and stern about it too, something that speaks of the lash, of the child torn from its mother's bosom, of the body riddled with bullets and swinging all night by the roadside.

Naturally one might expect to find this temper best revealed in those members of the race who were strong characters but untouched by the schools. So we do. Harriet Tubman was describing to an audience a great battle in the Civil War. "And then," she said, "we saw the lightning, and that was the guns; and then we heard the thunder, and that was the big guns; and then we heard the rain falling, and that was drops of blood falling; and when we came to git in the craps, it was dead men that we reaped."

Sojourner Truth, the old prophetess with inimitable wit, was speaking to one who came to see her in her last illness. "I isn't goin' to die, honey," she said; "I's goin' home like a shootin' star."

John Jasper, of Richmond, Virginia, became famous a few years after the Civil War by reason of his sermon, "De Sun do Move." Even before the war he was well known in the vicinity for his picturesque discourses; and he preached not only on his favorite theme but also on "Dry Bones in the Valley," "The Hebrew Children in the Fiery Furnace," "The Raising of Lazarus," and other subjects that gave scope for his imagination. The Reverend William E. Hatcher, who heard him preach more than once, has described for us the portrayal of the King in his beauty. Said he of Jasper: "His earnestness and reverence passed all speech, and grew as he went. The light from the throne dazzled him from afar. There was the great white throne, there the elders bowing in adoring wonder, there the archangels waiting in silence for the commands of the King, there the King in his resplendent glory, there in hosts innumerable were the ransomed. In point of vivid description it surpassed all I had heard or read. The old Negro seemed glorified. Earth could hardly hold him. He sprang about the platform with a boy's alertness; he was unconsciously waving his handkerchief as if greeting a conqueror; his face was streaming with tears; he was bowing before the Redeemer; he was clapping his hands, laughing, shouting and wiping the blinding tears out of his eyes. It was a moment of transport and unmatched wonder to every one, and I felt as if it could never cease, when suddenly in a new note he broke into his chorus, ending with the soul-melting words, 'Oh, what mus' it be to be thar!' "

It is obvious, then, that if we would have at its best the element of which we have spoken, we must take the race without adulteration or sophistication. It happens that those who belong to the Negro people in the United States form the most variegated group in the world. Ray Stannard Baker said thirty years ago that he had not been studying the South very long before he was forced to ask just what was a Negro. The statement of some persons that they belonged to the race he accepted against the testimony of his own senses. Some had blue eyes and flaxen hair. That is true; and because the persons of fairer hue have generally had better economic and cultural opportunity than others, it was a favorite diversion of some men in the nineteenth century to assert and try to prove that the ability of individuals was in direct proportion to their infusion of white blood.

In some cases this may have been true; but so far was it from being the general truth that we may now affirm that such distinction as the Negro has won in the arts is due primarily to the black rather than the mixed element in the race. People of mixed blood have given us the college presidents, the administrators, the Government employees; but the blacks are the singers and seers. Black slaves gave us the spirituals; modern composers of a lighter hue transcribe them. A modern author may reproduce in verse the sermons of the old exhorters, but it would hardly do to ask him to preach one of them. In other words, the mixed element in the race may represent the Negro's talent, but it is upon the black element that he must rely for his genius.

Let us not be misunderstood. In our emphasis on achievement in the arts, we do not mean to say that the Negro can not rise to distinction in any other sphere. He has recently made notable advance in scholarship, and some of the younger men have been especially brilliant in science. We do suggest, however, that every race has its peculiar genius and that, as far as we can at present judge, the Negro, with all his manual labor, is destined to reach his greatest heights in the field of the artistic. On every hand we have proof of this tendency.

For a long time this inclination was discounted or disregarded. The public associated the Negro simply with minstrelsy, burlesque, and a few stereotyped characters. Then, in 1867, a sympathetic article on the spirituals by Thomas Wentworth Higginson in the *Atlantic* commanded attention, and within the next decade the Fisk Jubilee Singers were received with acclaim. At the close of the century Paul Laurence Dunbar won such success as was never before achieved by a Negro author. Two decades later, in connection with the World War and after, the change in attitude became general. Where formerly the Negro was ignored, he mounted to the crest of the wave. It became the popular thing to attend night clubs in Harlem. Publishers who formerly had frowned upon Negro novels were now eager to have one or two such books on their lists. By 1925 the new fad was in full career. In literature there was a so-called renaissance.

About the origin of jazz, which was now popular, there was much discussion. Some writers have insisted that the word is primarily a verb rather than a noun. That means, as Sigmund G. Spaeth reminded us *(Forum,* August, 1928), that "jazz is not a form of music. It is a treatment applied to music, and, incidentally, to all the arts, and to modern life in general. The jazz treatment, in brief, is a distortion of the conventional, a revolt against tradition, a deliberate twisting of established formulas. As such, it is thoroughly characteristic of the civilization of today." That may be, but it was generally understood that what was known as jazz in music originated in Negro slums; and it called for serious consideration in view of its far-reaching connections in modern art.

Whether the new impulse was an unmixed good, and whether it tended toward the development of what is best in literature, is an open question. Again we are primarily concerned with a fact. A change had taken place and as never before attention was directed to Negro life and Negro themes. It happened that interest was chiefly in life on the lowest plane, writers seeming to be moved by one or the other of two appeals. One was that of the sensational. Prostitutes and gamblers had to be featured by all means, and a whole stream of novels followed in the wake of Carl Van Vechten's *Nigger Heaven*. The other appeal was that of primitivism. This was more provocative.

It was about 1907 that some modernistic painters in Paris—Picasso, Derain, Matisse, and Vlaminck—in their endeavor to produce certain new effects on canvas, observed that similar effects had been achieved centuries before in primitive African art. About some samples of wood-carving that they found they realized that "these figures were not mere childish attempts to make our kind of statue; they were successful attempts to make an entirely different kind of statue." In some ways they were even "a stage in advance of European evolution." Clive Bell, writing in 1920, said of the efforts of the artists and their literary apostle, Guillaume Apollinaire, to find pieces of African workmanship in old shops: "Thus a demand was created which M. Paul Guillaume was there to meet and stimulate. The part played by that enterprising dealer is highly commendable; it was he who put the most sensitive public in Europe—a little cosmopolitan group of artists, critics, and amateurs—

in the way of seeing a number of first-rate things." In 1926, with the co-operation of the Barnes Foundation of Merion, Pennsylvania, Paul Guillaume and Thomas Munro produced *Primitive Negro Sculpture,* a book that became almost the bible of the new movement. It called attention to the fact that Negro sculpture offered a compromise between representation and design, and concluded: "In an age when more than one voice has been heard to say that sculpture is obsolete, and the plastic arts exhausted, Negro art has brought creative forces that may prove to be inexhaustible."

To some extent that statement was a challenge, and there were not lacking those willing to take up the gauntlet. To many it not only seemed that the fad was overdone, and largely promoted by commercialism, but that a fundamental question was raised as to the extent to which primitive African art had anything whatsoever to do with the achievement of Negro artists in America. Some Negroes were opposed to the fad by reason of its social and political implications. They felt that effort in connection with it was a subtle attempt to set them apart and fit them into a groove in American life, and they insisted that for the Negro in the United States the influence of nationalism was stronger than that of race. Even Paul Laurence Dunbar twenty years previously had taken this position. A reporter once asked him about the poetry written by Negroes as compared with that of white people. Dunbar replied, "The predominating power of the African race is lyric. In that I should expect the writers of my race to excel. But, broadly speaking, their poetry will not be exotic or differ much from that of the whites. For two hundred and fifty years the environment of the Negro has been American, in every respect the same as that of all other Americans." George S. Schuyler, writing under the title "The Negro-Art Hokum" in the *Nation* (June 16, 1926), said: "Because a few writers with a paucity of themes have seized upon the imbecilities of the Negro rustics and clowns and palmed them off as authentic and characteristic Aframerican behavior, the common notion that the black American is so 'different' from his white neighbor has gained wide currency. . . . Negro art has been, is, and will be among the numerous black nations of Africa; but to suggest the possibility of any such development among the ten million colored people in this republic is self-evident foolishness."

This attitude of protest is of course largely negative; it does not encourage a distinctive art. On the other hand one might note the position of Langston Hughes, who has also written in the *Nation* (June 23, 1926). Says he: "We younger Negro artists who create now intend to express our individual dark-skinned selves without fear or shame. If the white people are pleased, we are glad. If they are not, it doesn't matter. We know we are beautiful. And ugly too. The tom-tom cries and the tom-tom laughs. If colored people are pleased, we are glad. If they are not, their displeasure doesn't matter either. We build our temples for to-morrow, strong as we know them, and we stand on top of the mountain, free within ourselves."

To some extent the temples have begun to be erected, but there is a shortcoming not always recognized by writers of the school of Mr. Hughes. In their protest against the smugness and the self-consciousness of the bourgeoisie, they laud "the so-called common element," the "lowdown folks," who "live on Seventh Street in Washington or State Street in Chicago," and they present again and again the roustabout, the gambler, and the prostitute. They protest against the older stereotypes; yet, if they do not watch, they will give us new stereotypes hardly better than the old.

It thus appears that in speaking of the Negro Genius we enter a field beset with explosives. At any turn one may run into a contradiction or an inconsistency. We can not reconcile all the differences of opinion, but about one thing at least we must be clear: we emphasize no connection between primitive African art and that of the Negro in America to-day. An individual sculptor may indeed receive some suggestion or inspiration from a piece of African carving, but that would not say that his own culture was basically African. We recall that the English drama, an indigenous growth, at the time of Elizabeth received stimulus from Plautus and Seneca, but that stimulus did not make the English drama Latin. So we shall not attempt to overstate the present case. We do think, however, that the main observation will hold: The temperament of the American Negro is primarily lyrical, imaginative, subjective; and his genius has most frequently sought expression in some one of the arts.

I

THE PIONEERS

JUPITER HAMMON—PHILLIS WHEATLEY—GUSTAVUS VASSA

FOR a long time it was supposed that Phillis Wheatley was the first person of African descent whose work appeared in print in America, but investigation has shown that there was another writer of verse, Jupiter Hammon, whose first published poem antedated hers by a full decade. As early as 1760 also a Negro with the same surname published in Boston *A Narrative of the Uncommon Sufferings and Surprising Deliverance of Briton Hammon.* This told how the author, with his master's consent, left his home in Massachusetts to go to Jamaica, suffered captivity at the hands of the Indians and Spaniards and escaped to England, at last finding his master on a ship returning to America; but the story is not nearly as good as its material might suggest and in human interest falls far below some later narratives.

JUPITER HAMMON

Jupiter Hammon was born probably soon after 1720 and died about 1800, but there is no definite evidence on either point. He was first owned by Henry Lloyd, of Lloyd's Neck, Long Island, New York. This master, dying in 1763, left him in the portion of the inheritance that fell to Joseph, one of his four sons. A third owner was John Lloyd, Jr., nephew of Joseph. Hammon was a dutiful and trusted servant, so highly regarded by the members of the Lloyd family that they assisted him in placing his verses before the public.

"An Evening Thought. Salvation by Christ, with Penetential Cries: Composed by Jupiter Hammon, a Negro belonging to Mr. Lloyd, of Queen's Village, on Long Island, the 25th of December, 1760," was printed as a broadside in New York in 1761. The poem consists of twenty-two four-line stanzas, and shows the influence of the evangelical hymns of Charles Wesley, William Cowper, and John Newton. The author's habit of using again and again a word that appealed to him may be seen from the following:

Dear Jesus, unto Thee we cry,
  Give us the Preparation;
Turn not away thy tender Eye;
  We seek thy true Salvation.

Salvation comes from God we know,
  The true and only One;
It's well agreed and certain true,
  He gave his only Son.

Lord, hear our penetential Cry:
Salvation from above;
It is the Lord that doth supply,
With his Redeeming Love.

Of more personal interest was the second piece, "An Address to Miss Phillis Wheatly," dated Hartford, August 4, 1778, also in broadsheet form. Then appeared "An Essay of the Ten Virgins" (1779) and "A Winter Piece" (1872). This last production was mainly a sermon in prose, but contained on the last two pages "A Poem for Children, with Thoughts on Death." "An Evening's Entertainment," written about the close of the Revolutionary War, includes a dialogue in verse entitled "The Kind Master and the Dutiful Servant."

Significant perhaps beyond any of the poems was "An Address to the Negroes of the State of New York," originally presented to the members of the African Society in the city of New York September 24, 1786, and printed in New York early in the next year. This shows Hammon as feeling it his personal duty to bear slavery with patience but as strongly opposed to the system and insistent that young Negroes be manumitted. He had to receive editorial assistance before the Address could be issued, but the strong style is his own. The Pennsylvania Society for Promoting the Abolition of Slavery ordered a reprinting immediately, and there was a third edition after the author's death. It is also worth

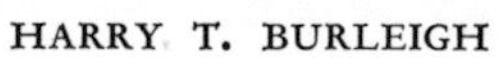
HARRY T. BURLEIGH

while to note that in his will in 1795 John Lloyd, Jr., ordered that certain of his slaves be set free on arriving at the age of twenty-eight; and the Address doubtless had something to do with the fact that in 1799 the state of New York took formal action looking toward gradual emancipation.

Jupiter Hammon came on the scene long before the recent day of Negro self-expression in verse, and he could only follow such models as he knew. As he was a slave without formal education, his poems naturally show much faulty syntax and many forced rhymes and strained metrical effects. Even so there is in his work an earnestness that gives suggestion of originality and that keeps him in touch with the people of whom he was so early a representative.

PHILLIS WHEATLEY

Because her work was largely imitative, with almost nothing distinctively racial in it, Phillis Wheatley has suffered more than most from discount in recent years. However, she not only had an unusual career and published the first book brought out by an American Negro, but for decades before other poets were heard of she was a shining example of Negro genius. Before 1840 a dozen editions of her poems were issued, and the abolitionists cited her as proof of the Negro's powers. She thus has historical importance far beyond what the intrinsic merit of her verses might warrant.

She was first seen in America as a little girl on a slave ship that had just come to Boston from Senegal. At the time she was probably in her eighth year; the poem on Whitefield published in 1770 said on the title-page that she was seventeen years old. Mrs. Susannah Wheatley, wife of John Wheatley, a tailor, desiring to have a girl who might be trained as her personal attendant, and attracted by the bright eye and gentle demeanor of the child, bought her, took her home, and gave her the name *Phillis,* which was always spelled thus. When the young slave became known to the world, she also used the name of the family to which she belonged.

Mrs. Wheatley was well known to the people of culture in Boston. King Street (now State) was then as notable for its residences as it is now famous for its banking houses. When Phillis entered the home the family consisted of four persons, the parents and their twin children, Nathaniel and Mary. Three other children had died early. Mary Wheatley accordingly was the only daughter of the family that Phillis knew, and she was eighteen years old when her mother brought the child to the house. Thanks to her teaching, Phillis was able within sixteen months to read the most difficult parts of the Bible. In course of time she also mastered the greater Latin classics. Mrs. Wheatley strove to cultivate her pious disposition, exacted of her no hard labor, and gradually came to regard her as a companion rather than as a slave.

Pope's translation of Homer was the favorite English classic of the young student, and more and more she felt that she too could write poetry. After a while, whenever an unusual event, especially a death, occurred in the circle of the family's acquaintance, she would be moved to express her feeling in verse.

In 1770 appeared "A Poem, by Phillis, a Negro Girl, on the Death of the Reverend George Whitefield," this taking up four pages of large print. The dedication was to Selina Shirley, Countess of Huntingdon. That lady, by the time she was forty, had lost her husband and her children, and thenceforth was devoted to good work. She was in touch with the Calvinistic Methodists and Whitefield had served as her chaplain.

On August 18, 1771, Phillis became a communicant of the Old South Meeting House in Boston, her membership being "an exception to the rule that slaves were not baptized into the church." All through the next year her health was uncertain. By the spring of 1773 Mrs. Wheatley was greatly concerned about her, and the family physician advised that she try the air of the sea. As Nathaniel Wheatley was just then going to England, it was decided that she should go with him. Before leaving she was formally manumitted.

The poem on Whitefield served as an introduction to the Countess of Huntingdon, who received the young visitor as her guest. Phillis met other ladies and made friends by her modesty and bright conversation. Presents were showered upon her. One that has been preserved is a copy of the 1770 Glasgow folio edition of *Paradise Lost*, given by Brook Watson, Lord Mayor of London. This book is now in the Harry Elkins Widener Library at Harvard. At the top of one of the first pages, in the handwriting of the recipient, are the words, "Mr. Brook Watson to Phillis Wheatley, London, July, 1773." At the bottom of the same page, in the handwriting of the donor to the University, one finds: "This book was given by Brook Watson formerly Lord Mayor of London to Phillis Wheatley & after her death was sold in payment of her husband's debts. It is now presented to the Library of Harvard University at Cambridge, by Dudley L. Pickman of Salem. March, 1824."

While Phillis was in London arrangement was made for the publication of her volume, *Poems on Various Subjects, Religious and Moral.* This was "Printed for A. Bell, Bookseller, Aldgate." As it had been suggested that some readers might have doubts about the authorship, attestation as to authenticity was secured from "the most respectable characters in Boston," among them Governor Thomas Hutchinson, Lieutenant-Governor Andrew Oliver, the Reverend Samuel Cooper, the Reverend Samuel Mather, James Bowdoin, John Hancock, and John Wheatley. While a few other single pieces have been preserved, this book is the only collection of poems by Phillis Wheatley ever published. Another collection was contemplated, and indeed announced in the Boston *Evening Post and the General Advertiser* for October 30, 1779, but the Revolutionary War was on, subscriptions were slow, and the second book never appeared.

The visit to England marked the highest point in the career of the young author. By the early autumn she was back in Boston, her return being hastened by the illness of Mrs. Wheatley. On October 30 she wrote to Obour Tanner, a friend living in Newport: "I hear of your welfare with pleasure; but this acquaints you that I am at present indisposed by a cold, and since my arrival have been visited by the asthma." She wrote again the next March to tell of the death of her best friend, Mrs. Wheatley. After that event she seems not to have lived regularly at the old home; for a while at least in 1775 she was in Providence. It was in this darkening period of her life that she wrote to General George Washington a letter enclosing a complimentary poem. Washington replied after a few weeks, apologizing for his delay in answering and saying, "If you should ever come to Cambridge or near headquarters, I shall be happy to see a person so favored by the muses, and to whom Nature has been so liberal and beneficent in her dispensations." A little later Phillis accepted the invitation and was received with courtesy by the General and his officers. The poem was published in the *Pennsylvania Magazine* for April, 1776, while Thomas Paine was editor.

Mary Wheatley in 1771 had become the wife of the Reverend John Lathrop of Boston. Her brother was living abroad. The old home was finally broken up by the death of John Wheatley in March, 1778. Mrs. Lathrop followed her father after six months. It was in April of this year of disaster that Phillis Wheatley entered into her ill-starred marriage to John Peters. The first we hear of this man is in one of the letters to Obour Tanner, in which he is described as "very complaisant and agreeable." He is variously reported to have been a baker, a barber, a grocer, a doctor, and a lawyer; but one thing he did not have, and that was the ability to earn a living. He wore a wig, sported a cane, and in general felt himself superior to labor. His wife soon realized that she had married a ne'er-do-well at a time when the most industrious man found the way difficult. When Boston fell into the hands of the British, Mrs. Peters went with her husband to Wilmington, a town twenty miles to the north. There she suffered great poverty. After the evacuation of Boston she returned to the city and was received under the roof of a niece of Mrs. Wheatley, a widow who had lost a son in the war and who kept a little school to support herself. With this friend she remained for six weeks, having with her two children whose mother she had become; then she went to a place that her husband provided. Somewhat later another relative of Mrs. Wheatley sought for her and found that the two older children were dead and that a third child, an infant, was sick. That seems to have been in the winter of 1783-84. The outlook did not improve for the mother, and at length she worked for her board in a cheap lodging-house. Her disease made rapid progress, and she died December 5, 1784. Her last baby died within a few hours and was buried with her.

When she first appeared Phillis Wheatley was regarded as a prodigy, but her vogue was more than temporary, and editions of her poems in 1793, 1802, and 1816 found ready sale. Some of the pieces found their way into school readers. From the first, however, there were those who discounted her poetry; Thomas Jefferson said it was beneath the dignity of criticism. Interest greatly revived at the time of the anti-slavery agitation. When, then, Margaretta Matilda Odell, who was related to the Wheatley family, republished the poems with a memoir in 1834, there was such a demand for the book that two more editions were called for within four years.

Poems on Various Subjects lists thirty-eight titles, aside from "A Rebus by I. B.," to which one of the pieces is a reply. Fourteen of the poems are elegiac, and at least six others were called forth by special occasions. Two are paraphrases from the Bible. We are thus left with sixteen poems to represent the best that Phillis Wheatley had produced by the time she was twenty years old. One of the longest of these is "Niobe in Distress for her Children Slain by Apollo, from Ovid's Metamorphoses, Book VI, and from a View of the Painting of Mr. Richard Wilson." This contains two interesting examples of personification neither of which seems to be drawn from Ovid, "fate portentous whistling in the air" and "the feather'd vengeance quiv'ring in his hands," though the point might easily be made that these are but the stock-in-trade of pseudo-classicism. "To S. M., a Young African Painter, on Seeing his Works" was addressed to Scipio Moorhead, servant of the Reverend John Moorhead, who exhibited some talent with the brush and one of whose subjects was the friendship of Damon and Pythias. The early poem, "On Being Brought from Africa to America," consisting of only eight lines, is one of the few pieces with autobiographical interest, and there is also a reference to race in the lines addressed to William, Earl of Dartmouth; but in general Phillis Wheatley is abstract, polite, restrained. "An Hymn to Humanity" is one of the most conventional pieces in the volume. One can but speculate upon what the author might have done if she had lived to see the French Revolution and to feel the glow of the romanticism of Wordsworth and Coleridge and Scott.

Yet, when all discount is made, when we have spoken of the influence of Pope and of the few examples of lyrical expression, we are still forced to wonder at the ease with which the young author, technically a slave, could chisel the heroic couplet.

Her achievement in this line is as amazing as it is unique. The poem "On Imagination" is one of her best, and the following lines are representative:

> Imagination! who can sing thy force?
> Or who describe the swiftness of thy course?
> Soaring through air to find the bright abode,
> Th' empyreal palace of the thundering God,
> We on thy pinions can surpass the wind,
> And leave the rolling universe behind:
> From star to star the mental optics rove,
> Measure the skies, and range the realms above.
> There in one view we grasp the mighty whole,
> Or with new worlds amaze the unbounded soul.

As a sample of the verse ten years later we might note the conclusion of "Liberty and Peace," independently published in 1784:

> Descending peace the power of war confounds;
> From every tongue celestial peace resounds:
> As from the east th' illustrious king of day,
> With rising radiance drives the shades away,
> So freedom comes array'd with charms divine,
> And in her train commerce and plenty shine.
> Britannia owns her independent reign,
> Hibernia, Scotia, and the realms of Spain;
> And great Germania's ample coast admires
> The generous spirit that Columbia fires.
> Auspicious Heaven shall fill with fav'ring gales,
> Where'er Columbia spreads her swelling sails:
> To every realm shall peace her charms display,
> And heavenly freedom spread her golden ray.

Phillis Wheatley triumphed over the most adverse circumstances. A child of the wilderness and a slave, she satisfied the culture of Boston and of England. Her manner was refined, her conversation gracious, and her faith infinite. More and more as one studies her career he becomes aware of her sterling character. In a dark day she caught a glimpse of the light, and it was meet that the first Negro woman in American literature should be one of unerring piety and high ideals of artistic achievement.

GUSTAVUS VASSA

One of the earliest and still one of the most engrossing of the narratives of slave life was that of Gustavus Vassa (1745-1801?). This man was born in Benin in Southern Nigeria, was kidnapped at eleven and taken to America, served on a plantation in Virginia and then as attendant to a British officer, and later was owned by a merchant in Philadelphia. This last master was considerate, took him as a helper on trips to the West Indies, and assisted his effort to purchase his freedom. Vassa was converted to Methodism and finally settled in England to engage in anti-slavery work. He came in touch with liberal spirits, in 1790 presented to Parliament a petition for the suppression of the slave trade, and was for some time a guest in the home of Thomas Hardy, secretary of the radical organization, the London Corresponding Society. From the *Memoir* of Hardy it appears that he put that earnest worker in touch with liberals he knew in Sheffield and other cities.

The Interesting Narrative of the Life of Oloudah Equiano, or Gustavus Vassa first appeared in two volumes in London in 1789, but within five years was in its eighth edition. The first few paragraphs give a typical high-sounding eighteenth century introduction and at the close is a formal argument. It seems quite certain that these portions of the work and the title are from the pen of an editor, but the heart of the narrative is Vassa's own, and it is in a vivid naive style that carries conviction. The following is the account of the kidnapping in Benin:

Generally, when the grown people in the neighborhood were gone far in the fields to labour, the children assembled together in some of the neighbors' premises to play; and commonly some of us used to get up a tree to look out for any assailant or kidnapper that might come upon us; for they sometimes took those opportunities of our parents' absence, to attack and carry off as many as they could seize. One day, as I was watching at the top of a tree in our yard, I saw one of these people come into the yard of our next neighbor but one, to kidnap, there being many stout young people in it. Immediately, on this, I gave the alarm of the rogue, and he was surrounded by the stoutest of them, who entangled him with cords, so that he could not escape till some of the grown people came and secured him. But alas! ere long it was my fate to be thus attacked, and to be carried off, when none of our grown people were nigh. One day, when all our people were gone out to their works as usual, and only I and my dear sister were left to mind the house, two men and a woman got over our walls, and in a moment seized us both; and without giving us time to cry out, or make resistance, they stopped our mouths and ran off with us into the nearest wood. Here they tied our hands, and continued to carry us as far they could, till night came on, when we reached a small house, where the robbers halted for refreshment, and spent the night. We were then unbound, but were unable to take any food; and, being quite overpowered by fatigue and grief, our only relief was some sleep, which allayed our misfortune for a short time. The next morning we left the house, and continued traveling all the day. For a long time we had kept the woods, but at last we came into a road which I believed I knew. I now had some hopes of being delivered; for we had advanced but a little way when I discovered some people at a distance, on which I began to cry for their assistance; but my cries had no other effect than to make them tie me faster and stop my mouth, and then they put me into a large sack. They also stopped my sister's mouth and tied her hands; and in this manner we proceeded till we were out of the sight of these people.

OTHER WRITERS

There is record of several Negroes besides Jupiter Hammon, Phillis Wheatley, and Gustavus Vassa who were interested in giving of their best thoughts to the public in the closing years of the eighteenth century. A writer of verse named Cæsar is said to have lived in North Carolina, but nothing that he wrote has come down to us. Prince Hall, the early leader of

Negro Masons, in a *Charge* to the lodge at Menotomy, Massachusetts, in 1797, mingled a dark portrayal of the lot of the Negro and a call to patience with the suggestion of resistance to oppression after the manner of that of the Negroes in Hayti. Beyond other occasional papers and addresses are two by the noted mathematician and astronomer, Benjamin Banneker (1731-1806), who issued an almanac for each year in the period 1792-1802. A copy of the first almanac he sent in 1791 to Thomas Jefferson, then Secretary of State, with a letter making a manly plea for freedom in accord with the principles on which the country was founded. In the almanac for 1793 appeared "A Plan of Peace-Office for the United States," which showed the author as opposed to capital punishment and militarism and as generally in line with the most advanced humanitarianism of the age.

II

THE ERA OF EFFORT FOR FREEDOM

DAVID WALKER—JAMES MC CUNE SMITH—HENRY HIGHLAND GARNET—FREDERICK DOUGLASS—WILLIAM WELLS BROWN

THE first three decades of the nineteenth century were comparatively barren of Negro literary effort, but the anti-slavery struggle within the next three called several men into prominence and gave vitality to what they had to say. Protest in the earlier decades took the form of armed revolt. There were several insurrections, the most memorable being the carefully planned attempt of Gabriel Prosser in Richmond, Virginia, in 1800; the deeply laid scheme of Denmark Vesey in Charleston, South Carolina, in 1822; and the bloody outbreak of Nat Turner in Southampton County, Virginia, in 1831. After 1830 the abolitionists were active. William Lloyd Garrison began the publishing of the *Liberator* in Boston January 1, 1831, and among the features of the first year were reprints of several of the poems of Phillis Wheatley. The American Colonization Society also helped. When this organization was founded at the close of 1816 the leading spirits were slaveholders, and the conviction of many persons was that the intention was to get the free Negroes out of the country in order that the chains of bondage might be more securely fastened on the slaves. Negro leaders accordingly were united in their opposition. After thirty years, however, there was a shift of emphasis. The futility of attempting to take great hosts of people to another country was apparent; meanwhile more liberal spirits came into the Society. Effort now took the form of helping Liberia to become a model republic and of assisting promising young men in their preparation for service there.

Inspiration also came from the Negro church. It was through this agency that such a man as Bishop Daniel A. Payne found himself best able to work. The first Negro minister who left writings that we may read to-day was Lemuel B. Haynes (1753-1833), a pioneer in the Congregational denomination. Although clearly of Negro descent, Haynes became pastor of several white churches in New England and closed his ministry in Granville, New York. He was an able disputant; a finely ironical discourse of his, *Universal Salvation,* which grew out of a controversy with Hosea Ballou, ran through numerous editions. Peter Williams, Jr., was prominent as rector of St. Philip's Episcopal Church in New York from 1820 until his death in 1840. In his later years he lost the heart of his people by his failure to take an aggressive stand on questions affecting the Negro. He is remembered for three discourses, *An Oration on the Abolition of the Slave Trade* (1808), *A Discourse Delivered on the Death of Capt. Paul Cuffe* (1817), and *Discourse Delivered for the Benefit of the Coloured Community of Wilberforce, in Upper Canada* (1830). The first of these is in a highflown ejaculatory style; the second also begins in stilted fashion but fortunately changes into a smooth and clearcut account of the life of the seaman and philanthropist who had recently died.

Agitation naturally led to activity in the press. Negro periodical literature began with the appearance in March, 1827, of the first number of *Freedom's Journal*, a weekly edited by Samuel E. Cornish, a Presbyterian minister, and John B. Russwurm, soon to be a graduate of Bowdoin. Support was inadequate and the two editors differed on the vital matter of colonization. In the issue for September 5, 1827, Russwurm assumed an attitude that seemed to support the project, and Cornish resigned the next week. Russwurm continued in charge until February, 1829, when he left to superintend the system of education in Liberia. Later he became governor of the district around Cape Palmas known as Maryland in Africa. Cornish now became sole editor and for twenty months issued the periodical under the name *Rights for All*. In 1841 he became the first of the editors of the *Colored American*, a paper that endured for four years. There were several other early periodicals, but of more than usual importance was the *North Star*, which Douglass began to issue in Rochester in 1847, the name being changed three years later to *Frederick Douglass' Paper*. Outstanding among the magazines was the *Anglo-African*, which began publication in New York in January, 1859, and appeared regularly for fifteen months. The editor was Thomas Hamilton, and though there was no remuneration for articles, the list of contributors reads like a "Who's Who" of the Negroes of the day, among the names being James McCune Smith, Martin R. Delany, Alexander Crummell, and Edward W. Blyden.

One man of Negro descent in another country especially thrilled black men in America by the splendor of his achievement. This was Toussaint L'Ouverture, the military chieftain and statesman of Hayti, who gave to the Negro his first independent government in any land beyond the bounds of Africa.

François Dominique Toussaint (1743-1803) was a full-blooded Negro born near Cape François in Hayti. When the French Revolution broke out he was forty-six years of age and serving as overseer to his master. The French Constituent Assembly, having received from the mulattoes in Hayti a gift of six million francs and a pledge toward the payment of the national debt, with the request that their disabilities be removed, gave to all such persons of color the full privilege of French citizenship. The white planters on the island did everything in their power to delay the execution of the decree, and on August 23, 1791, the Negro slaves became a factor by rising in a fierce insurrection. By August, 1793, Toussaint had become the real leader of his people. The English had taken Port au Prince and were besieging the French governor, Laveaux. Toussaint went to the latter's assistance and his exploits led Laveaux to exclaim, "*Mais cet homme fait l'ouverture partout,*" thus giving him the name by which he was later known. He forced the surrender of the English and starved out the garrison of his rival, the mulatto, Rigaud, who had to consent to leave. Then, as general-in-chief, he imprisoned Roume, the agent of the Directory, assumed civil as well as military authority, and seized the Spanish part of the island, which had been ceded to France some years before but never actually surrendered. Toussaint next, in May, 1801, gave to Santo Domingo a constitution by which he assumed supreme authority and had the privilege of naming his successor. All the while he was awakening the admiration of the world by his bravery, his moderation, and his instinct for government. In 1802 he was treacherously seized while in a conference on a French vessel and taken to France, where within a year, in the dungeon of Joux, he died of pneumonia. The deeds of this leader were celebrated in prose and verse down to the Civil War. Wordsworth wrote a sonnet, Whittier a longer poem, and Wendell Phillips made him the subject of a brilliant address. Among Negro men the tributes were innumerable.

Two other men of African descent in the period who might be supposed to have had more influence than they exerted were the Russian poet Pushkin and the elder Dumas in France. William Wells Brown was interested in seeing Dumas in Paris, but in general the two famous European writers were little more than names to American Negroes before the Civil War. We recall both, however, for, aside from any touch they may have had with America, each is an eminent representative of the main idea of this book, one by reason of the lyrical quality of his genius and the other because of the resources of his imagination. They have the additional interest of showing the possibilities of the Negro genius in countries where the color line is not a barrier.

Alexander Sergeyevich Pushkin (1799-1837), greatest of the poets of Russia, was descended from Abram Petrovich Gannibal, an Ethiopian prince who, while a hostage in Constantinople, was bought or stolen by the Russian envoy, and later, under the patronage of Peter the Great, became a general in the War of the Spanish Succession, his second wife being a Russian noblewoman, the great grandmother of the poet. Pushkin always spoke of himself as a Negro. When twelve years of age he entered the Imperial Lyceum at Tsarskoe Selo, where his bold epigrams and poetic endowment soon marked him as above the average student. Even in those days he wrote an "Ode to Liberty" in which he warned "crowned criminals" of the wrath to come. After completing his course he became a clerk in the Ministry of Foreign Affairs. A revolutionary movement in 1825 caused several of his friends to be hanged or sent to Siberia, but he himself, already popular as a poet, was sent to a colonizing bureau in South Russia. The life in Bessarabia, the Crimea, and Odessa stimulated him; he came under the spell of Byron; and the next few years were among the most productive in his life. Although eminently subjective, he became distinguished in dramatic as well as lyric poetry. *Evgeni Onegin* is a novel in verse with a hero reminiscent of Don Juan; *Boris Godunov* is a tragedy based on Russian history which shows a veering toward Shakespeare; and *The Bronze Horseman,* commonly considered the highest achievement in Russian poetry, is concerned with the rights of the individual as opposed to those of the Empire. Pushkin was married to Nathalie Goncharova, a beautiful but foolish woman, and his life was cut short by a duel in which he engaged on her account with Georges d'Anthes, a cousin by marriage.

> There is intoxication in battle,
> And on the edge of a dark abyss,
> And in a furious ocean
> Amid menacing billows and stormy darkness,

And in the Arabian hurricane,
And in the breath of the Plague.

All, all that menaces with ruin
Contains for the heart of Mortals
Ineffable delight;
The token maybe of immortality.
And happy he who in the midst of excitements
Was able to discover and to know it.

Alexandre Dumas (1802-1870) was the grandson of Marquis Alexandre Davy de la Pailleterie and Marie Cessette Dumas, a Negro woman of Hayti. His father, Alexandre Davy de la Pailleterie Dumas, married a French woman, Marie Elisabeth Labouret, in 1792, and became a general under Napoleon, but died early, leaving his wife in straitened circumstances. The gifted son thought first of the law and engaged in the Revolution of 1830, but soon conceived the idea of a series of works that would "exalt history to the height of fiction." Thus arose the *Chroniques de France*, extending to nearly a hundred volumes, with little insight into history and perhaps even less into character, but with such treatment of incidents and episodes as aroused the greatest curiosity in a reader. Dumas now began to operate what has been called his factory. He would supply the main idea of a book and let an assistant attend to the mechanics, or even otherwise use as his own the talents of others. Yet, when all discount is made, the fact remains that he thrilled his generation as did no other author and that he won for French fiction an audience such as it never had before. The returns from his work were enormous, but he was not thrifty and was frequently involved in lawsuits. While other books show his extraordinary gifts, he seems destined to be remembered chiefly in connection with *The Three Musketeers* and *The Count of Monte Cristo.* His son, Alexandre Dumas *fils,* became distinguished among French dramatists not only for his emphasis on romantic love but also for his attention to the modern problem play.

DAVID WALKER

When we pass from Pushkin and Dumas to David Walker (1785-1830), the first American Negro in the period to be considered, we come to a different order of literary achievement but also to such earnestness as could hardly be excelled. Walker was born in Wilmington, North Carolina, his mother being a free woman and his father, who died early, a slave. Having realized the lack of opportunity in the South at the time, he set out for the North while still a young man and at length succeeded in reaching Boston. In 1827 he opened a clothing store and the next year married. In 1829 he published his famous *Appeal.* This impressed the South as incendiary, and even the abolitionist, Benjamin Lundy, felt that it would hurt rather than help the cause of freedom. The governors of Virginia and North Carolina sent messages to their legislatures about it, and the governor of Georgia wrote to the mayor of Boston, Harrison Gray Otis, to ask that it be suppressed. Otis replied that he did not personally approve of all the sentiments expressed in the pamphlet, but that the author had not done anything that made him amenable to the laws and could not be denied the right of free speech. A reward of a thousand dollars was then placed on Walker's head, the amount to be ten times as much if he was taken alive. His wife and friends urged that he go to Canada, but he refused to leave, feeling that someone had to die in the cause. Before the end of 1830 he was dead. He was a man six feet in height, slender, well proportioned and dark, with loose hair. Those who knew him best were impressed by his public spirit and many who were in need found succor in his home.

Walker's Appeal, in Four Articles; together with a Preamble, to the Coloured Citizens of the World, but in Particular and very Expressly to Those of the United States of America sold so rapidly that within seven months it was in the third edition, the language being increasingly bold and vigorous. Article I the author headed "Our Wretchedness in Consequence of Slavery." A trip over the United States had convinced him that the Negroes of the country were "the most degraded, wretched and abject set of beings that ever lived since the world began." "The whites," he asserted, "have always been an unjust, jealous, unmerciful, avaricious and bloodthirsty set of beings, always seeking after power and authority." As heathen they had been cruel enough, but as Christians they were ten times more so. Next was considered "Our Wretchedness in Consequence of Ignorance." The writer maintained that his people as a whole did not have sufficient intelligence even to realize their degradation. In the South or West a son would, at the command of a tyrant, take even his mother and apply the cowhide to her until she fell a victim to death in the road. In Article III Walker considered "Our Wretchedness in Consequence of the Preachers of the Religion of Jesus Christ." Here was a fertile field, one only partly developed. The writer did not have at hand the recent statements of some Southern ministers that might have served as a point of attack, but he did point out the general failure of preachers to live up to the Sermon on the Mount. Hypocrisy could hardly go further than that of those who could not see the evils at their door but who still could send out missionaries to convert the heathen. Article IV was headed "Our Wretchedness in Consequence of the Colonizing Plan." This was a bitter arraignment, especially directed against Henry Clay. As to the idea of colonization Walker said: "Here is a demonstrative proof of a plan got up by a gang of slaveholders to select the free people of color from among the slaves, that our more miserable brethren may be the better secured in ignorance and wretchedness, to work their farms and dig their mines, and thus go on enriching the Christians with their blood and groans. What our brethren could have been thinking about, who have left their native land and gone away to Africa, I am unable to say. . . . The Americans may say or do as they please, but they have to raise us from the condition of brutes to that of respectable men, and to make a national acknowledgment to us for the wrongs they have inflicted on us. . . . You may doubt, if you please. I know that thousands will doubt—they think they have us so well secured in wretchedness, to them and their children, that it is impossible for such things to occur. So did the antediluvians doubt Noah, until the day in which the flood came and swept them away. So did the Sodomites doubt, until Lot had got out of the city, and God rained down fire and brimstone from heaven upon them and burnt them up. So did the king of Egypt doubt the very existence of God, saying, 'Who is the Lord, that I should let Israel go?' . . . So did the Romans doubt, but they got dreadfully deceived."

This document, as has been shown, created the greatest consternation. The language was often colloquial and the style ejaculatory, but no one could doubt the sincerity of the utterance. All told, it was a worthy prelude to the agitation that became heated within the next few years and that did not cease until the Civil War was over.

JAMES MCCUNE SMITH

Prominent for more than two decades in the period now under review was James McCune Smith, a physician who was also a man of letters. The work of this writer was somewhat miscellaneous, but he was well educated, his approach to any subject was scholarly, and the rhetoric of his prose was never overdone. Well known Negroes were pleased to have him formally present them to the public, and the abolitionists referred to him as an example of the possibilities of those for whom they labored. All felt a loss when he died in mid-career.

While the chief facts in the life of Smith are fairly well known, biographers have been uniformly hazy about his early and his last years. Williams, the historian, tells of a visit of La Fayette to the African Free School in New York in 1824, on which occasion "Master James M. Smith, aged eleven years, stepped forward and gracefully delivered" a brief address of welcome. If, as seems likely, the pupil thus referred to became the man we have in mind, James McCune Smith was born in 1813. After completing his early training in New York, he made his way to Scotland and in 1837 received the degree of Doctor of Medicine at the University of Glasgow. On his return to the country he was given a warm welcome by the

Negroes of New York and became a physician in that city. The start that he thus had may be seen from the situation of some other men in 1837. Frederick Douglass had still a year to serve before his escape from slavery; Henry Highland Garnet was a student at Oneida Institute; Daniel A. Payne, just two years from the South, was completing his course at the Lutheran Seminary in Gettysburg; and William Wells Brown, twenty-two years of age, was working on a boat on Lake Erie. Smith was short and thickset in stature, but he had unusually bright eyes, was considerate of others, and readily made friends. On the *Colored American* he became a valiant helper, and to him and two other leaders the wealthy abolitionist, Gerrit Smith, applied for names when he thought of colonizing Negroes in some of the southern counties of New York. Payne, in his *Recollections of Seventy Years* (pp. 324-326) says that Smith was called to Wilberforce when that institution came under African Methodist auspices and given the choice of any chair he cared to fill. After he selected that of anthropology, the post and a home were held in reserve for him for twelve months, but in the course of the year he died of heart disease. That was in or about 1864.

Smith left no one well rounded work; thus he has to be judged on the basis of his scattered writings. He wrote the introductions for Douglass' *My Bondage and My Freedom* and Garnet's *Memorial Discourse.* In the *Liberator* (June 1, 1838, and February 16 and 23, 1844) one may find a speech that he delivered before the American Anti-Slavery Society soon after his return from Glasgow, and two letters on Freedom and Slavery first contributed to the *Tribune.* To the *Anglo-African Magazine* (January, 1859) he contributed a paper, "Civilization: Its Dependence on Physical Circumstances." To *Autographs for Freedom,* an annual edited for two years by Julia Griffiths, secretary of the Rochester Ladies' Anti-Slavery Society, he gave in 1853 a paper on John Murray, an abolitionist of Glasgow, and to the issue for 1854 a paragraph entitled "Freedom—Liberty," which may be taken as representative of his style.

Freedom and Liberty are synonyms. Freedom is an essence; Liberty, an accident. Freedom is born with a man; Liberty may be conferred on him. Freedom is progressive; Liberty is circumscribed. Freedom is the gift of God; Liberty, the creature of society. Liberty may be taken away from a man; but, on whatsoever soul Freedom may light, course of that soul is thenceforth onward and upward; society, customs, laws, armies, are but as wythes in its giant grasp, if they oppose, instruments to work its will, if they assent. Human kind welcome the birth of a free soul with reverence and shoutings, rejoicing in the advent of a fresh off-shoot of the Divine Whole, of which this is but a part.

HENRY HIGHLAND GARNET

The spiritual successor of David Walker and one of the foremost advocates of full enfranchisement for the Negro was Henry Highland Garnet (1815-1882), whose militant addresses caused him to be regarded as one of the most extreme of radicals.

Garnet was born a slave in Maryland but received his early schooling in New York, his father having escaped to that city with his family. When fourteen years of age he helped as a cook on a schooner plying between New York and Washington. One day he returned from a trip to find that slave hunters had invaded the home; his father and mother had barely escaped, and a sister who had been seized was forced to prove an alibi in court. In 1833 he began to attend the Sunday School of the First Colored, the Shiloh Presbyterian Church. The pastor, Theodore S. Wright, became his friend and adviser, and some years later he himself became pastor of the church.

In 1835, with young Alexander Crummell and Thomas S. Sydney, Garnet, then twenty years of age, went to Canaan, New Hampshire, to attend an academy that had been opened by the abolitionists. So hostile was the community that the building was pulled from its place and destroyed. Garnet then entered Oneida Institute at Whitesboro, New York, presided over by Beriah Green. On graduating in 1840 he was employed as an agent of the American

Anti-Slavery Society. He also threw himself into the Convention Movement of Negro men. In 1843, at the convention in Buffalo, he read *An Address to the Slaves of the United States of America.* This did not win formal approval because several delegates felt that it tended to promote insurrection and would make it difficult for men from the border states to return home. Frederick Douglass, the rising leader, was one of those who took this point of view. Garnet next became pastor of Liberty Street Presbyterian Church in Troy, New York. Later he went to Jamaica as a missionary of the United Presbyterian Church of Scotland, but he returned to New York to become pastor of Shiloh. In 1864 he went to the Fifteenth Street Presbyterian Church in Washington. In both Troy and New York he was frequently quoted in the press, and while in Washington, on the invitation of the Reverend William H. Channing, chaplain of the House of Representatives, he delivered in the House on Sunday, February 12, 1865, an address memorializing the thirteenth amendment to the Constitution. A desire to see Africa at last saw fulfilment in his appointment as minister to Liberia, but he died two months after his arrival.

In spite of the political objections brought against it, the address of 1843 is, in both substance and style, probably the strongest that Garnet ever delivered. He suggested both a labor strike and an appeal to arms, and even to-day one can feel the fervor of his message. "Your condition," he said, supposedly to the slaves, "does not absolve you from your moral obligation. The diabolical injustice by which your liberties are cloven down, neither God, nor angels, or just men command you to suffer for a single moment. Therefore it is your solemn and imperative duty to use every means, both moral, intellectual, and physical, that promises success. It is as wrong for your lordly oppressors to keep you in slavery as it was for the man thief to steal our ancestors from the coast of Africa. You should therefore now use the same manner of resistance as would have been just in our ancestors, when the bloody footprints of the first remorseless soul-thief was placed upon the shores of our fatherland." Recalling well known insurrectionists Garnet said: "Brethren, arise, arise! Strike for your lives and liberties. Now is the day and the hour. Let every slave throughout the land do this, and the days of slavery are numbered. You can not be more oppressed than you have been; you can not suffer greater cruelties than you have already. *Rather die freemen than live to be slaves.*"

A discourse, *The Past and Present Condition, and the Destiny of the Colored Race,* delivered in Troy in 1848 on the fifteenth anniversary of the Female Benevolent Society, has much of the flavor of an old lyceum address but also touches upon vital matters. Garnet paid tribute to Placido, the Cuban poet who was a martyr to freedom, and said that resistance to tyranny must be the basis of all popular demonstrations; then he spoke of the future as follows: "This western world is destined to be filled with a mixed race. Statesmen, distinguished for their forecast, have gravely said that the blacks must either be removed or such as I have stated will be the result. It is a stubborn fact that it is impossible to separate the pale man and the man of color, and therefore the result which to them is so fearful is inevitable. All this the wiser portion of the Colonizationists see, and they labor to hinder it. It matters not whether we abhor or desire such a consummation; it is now too late to change the decree of nature and circumstances."

The *Memorial Discourse* of 1865 had the interest of marking the first time that a Negro spoke on any occasion in the National Capitol. Thirty-eight men of color in Washington and the vicinity were so impressed that they asked for a copy for publication, and James McCune Smith wrote a lengthy introductory sketch. However, the address does not show Garnet in his most dynamic vein. A review of history cast in the form of a sermon hardly gave the best opportunity for the play of his emotion. In opposing slavery he could be unflinching and rise to nobility, but he had no ringing message for the new era upon which the country had embarked.

FREDERICK DOUGLASS IN 1855

FREDERICK DOUGLASS

Frederick Douglass (1817-1895), the foremost man of the period, is still regarded by many as the greatest of American Negroes. Of massive physique and leonine appearance, and master of a high order of eloquence, he made an indelible impression upon his time.

Some incidents in his youth foreshadow the man. As a young slave in Maryland he somehow learned his letters. Later he realized that it might also be worth while to know how to write in case one needed to show a pass. When thirteen years of age he purchased for fifty cents a copy of a book, *The Columbia Orator,* whose appeals for liberty woke in him something he never lost. Three years later, while at work on a farm, he had to suffer much from the man to whom he was bound; but one day he resisted physical punishment and never again was an attempt made to whip him. When eighteen years old he planned with some others to escape, but the plot was divulged and he was placed in jail. At last when he was twenty-one and working as a calker in Baltimore, he succeeded in getting away in the disguise of a sailor. In New York he found David Ruggles, secretary of the Vigilance Committee, who advised him to go on to New Bedford. There he worked about the docks until 1841, when he was twenty-four years of age.

Formerly the young man had used the surname of

his slave mother, Harriet Bailey, but Nathan Johnson, a Negro citizen of New Bedford to whom he brought from New York a letter of introduction, suggested from a reading of *The Lady of the Lake* the name *Douglas*. This was immediately adopted, though always spelled with a double *s*.

Douglass soon became an earnest reader of the *Liberator* and regularly attended anti-slavery meetings. One day, feeling the need of a brief rest, he left his work in the brass foundry where he was employed in order to attend an abolition convention in Nantucket, Massachusetts. William C. Coffin, who had heard him speak to the Negro people in New Bedford, sought him out in the crowd and asked if he would not say a few words. Douglass later wrote that he could hardly stand erect or say anything without stammering; but William Lloyd Garrison, who was the next to speak, took him as a theme, delivering an address of tremendous power. So strong was the impression that the young man had made that at the close of the meeting John A. Collins, general agent of the Massachusetts Anti-Slavery Society, urged that he become an agent of that organization. Douglass demurred, as he was conscious of his lack of training and questioned the wisdom of exposure to discovery, but finally consented to serve for a trial period of three months. He served for fourteen years, and so rapid was his advance that after three or four years some people doubted that he had ever been a slave.

In 1845 he went to England. There, breathing a freer air and meeting distinguished liberals, he grew rapidly in mental stature. Before he sailed for home, one hundred and fifty pounds was raised for the formal purchase of his freedom. Even before he left America he had been restless under the restraint imposed upon him by the officials of his organization. They constantly urged upon him to tell his story whereas he felt impelled more and more not simply to narrate but also to denounce the wrongs he had known. When he returned in 1847 the days of tutelage were over and he adopted a new policy. Separating from Garrison and others who would not use direct political action, he now threw his influence with those who sought to do away with slavery by constitutional means. Settling in Rochester, New York, he began the publication of the paper of which we have spoken, the *North Star,* later known as *Frederick Douglass' Paper.* In 1858 he also began *Douglass' Monthly,* a little magazine. With this the weekly was merged in 1860, when the editor's connection with John Brown caused him to go again to England; and so it continued until early in 1863.

As a member of the Liberty Party and an orator as well as an editor, Douglass was now in constant demand as a speaker. On July 5, 1852, he delivered at Rochester one of the greatest of his addresses on the theme, "What to the slave is the Fourth of July?" In the course of the Civil War he was often in conference with President Lincoln, and assisted with enlistments for the Fifty-fourth and Fifty-fifth Massachusetts regiments of Negro men, his own sons being among the first recruits. After the war he spoke for the suffrage and civil rights, as in the address, "What the Black Man Wants," at the annual meeting of the Massachusetts Anti-Slavery Society in 1865. From 1869 to 1872 he conducted in Washington another weekly, the *New National Era,* meanwhile contributing to the *North American Review* and other periodicals. Later he was United States marshal, recorder of deeds for the District of Columbia, and minister to Hayti. Twice in his later years his utterances caused him to lose the heart of his people. The first was at the time of the rejoicing over the Fifteenth amendment when he wounded the religious sensibilities of many by asserting that he would not indulge in the cant of thanking God for a deliverance "wrought out through our common humanity." The second time was when he opposed the Negro Exodus of 1879. That one who had escaped from slavery to live in the freer air of the North should oppose the movement of other black men who sought to escape from peonage or midnight violence, hardly carried conviction.

The works of Douglass have never been fully collected. Naturally of most importance is his account of his own career. This appeared in various forms. In 1845 was published in Boston the first edition of the *Narrative of the Life of Frederick Douglass,* called forth by the attitude of those who regarded the amazing young speaker as an impostor and demanded a full statement of facts. Garrison and Phillips were among the friends who questioned the wisdom of the publication, but both finally wrote introductions. *My Bondage and My Freedom,* a much larger work, appeared in 1855, and this time the introduction was by a member of the author's own race, James McCune Smith. In 1881 appeared the third form of the autobiography, *Life and Times of Frederick Douglass,* with an introduction by George L. Ruffin, a man of color prominent as a judge in Boston. This was enlarged in 1892. There was also an English edition with an introduction by John Bright. The "Times" in the third title indicates to some a weakness, for the narrative has not the continuous flow of *My Bondage and My Freedom.*

Douglass could be tender at times. He showed deep feeling when speaking of such friends of the oppressed as Garrison, Theodore Parker, and Elizabeth Barrett Browning, and when he touched upon the folk songs of his people. That, however, was not the typical Douglass—the man of invective, of fearless denunciation of wrong, and majestic presence. For that man we have to go to such a thing as the letter written to Garrison from England (January 1, 1846), this holding up to scorn the churches and the supposedly free institutions of America, all of which were overladen with prejudice. At Rochester he said, "This Fourth of July is *yours*, not *mine*. *You* may rejoice, *I* must mourn. To drag a man in fetters into the grand illuminated temple of liberty, and call upon him to join you in joyous anthems, were inhuman mockery and sacrilegious irony." He quoted with telling effect Psalm 137: "By the waters of Babylon, there we sat down. Yea! we wept when we remembered Zion. We hanged our harps upon the willows in the midst thereof. For there, they that carried us away captive, required of us a song; and they who wasted us required of us mirth, saying, Sing us one of the songs of Zion. How can we sing the Lord's song in a strange land?" Then he said: "I shall see this day and its popular characteristics from the slave's point of view. Standing there identified with the American bondman, making his wrongs mine, I do not hesitate to declare, with all my soul, that the character and conduct of this nation never looked blacker to me than on this 4th of July. America is false to the past, false to the present, and solemnly binds herself to be false to the future."

"What the Black Man Wants" was suggested by the attitude of those even in the North who, like General Nathaniel P. Banks, favored such tutelage and oversight of the Negro as would practically remand him to slavery. "It may be objected," said Douglass, "that this pressing of the Negro's right to suffrage is premature. Let us have slavery abolished, it may be said, let us have labor organized, and then, in the natural course of events, the right of suffrage will be extended to the Negro. I do not agree with this. The constitution of the human mind is such that if it once disregards the conviction forced upon it by a revelation of truth, it requires the exercise of a higher power to produce the same conviction afterward." In the course of his conclusion he said: "The American people have always been anxious to know what they shall do with us. General Banks was distressed with solicitude as to what he should do with the Negro. Everybody has asked the question, and they learned to ask it early of the Abolitionists, 'What shall we do with the Negro?' I have had but one answer from the beginning. Do nothing with us! Your doing with us has already played the mischief with us. Do nothing with us! If the apples will not remain on the tree of their own strength, . . . let them fall! I am not for tying or fastening them on the tree in any way, except by nature's plan, and if they will not stay there, let them fall. And if the Negro can not stand on his own legs, let him fall also. All I ask is, give him a chance to stand on his own legs! Let him alone! If you see him on his way to school, let him alone,—don't disturb him. If you see him going to the dinner table at a hotel, let him go! If you see him going to the ballot-box, let him alone,—don't disturb him! If you see him going into a workshop, just let him alone,—your interference is doing him a positive injury. If the Negro can not live by the line of eternal justice, the fault will not be yours; it will be his who made the Negro, and established that line for his government. Let him live or die by that."

One of the best of the later addresses was that on John Brown, delivered at various places and finally at Harper's Ferry in 1881, with the district attorney who had prosecuted Brown a listener on the platform. After an elaborate introduction Douglass gave a succinct review of the events of the raid and his own meetings with the martyr. The speech was notable not only for its deep feeling but also for the firm handling of its material.

Frederick Douglass was essentially an orator, not a logician or a debater. In a formal encounter he was sometimes worsted by a trained man sure of his ground, as when he was opposed on the subject of the Negro Exodus by Richard T. Greener, the first man of color to be graduated at Harvard. After all, it was not the work of his later years that made him great, but that of his young manhood, when he had a story to tell and when no one who heard him could fail to be impressed. Greater than anything he said was himself, the supreme exhibit from the house of bondage. For years

> He, above the rest
> In shape and gesture proudly eminent,
> Stood like a tower.

WILLIAM WELLS BROWN

William Wells Brown (1815?-1884) was in his day the most voluminous Negro writer in the United States, and the most successful. He attempted more different things than any other, being the first man of the race to write a novel, a drama, and a book of travel, and in his later years was regarded as an historian. With keen zest for living, some insight into character, and an eye for effect, he seldom failed to be interesting. On the other hand he had not a sound education, he depended largely on sensational material, and was hasty and superficial in method. Against few authors has there been so strong a reaction. To-day his importance is mainly historical.

The boy known first simply as William was born a slave in Lexington, Kentucky, but when very young was taken to St. Louis. When ten years old he worked about the cabin on a boat on the Mississippi, and two years later was employed in the office of Elijah P. Lovejoy, then editor of the *St. Louis Times*. Soon he was again on a boat, but in 1834, while in Cincinnati, escaped, being then about nineteen years of age. As he made his way to Canada he was befriended by a Quaker, Wells Brown, whose name he adopted.

Brown now found employment on a boat on Lake Erie, and within the next few years, working as a steward, assisted many fugitives on their way to freedom, about sixty or seventy a year. Meanwhile he was making advance in education and public speaking, so much so that he was engaged first by the Western, then by the Massachusetts Anti-Slavery Society. In 1849 he went to England, where he met George Thompson, Richard Cobden, and other liberals. At the Peace Congress in Paris he represented the American Peace Society, winning the warm approval of the president, Victor Hugo, by a speech he made. As the Fugitive Slave Law made it inadvisable for him to return to the United States at this time, he remained abroad until the autumn of 1854, giving much of his time to the study of medicine. On his return, having been formally manumitted, he resided in Cambridge, then in Chelsea, Massachusetts, practicing his profession but also going forward with his writing. In his later years he showed interest in woman suffrage, prison reform, and the cause of temperance.

The *Narrative of William W. Brown,* published in 1847, sold through three editions in eight months, at the rate of a thousand copies every four weeks. Just a year later appeared a small collection entitled *The Anti-Slavery Harp,* one of the poems being "Jefferson's Daughter." This was based on the story that a daughter of the former president had been sold for a thousand dollars, a theme later used in *Clotel. Three Years in Europe,* containing some of the author's bright comment on the things he saw abroad, was issued in London in 1852, an enlarged edition being brought out in America three years later under the title, *Sketches of Places and People Abroad*. *Clotel, or The President's Daughter* (London, 1853) is a crowded, harrowing story introducing many situations incident to slavery, even events like Nat Turner's Insurrection that have no connection with the main theme. An attractive woman of color, Jefferson's housekeeper, had two daughters. One of these, the heroine, at last ends her sorrows by drowning herself in the Potomac in sight of the Capitol. There were American editions in 1864 and 1867, but in these any reference to Jefferson was omitted, the title being simply *Clotelle: A Tale of the Southern States*. *The Escape*, a drama in five acts, appeared in Boston in 1858. A slave master makes advances to the young woman Melinda, but she repels him and with her husband, Glen, succeeds eventually in escaping to Canada. With the fresh setting incident to slavery this old trio of the hero, heroine, and villain might have been worked up into a strong melodrama, but for the most part the speeches are in a stilted, self-conscious vein, with an excess of moralizing. Only occasionally, as when the mistress reveals her jealousy of Melinda, is there a flash of genuine drama.

Brown's work in history and biography began with *The Black Man: His Antecedents, his Genius, and his Achievements*, which appeared just after the Emancipation Proclamation in 1863. One who looks into the book to-day is likely to be surprised by the incompleteness and inadequacy of the sketches, but within a year it was in the third edition. Four years later was issued *The Negro in the American Rebellion: His Heroism and his Fidelity,* a work that even more than others showed the lack of careful research but that succeeded by reason of its human interest. Both books contributed to and were superseded by *The Rising Son* (1874), in which Brown attempted to give a comprehensive treatment of the history of the Negro from Africa to America. It is said that ten thousand copies were sold within a year. In 1880 appeared *My Southern Home, or The South and its People,* in which the strength suggested in the main title is lessened by the implications of the sub-title. The book is made up of a series of sketches. Some of these recount incidents of the harsher side of slavery and others are broadly humorous, as when a slave prays in the presence of his master that heaven will not let this man fall into *too* hot a fire; but the book is weighed down by an excess of sermonizing. As for the bits of folklore included, one can but remember that it was in the very next year that Joel Chandler Harris produced *Uncle Remus* and that Charles W. Chesnutt was just over the horizon. So it was also that when *The Rising Son* appeared, Williams' *History of the Negro Race in America* was less than a decade in the future. Brown had lingered into an age in which higher standards than his were demanded. He was deeply interested in his people and did much to popularize their history, but his final place is that of an alert pioneer who started many things that those who came after were to do a little better.

SLAVE NARRATIVES

The accounts of their lives written by Douglass and Brown were only representative of a flood of slave narratives in the two decades just before the Civil War. In literary quality these range all the way from dull monotonous chronicles to stories of enthralling interest. Sometimes there was much editorial assistance, at other times almost none. The narratives here recalled are only a few of the better known.

Lunsford Lane was a thrifty and industrious Negro of Raleigh, North Carolina, who had learned from his father the secret of making a special brand of smoking tobacco. Hiring his time from his master, he began to manufacture the product for market. The master dying, he undertook to purchase his freedom from his mistress for $1,000. He now became involved in a chain of legal technicalities. As a slave he could not make a contract; accordingly he entrusted the matter to the master of his wife, one Mr. Smith. As by law a slave in North Carolina could be manumitted for meritorious service only, the best thing Smith could do was to take Lane with him to New York and have the freedom papers issued there. Later Smith charged him $2,500 for the wife and six children, though eight years previously he had purchased the wife and two children for $560. Some men, jealous of Lane's success in business, recalled an old act that forbade free Negroes from other states to come to North Carolina, and he was forced to leave. Later, having given Smith $560 in cash and his house and lot, he undertook to raise the remainder of the sum required by delivering lectures in the North. On his return to Raleigh to close up his business he was arrested on the charge of having given abolition lectures in the State of Massachusetts. In court he recounted with pathos the whole story of his life and the case was dismissed; but later his trunk was searched and he was tarred and feathered. The soldiery at last came to his protection, and he left with his family for Philadelphia. All this and more he told in *The Narrative of Lunsford Lane, formerly of Raleigh, N. C.*, published in Boston in 1842. Garrison spoke of the author as a "modest, intelligent man, and very prepossessing in his appearance."

Lewis Clarke and Henry Bibb were both men of more than average intelligence. Clarke, who was so fair of complexion that he escaped from slavery by posing as a white man and who gave Harriet Beecher Stowe some suggestion for her character George Harris, published in the *Narrative of the Sufferings of Lewis Clarke, during a Captivity of More than Twenty-five Years among the Algerines of Kentucky* (1845), perhaps the most bitter and vindictive of all the accounts written by former slaves. The *Narrative of the Life and Adventures of Henry Bibb, Written by Himself* (1849) is in very simple diction and faulty in syntax, but has the merit of setting forth vividly the life and customs of slaves in the South. Among the superstitions recalled was one saying that if an amorous swain would win a young woman's love, he must pull out a lock of her hair and wear it in his shoe. Accordingly the author sought to emulate Lord Petre in *The Rape of the Lock,* with results that indicated anything but success. After serving as an anti-slavery lecturer, Bibb settled in Canada, where he edited a paper, *The Voice of Freedom.*

Josiah Henson, the original of Uncle Tom, was born a slave in Maryland but, when forty-five years of age, escaped to Canada, where, as a Methodist preacher, he endeavored to found a community and establish an industrial school. He assisted in the work of the "underground railroad," was awarded a bronze medal for some walnut boards he exhibited at the World's Fair in London in 1851, and on a third visit to England in 1876 was received in audience by Queen Victoria. *The Life of Josiah Henson, formerly a Slave, now an Inhabitant of Canada, as Narrated by Himself* appeared in 1849 as a pamphlet of seventy-six pages, the work having been dictated to an editorial helper. This did not attract much attention, but Mrs. Stowe was impressed by it, talked with Henson, and herself wrote the introduction for the enlarged work, *Truth Stranger than Fiction: Father Henson's Story of his Own Life* (1858). In England in 1876 was issued still another version, *An Autobiography of Josiah Henson (Mrs. Harriet Beecher Stowe's "Uncle Tom")*, the cover reading *Uncle Tom's Story of his Life*, and an enlarged edition of this appeared two years later. All of the books after the first had extraordinary success. Any student of Henson's career is likely to be exasperated by his tendency to exploit himself, but this must not blind one to the merits of the earlier portion of his narrative, as when he describes the beating in which an arm and both of his shoulder blades were broken, or tells of the difficulties he had to face when conducting a number of slaves from Maryland to Kentucky.

Samuel Northup's *Twelve Years a Slave* (1853) is a story of trials and suffering, hope deferred and at last realized, that reads like a well constructed novel. The author, living in Saratoga, New York, was happily married and the father of three young children. An expert player on the violin, he was enticed away to New York by two men who professed to be connected with a circus. A day or two later he found himself in a slave pen in Washington. He was taken to New Orleans and sold, and then, under the name Platt, spent years on a plantation on the Red River in Louisiana. At length, through the assistance of a Canadian named Bass, a carpenter in the vicinity, the wheels of the law were set in motion for his release and he was reunited with his family. "O Platt," cried the young woman Patsey whom he had befriended, "you're goin' to be free—you're goin' way off yonder, where we'll nebber see ye any more. You've saved me a good many whippin's, Platt; I'm glad you're goin' to be free—but oh! de Lord! de Lord! what'll become of me?"

Comparatively late was *The Autobiography of a Fugitive Slave: His Anti-Slavery Labours in the United States, Canada, and England* (1855), by Samuel Ringgold Ward, a work that is hardly adequately represented by its title, as the autobiographical portion takes up but a small portion of the whole. The book is in a firm and vigorous style, is replete with incident and anecdote, and launches out into a general discussion of matters pertaining to the Negro. The author, a black man, was very eloquent and for some years was a rival of Douglass on the lecture platform. A Congregational minister, he served for some time as pastor of a church in South Butler, New York, of which all the members were white people. His book was written in England. Soon after its publication he went to Jamaica, where he died a few years later.

OTHER WRITERS

Three other men who were prominently on the scene during the period and who were interested in the past and the future of the Negro were James W. C. Pennington, Martin R. Delany, and William C.

Nell. Pennington, born a slave on a plantation in Maryland, escaped on becoming of age, made his way to Heidelberg, where he received the degree of Doctor of Divinity, and later served as a Presbyterian minister in New York. He published *A Text Book of the Origin and History of the Colored People* (1841), made several contributions to periodical literature, and added to the number of slave narratives with *The Fugitive Blacksmith* (1849), all of his writing being in a crisp, didactic style. Martin R. Delany, an eager, restless spirit, was editor, lecturer, physician, explorer, a major in the Army, an employee in the Freedmen's Bureau, and finally a customs-house inspector and a trial justice in Charleston, South Carolina. His interests took him at one time or another to Canada, to England, and Africa. To his children he gave the Christian names, Toussaint L'Ouverture, Charles Lennox Remond, Alexandre Dumas, Saint Cyprian, Faustin Soulouque, Rameses Placido, and Ethiopia Halle Amelia. He wrote much, but is chiefly remembered for a little book entitled *The Condition, Elevation, Emigration, and Destiny of the Colored People of the United States, Politically Considered* (1852), which is a mine of information about the Negro in the period. Nell was a man of quiet, pleasant manner and the temperament of a scholar. Born in Boston, he became an assistant of Garrison in the editing and printing of the *Liberator,* and for some time helped Douglass in Rochester with the *North*

Star. His mature years were given mainly to research in the sources of Negro history, and he is best represented by *The Colored Patriots of the American Revolution, with Sketches of Several Distinguished Colored Persons: to which is added a Brief Survey of the Condition and Prospects of Colored Americans* (1855). The book is not smooth in style but in the main showed the author as working along the right line and is far more reliable than the historical productions of William Wells Brown a few years later.

Somewhat apart from other works of the period was a book that appeared in London in 1857 under the patronage, at least in the second edition, of Harriet Beecher Stowe. This was *The Garies and their Friends*, a novel, by Frank J. Webb. Garie is a wealthy Southerner who comes with his wife, a woman of color, and his children to Philadelphia. Even here peace is denied him. He loses his life when a mob attacks his home, his wife dies during the excitement, and tragedy hangs over his offspring. Against this group is placed as a foil a Negro family that fights its way through poverty and proscription to some measure of success. The book is a long one, but is not well co-ordinated, and, like some later works, depended unduly upon sensational effects.

III

POETRY AND THE ARTS, 1830-1865

GEORGE MOSES HORTON—DANIEL A. PAYNE—JAMES WHITFIELD—GEORGE B. VASHON—JAMES MADISON BELL—EARLY ARTISTS—THE STAGE: IRA B. ALDRIDGE—MUSIC: JUSTIN HOLLAND, ELIZABETH TAYLOR GREENFIELD, THOMAS J. BOWERS

THE period covered by the present chapter is the same as that of the last, but with the writers there is a shift of emphasis. David Walker, Henry Highland Garnet, and Frederick Douglass were primarily concerned with the wrongs of slavery and expressed themselves in vigorous prose. James Whitfield also wrote about slavery and James Madison Bell about the triumph of liberty, but these authors used the medium of verse. George Moses Horton developed a vein of humor that had nothing to do with his being a slave, and Daniel A. Payne worked with a devotional temper. In some measure poetry was for the men we are now to consider a means of escape. Taken all together, their writings mark a notable advance.

There were also now appearing beginners in fields other than literature. Ira Aldridge was a tragedian acclaimed in Old World capitals, while Elizabeth Taylor Greenfield needed only a little more training to be one of the greatest singers of the century. In painting, sculpture, and engraving there were at least a few workers who would not have had to fear comparison with those of a later day.

GEORGE MOSES HORTON

George Moses Horton (1797-1883?) is an isolated figure. Because he had an unusual career and offers interesting questions for the literary student, he has received much attention within recent years; but hardly any of his efforts went beyond promise. In spite of an auspicious beginning, his life was not one of "high seriousness," and he was most original when in a humorous or bantering vein.

For most of his life and until the close of the Civil War Horton was a slave. He was born in Northampton County, North Carolina, the property of William Horton. At the death of this master in 1815 he passed to James Horton, a son, and seventeen years later to Hall Horton, son of James. It was the second of these masters who knew him as a young man and encouraged his early striving. The third, seeing that he was not the best of field hands, permitted him to go to Chapel Hill to hire his time. There for thirty years he was a janitor at the University of North Carolina. Someone who knew him remarked that he owned his master and very nearly owned the president of the University. He executed small commissions in verse for the students, but took to drink and in time capitalized his distress, appealing to any who would hear to "lend a helping hand to the old, unfortunate bard." In 1865 he went to Philadelphia with a United States cavalry officer, Captain Will H. S. Banks, and there spent his last years. He was described as "of medium height, dark but not black," and of courteous manner.

Horton was largely self-taught. He learned to read mainly by studying the evangelical hymns he heard, and these naturally influenced his early verse. Some of his poems appeared in the *Raleigh Register* and papers in Boston before he brought out his first booklet, *The Hope of Liberty* (1829). He thought that from the proceeds he might be able to purchase his freedom and go to Liberia, but this dream was never realized. In 1837 the booklet was reprinted in Philadelphia as *Poems by a Slave,* and under this title was again printed and bound with the 1838 edition of the poems of Phillis Wheatley. We read of other collections within the next few years, but most of these are not now accessible. Important, however, is *Naked Genius* (1865), a book of a hundred and sixty pages. The contents are miscellaneous, but there is quite enough to show that the author has now struck his true vein. There is much about the fickleness of woman, also much about hunting in North Carolina. "The Creditor to his Proud Debtor" is typical of the lighter pieces, and "Jefferson in a Tight Place" satirizes the president of the Confederacy, with pointed reference to the disguise in which he is said to have tried to escape. Horton had not the sure taste of Phillis Wheatley, but he had a more lively imagination and at his best gave a suggestion of power. The following stanzas are from the early poem, "On Hearing of the Intention of a Gentleman to Purchase the Poet's Freedom":

When on life's ocean first I spread my sail,
I then implored a mild auspicious gale;
And from the slippery strand I took my flight,
And sought the peaceful haven of delight.

At length a golden sun broke through the gloom,
And from his smiles arose a sweet perfume—
A calm ensued, and birds began to sing,
And lo! the sacred muse resumed her wing.

'Twas like the salutation of the dove,
Borne on the zephyr through some lonesome grove,
When Spring returns, and Winter's chill is past,
And vegetation smiles above the blast.

'Twas like the evening of a nuptial pair,
When love pervades the hour of sad despair—
'Twas like fair Helen's sweet return to Troy,
When every Grecian bosom swell'd with joy.

The silent harp which on the osiers hung,
Was then attuned, and manumission sung;
Away by hope the clouds of fear were driven,
And music breathed my gratitude to Heaven.

Thus on the dusky verge of deep despair,
Eternal Providence was with me there;
When pleasure seemed to fade on life's gay dawn,
And the last beam of hope was almost gone.

DANIEL A. PAYNE

Daniel Alexander Payne (1811-1893) wrote a great deal, verse in his earlier years, then sermons and addresses, and finally works bearing on the history of his denomination; but if he had written nothing at all, he would still deserve consideration by reason of his effort for light and learning. He felt the wrong of slavery and spoke against it, but was not a professional agitator, his chief concern being ever with the spiritual and cultural development of his people.

Payne was born of free parents in Charleston, South Carolina. When not more than eighteen years of age he began to teach, but in 1835, when he was twenty-four, was forced by adverse legislation in the state to close his school. Going to New York, he was advised to enter the Lutheran Seminary in Gettysburg, Pennsylvania, where he remained two years. Joining the African Methodist Episcopal Church, he encountered storms by reason of his insistence upon an educated ministry and intelligent modes of worship; but, in spite of his small stature, shrill voice, and dictatorial manner, he conquered by reason of his zeal and integrity, being elected bishop in 1852. In 1863 he assumed responsibility for the purchase of

Wilberforce University by his church, and for sixteen years was president of the institution. After the war he led in organizing conferences in the South and as senior bishop labored even more than before for a ministry with high standards of character.

In his longing for righteousness, his severe judgment of himself, and his communion with the infinite, Payne was like Francis of Assisi or John Henry Newman. His diary reveals a heart ever seeking the divine. In 1835, soon after entering the Seminary, he wrote: "When, my Redeemer, shall I be sanctified through thy word? Oh, when shall the thoughts of my heart and all the intentions thereof be cleansed by the inspiration of the Holy Spirit? O draw near, my Crucified Saviour, and make me clean. Then shall I love thee supremely above all things."

With this spirit he went to work, ever taxing himself to the utmost and encouraging others to do their best. Among other things he led in organizing musical and literary societies. For the dedication of New Bethel in Philadelphia December 23, 1841, he wrote an ode of twelve stanzas, and soon thereafter, with the consent of the pastor and the bishop, organized a choir, placing it in the gallery opposite the pulpit. Six years later Bethel in Baltimore, while he was pastor, became the first church of the denomination to countenance instrumental music. In 1848, when a new edifice was being erected, Payne, to assist in raising funds, went to Washington and persuaded James

Fleet, the ablest musician in the District, to come to Baltimore and give a sacred concert. Fleet engaged Eliza Euston, the best soprano of the race in the District, Fannie Fisher, the best alto, and James Wormley, the best if not the only bass viol, while Mrs. Fleet served as pianist. In order that there might not be on the program anything unsuited to the house of God, the pastor himself wrote the lyrics for the occasion. The novelty of the performance proved a powerful attraction; the church was filled to overflowing, and the evening was a financial as well as an artistic success. At a second concert seven stringed instruments were used, the conductor being William Appo, one of the most learned musicians of the race at the time; and the soloist for the occasion was Elizabeth Taylor Greenfield, then just entering upon her larger fame.

Actuated as he was by such ideals as these activities suggest, it was inevitable that Payne should set his face against what were known at the time as "praying bands," and quite natural that he should awaken opposition in so doing. In a "praying band" about the middle of the last century a group of people would form a ring, and then proceed to sing, clap their hands, and stamp their feet or march around under the leadership of a man who kept time with a handkerchief in his hand. Representative of the cornfield ditties used were

Ashes to ashes, dust to dust,
If God won't have us, the devil must.

I was way over there where the coffin fell;
I heard that sinner as he screamed in hell.

Such songs were frequently indulged in from eight until half past ten at night; in some places it was the custom to begin the dances after every evening service and to continue them until midnight. Payne opposed all such practices. When one young leader said to him, "Sinners won't get converted unless there is a ring," he replied, "Nothing but the Spirit of God and the Word of God can convert sinners." He was right of course; yet, while the praying bands are gone, the spirit that prompted them is still alive and in many places offers a problem to-day.

Payne's later productions include such works as *Recollections of Seventy Years* (1888), a book of absorbing interest, and *History of the African Methodist Episcopal Church* (1891). Just now, however, we are chiefly concerned with his verse. In the *Recollections* he included "The Mournful Lute, or The Preceptor's Farewell," a poem in eight-line stanzas running to six ordinary pages. This was suggested by the spiritual crisis through which he passed when forced to close his school in Charleston in 1835, and there can be no doubt about the sincerity of his feeling. In the *Liberator* for May 28, 1841, will be found "An Original Poem composed for the Soirée of the Vigilant Committee of Philadelphia, May 7, 1841." This is representative of Payne's verse when he had to deal with slavery, being earnest in temper but also largely objective. The author found his true vein in *The Pleasures and Other Miscellaneous Poems*, a booklet of forty-three pages issued in Baltimore in 1850.

About the title-piece in this collection is an eighteenth century flavor that Phillis Wheatley could hardly have exceeded. The dedication of the booklet is to the author's sister Caroline, "the open enemy of fashionable vice and the fearless advocate of holy virtue." "The Pleasures" opens with an invocation in pseudo-classic vein, then considers in detail the vices of drunkenness, gluttony, the use of tobacco, dancing, and excessive attention to personal adornment, the delights of which are declared to be vanity. Payne then takes up the pleasures of Virtue, Nature, and the worship of God, singing the praise of music and of love—not love degraded by coarseness, but pure and exalted, as at the altars of a sacred home. In the most subjective passage in the poem he praises his departed wife. The following lines are representative:

> Repent, ye fools! and listen while we sing
> Of pleasures sweeter than the flow'rs of Spring—
> Like the pure stream that gush'd from Horeb's side,
> It flows in currents, limpid, deep and wide,
> Through the parch'd deserts of this sin-curs'd vale.

Who wills may come and ev'ry sense regale;
May quench his thirst; may drink and ne'er be dry,
Nor lack a good beneath the bending sky;
Weave for himself a crown of endless life—
A crown! a throne! beyond the world of strife.
'Tis wisdom speaks—O hear her godlike voice!
Its melting tones will make the heart rejoice.

The "Miscellaneous Poems" are uneven in quality, but have pleasing sentiment, with a turn toward the religious. While he was not highly imaginative, Payne had at least a fair sense of versification. With him as with Milton poetry had to be subservient to the will of God. He is perhaps seen at his best in the hymn entitled "The Inspiration of Nature."

Father above the concave sky,
  Enthron'd in light profound,
At thy command the lightnings fly
  And thunders roar around.

Oh, who can see the beaming sun,
  The smiling moon at night,
The snowy clouds, the countless stars,
  Shedding their rays of light,

And yet refuse to sing thy praise,
  In sweetest notes of love?
Or echo to angelic lays
  Which fill the world's above?

Whene'er I tread the blooming plains,
  And pluck the fragrant flower,

The luscious fruits, the yellow grains,
I read thy matchless power.

What moves on earth or wings the air,
Or swims the swelling sea,
Is but a ray of life to point
Immortal Man to thee.

The sapient thought, the lucid eye,
Give to my gazing soul,
To see in all beneath the sky,
Thy power and wise control.

Then will my heart and tongue unite,
When Nature's works inspire,
Thy praise to sing at morn and night,
Upon the sacred lyre.

JAMES M. WHITFIELD

The dates of James M. Whitfield are not known with definiteness, but we hear of him in the decade just before the Civil War. Born in Boston, he went to Buffalo, and as a young man worked as a barber. In 1854, fired by the spirit of Delany, he attended the National Emigration Convention of Colored Men and had with Douglass a controversy about the wisdom of calling the meeting. When it was decided to study different places to which Negroes might go, he was commissioned to Central America. He died in San Francisco on his way thither, in or about the year 1858.

After contributing poems to different papers, Whitfield published a very small book, *America, and Other Poems* (1853), with a dedication to Delany. The influence of Byron is manifest in both temper and form. Several of the pieces seem to have been written at white heat. America is addressed as the "boasted land of liberty," again as the "land of blood, and crime, and wrong." Two of the most finished poems are "Lines on the Death of John Quincy Adams" and "The North Star." The beginning and the end of "How Long?" are fairly typical of the quality of Whitfield's work, and the lines are not only significant in connection with slavery but also have meaning for a troubled world to-day.

How long, O gracious God! how long,
  Shall power lord it over right?
The feeble, trampled by the strong,
  Remain in slavery's gloomy night?
In every region of the earth,
  Oppression rules with iron power;
And every man of sterling worth,
  Whose soul disdains to cringe or cower
Beneath a haughty tyrant's nod,
And, supplicating, kiss the rod
That, wielded by oppression's might,
Smites to the earth his dearest right,—
The right to speak, and think, and feel,
  And spread his uttered thoughts abroad,
To labor for the common weal,
  Responsible to none but God,—

Is threatened with the dungeon's gloom,
The felon's cell, the traitor's doom,
And treacherous politicians league
  With hireling priests, to crush and ban
All who expose their vile intrigue,
  And vindicate the rights of man.

. . . . .

How long, O Lord! shall such vile deeds
  Be acted in thy holy name,
And senseless bigots o'er their creeds
  Fill the whole world with war and flame?
How long shall ruthless tyrants claim
  Thy sanction to their bloody laws,
And throw the mantle of thy name
  Around their foul, unhallowed cause?
How long shall all the people bow
  As vassals of the favored few,
And shame the pride of manhood's brow,—
  Give what to God alone is due,
Homage to wealth and rank and power,
Vain shadows of a passing hour?
Oh, for a pen of living fire,
  A tongue of flame, an arm of steel!
To rouse the people's slumbering ire,
  And teach the tyrants' hearts to feel.
O Lord! in vengeance now appear,
  And guide the battles for the right,
The spirits of the fainting cheer,
  And nerve the patriot's arm with might;

Till slavery's banished from the world,
And tyrants from their power hurled;
And all mankind, from bondage free,
Exult in glorious liberty.

GEORGE B. VASHON AND HIS ASSOCIATES

About the year 1850 New York Central College, an abolitionist institution located at McGrawville, New York, had on its faculty three professors who were of Negro descent. They were William G. Allen, Charles L. Reason, and George B. Vashon. All three had received unusual training and did some writing. Allen was graduated from Oneida Institute, studied law in Boston, and then became professor of the Greek and German languages and rhetoric at Central College. He contributed several letters to the *Liberator* and an essay on Placido to the 1853 edition of *Autographs for Freedom*. That he could state a case clearly may be seen from his book, *American Prejudice against Color*, that he published in London in 1853 after his marriage to one of his white students had aroused a storm in the United States. Reason, a son of Patrick Reason, the engraver, thought first of the ministry, but, meeting with opposition when he applied for entrance at the Theological Seminary of the Protestant Episcopal Church, turned to teaching. Interested in mathematics, he began to work at Central College in 1849; in 1852 became principal of the Institute for Colored Youth in Philadelphia; and, after three years there, entered upon his long career as as a teacher in the public schools of New York City, being first connected with schools 6 and 3, then principal of 80. There he was serving as late as June, 1892; he died about 1898. Reason was a man of culture and unusually handsome, with a slight and graceful figure, clearcut features, and polished manner. One is surprised accordingly to find that his verse does not show more excellence, even more correctness. An ode entitled "Freedom," printed in 1847 with *A Eulogy on the Life and Character of Thomas Clarkson,* is in grandiloquent vein but without distinction; "Hope and Confidence," a poem in *Autographs for Freedom* for 1854, has some very faulty lines; and "The Spirit Voice, or Liberty Call to the Disfranchised" and "Silent Thoughts," included in Simmons' *Men of Mark,* hardly rise above mediocrity.

Somewhat more original was George B. Vashon. This author received the degree of Bachelor of Arts at Oberlin in 1844, remained there for a year in the Theological Seminary, and became Master of Arts in 1849, the degree being conferred by reason of his progress after leaving college. After serving for some time at Central College, he was admitted to the bar in New York City in 1847, and for the next three years was a teacher in College Faustin, Port-au-Prince, Hayti. Returning to the United States in the autumn of 1850, he contributed to various periodicals and began to practice in Syracuse, but soon became principal of the one school for Negro children in Pittsburgh. His application for admission to the bar in that city having been denied on account of color, he went to Washington and was admitted. He became a professor in Howard University and died of yellow fever in Mississippi in the autumn of 1878.

Vashon wrote a fairly long poem entitled "Vincent Ogé," which was printed in abridged form in *Autographs for Freedom* for 1853. This shows him as attempting a more sustained effort than any American Negro poet who had preceded him. He uses the rhythmic, discursive, and frequently subjective manner of Scott and Byron, and is surprisingly successful. Ogé was a mulatto, a native of Hayti educated in France, who was entrusted with a message of enfranchisement to the people of mixed blood on the island from the Convention in France. The planters in the island, who previously had monopolized the rights of citizenship, seized him and saw that he was drawn and quartered, the four parts of his body being hung up in the four leading cities of the island. As a martyr to liberty he was a forerunner of Toussaint L'Ouverture. "A Life-Day" is a shorter poem in three parts founded on fact. It tells the story of a young white man and a fair young woman of color who are sincerely in love. They marry and there are children, but after twelve years the father dies and the family is remanded to slavery. Vashon used provocative material but always managed to keep attention fixed on the characters with whom he had to deal. He is perhaps best represented by the opening lines of "Vincent Ogé":

There is, at times, an evening sky—
  The twilight's gift—of sombre hue,
All checkered wild and gorgeously
  With streaks of crimson, gold and blue;—
A sky that strikes the soul with awe,
  And, though not brilliant as the sheen,
Which in the east at morn we saw,
  Is far more glorious, I ween;—
So glorious that, when night hath come
And shrouded in its deepest gloom,
We turn aside with inward pain
And pray to see that sky again.
Such sight is like the struggle made
When freedom bids unbare the blade,
And calls from every mountain-glen—
  From every hill—from every plain,
Her chosen ones to stand like men,
  And cleanse their souls from every stain
Which wretches, steeped in crime and blood,
Have cast upon the form of God.
Though peace like morning's golden hue,
  With blooming groves and waving fields,
Is mildly pleasing to the view,
  And all the blessings that it yields
Are fondly welcomed by the breast
  Which finds delight in passion's rest,
That breast with joy forgoes them all,
While listening to Freedom's call.

Though red the carnage,—though the strife
Be filled with groans of parting life,—
Though battle's dark, ensanguined skies
Give echo but to agonies—
To shrieks of wild despairing,—
We willingly suppress a sigh—
Nay, gaze with rapture in our eye,
Whilst "Freedom!" is the rally-cry
That calls to deeds of daring.

JAMES MADISON BELL

James Madison Bell (1826-1902) is of interest in connection with John Brown, but his poetry has no technical excellence. Verse was to him simply a medium for the expression of his strong convictions about slavery. Born in Gallipolis, Ohio, he went to Cincinnati when sixteen years of age to live with a brother-in-law, and there became a plasterer. From 1854 to 1860 he lived in Canada. Having become a friend of John Brown, he assisted in getting men for the raid of 1859. After that event he went to California, but at the close of the Civil War removed his family from Canada to Toledo, Ohio, and for the next few years was active in the work of the Republican Party. He was an able speaker and would often read his poems with strong effect. Bishop B. W. Arnett, a personal friend, said that he would follow his trade in the summer and autumn, and travel and read his poems in the winter. "His logic was irresistible, like a legion of cavalry led by Sheridan."

While in California Bell published *The Day and the War* (1864), dedicated to the memory of John Brown, and *The Progress of Liberty* (1866), which celebrates the Emancipation Proclamation. In 1870 appeared *The Triumph of Liberty,* which recalled the background of the war, praised Lincoln and the Negro troops, and exulted in the new day of enfranchisement. These and many shorter pieces were brought together in 1901 as *The Poetical Works of James Madison Bell,* with a biographical sketch by Bishop B. W. Arnett. The following tribute to John Brown is from *The Triumph of Liberty.*

One decade back there lived a man,
A strict, unswerving Puritan;
And though as brave as Ammon's son,
No gods had he to serve but one,
The God of Justice, God of Truth,
Whom he had served from early youth.

His heart was not inured to wrong,
Though he had seen and felt it long;
Yet had he oft implored the time
When there should be an end to crime,
When Truth should rise, assert her claim,
And wrong sink down to whence it came.

At length he grew to feel inspired
To what his heart had long desired,

To strike one blow for Liberty,
Where it should end in victory;
Though he should perish in the deed,
He felt that he could plant the seed
From which the harvest would arise,
And shrank not from the sacrifice;
Him call enthusiast, if you will,
Fanatic, or something wilder still,
It will not blur his deathless name,
Nor bar his onward march to fame.

Although like Samson he was ta'en,
And by the base Philistines slain,
Yet he in death accomplished more
Than e'er he had in life before.
His noble heart, which ne'er had failed,
Proved firm, and e'en in death prevailed;
And many a teardrop dimmed the eye
Of e'en his foes who saw him die—
And none who witnessed that foul act
Will e'er in life forget the fact.

EARLY ARTISTS

Even as early as the middle of the eighteenth century there is record to indicate the interest of individual Negroes in the arts. Thomas Fleet, a printer of Boston, owned several Negroes, and of one we are told that he was "an ingenious man and cut, on wooden blocks, all the pictures which decorated the ballads and small books of his master." We have already spoken of Scipio Moorhead, the young Negro painter of Boston to whom Phillis Wheatley addressed a poem.

About the middle of the nineteenth century Patrick Reason, of New York, attracted attention by his portrait work. He was patronized by the abolitionists and engraved the frontispieces of several biographies of former slaves. Daniel Warbourg, a free man of color in New Orleans, was also an engraver. Eugene Warbourg (1825-1861), his brother, was a sculptor. He went to Europe in 1852 and there made his reputation, two of the best of his pieces being "Le Pecheur" and "Le Premier Baiser." Outstanding among the painters of the era was Robert Duncanson (1821-1871?), who received part of his training in Europe and was primarily concerned with landscapes. He was a friend of Tennyson and was thus led to paint "The Lotos Eaters." His "Evening" is a picture of unusual merit, and among his other titles are "Ellen Isle of Loch Katrine" and "Western Hunter's Encampment." To-day his work is preserved in New York, Philadelphia, and Cincinnati. Another painter was Robert Douglass, Jr., of Philadelphia, who was interested in portrait work.

THE STAGE: IRA F. ALDRIDGE

In spite of the far-reaching influence of the Negro on American life, it is only within recent years that this racial element has received serious attention in the theatre. Shakespeare's Othello was plainly said to be a Moor rather than a Negro, and the play that bears his name is the supreme English achievement in dramatic technique; yet he has been a constant source of embarrassment in the United States. Sometimes his color has been so lightened that one could only guess at his racial identity if he were not previously informed. When in 1696 Thomas Southerne adapted *Oroonoko* from the novel of Aphra Behn, still no one saw any reason why the Negro should not be a subject for tragedy. In 1768, however, a comic opera, *The Padlock,* was presented at Drury Lane, and a prominent character was Mungo, the degraded and profane slave of a West Indian planter. In the next century the development of Negro minstrelsy, and the antics of Topsy in *Uncle Tom's Cabin,* simply accelerated a movement that had already begun.

It was in this day of depreciation and of agitation against slavery that a Negro broke through to fame in the classic drama.

Ira Frederick Aldridge (*c.* 1805-1867) was born in Africa while his father, a native prince who in America had become an evangelist, was on a sojourn in the mother country. His early years were spent in Maryland, where he was apprenticed as a ship carpenter and learned to speak German. It was intended that he should enter the ministry, but he was employed as an attendant by Edmund Kean when that great actor visited the country; Kean was impressed by his ability and began to teach him. In 1826 Aldridge made his début as Othello at the Royalty

Theatre in London. Meeting with success, he made a tour of England and Ireland on which he played Othello to the Iago of Charles Kean, son of Edmund. A few years later he made a trip to America and played in Baltimore, but, not being well received, thenceforth forsook the country.

In 1833, his art having matured, Aldridge appeared at Covent Garden in London, and for the next thirty years was one of the great actors of the world. He played Macbeth and Lear as well as parts adapted to his color, but thrilled his audiences most as Othello. Often on the Continent he would speak in English while the other performers used their own language, and even with this arrangement he was successful. In the old Russian capital, St. Petersburg, so realistic was his portrayal that the actress playing Desdemona screamed with real fright. On another occasion in the same city, when he came to the speech in the last act beginning, "It is the cause, it is the cause, my soul," the house was so completely carried away that a young man in the audience leaped up, exclaiming, "She is innocent, Othello; she is innocent." The actor moved not a muscle but continued as if nothing had been said. The next day, while dining with a prince, he learned that a young man who had been present was so affected by the play that he became ill and died within a few hours.

Aldridge received tokens of the highest esteem. The King of Prussia gave him an autograph letter with a first class medal of the arts and sciences. The Emperor of Austria conferred the Grand Cross of Leopold. At Berne he was given the medal of merit, and at St. Petersburg honorary membership in the Imperial Academy of Beaux Arts. These souvenirs with others he treasured in a palatial residence near London, meanwhile evincing keen interest in anything affecting the welfare of the people with whom he was identified. He died in Lodz, Poland, while on his way to fill an engagement in Russia.

MUSIC: JUSTIN HOLLAND, ELIZABETH TAYLOR GREENFIELD, AND THOMAS J. BOWERS

In the two decades just before the Civil War appeared here and there in the United States, especially among the free people of color in Louisiana, a number of competent musicians. The fact that Negro fiddlers often assisted at balls doubtless helped in the general development. Several talented persons who rose in the far South left for foreign countries, where their color would not retard their progress. Most of those who rose to distinction flourished just after the war, but at least a few must be mentioned here.

Frank Johnson, of Philadelphia, about 1840 organized an orchestra that developed into a band specializing in martial music. This organization was made up of men who could read music at sight and met with sensational success. In England it gave concerts in all the principal cities. Queen Victoria was so pleased with a performance at court that she gave the leader a silver bugle. The general effect of Johnson's work was to elevate musical standards. He himself died in 1846, but the band continued to use his name for a number of years, being ably directed by Joseph G. Anderson.

Justin Holland was born in Virginia, but from the time he was fourteen until he was grown lived in Boston or Chelsea, Massachusetts. Having been inspired by Mariano Perez, a Spanish musician, and having the benefit of instruction from excellent teachers, he became a skillful performer on the guitar. In 1841, when twenty-two years of age, he went to Oberlin, where he made rapid advance in his studies. In 1845 he went to Cleveland, then a city of not more than nine thousand inhabitants, and his fine playing on his chosen instrument led to his being employed to teach in several prominent families. Thenceforth that city was his home, and he also became a finished performer on the piano and the flute. In order to study the best systems of guitar-playing abroad, he learned French, Spanish, and Italian; and at length, in 1874, through J. L. Peters and Company, of New York, published *Holland's Comprehensive Method for the Guitar*. Two years later a revision, *Holland's Modern Method for the Guitar,* was issued by Oliver Ditson, of Boston; and among the firms publishing the author's adaptations or arrangements were S. Brainard's Sons, of Cleveland, and John Church, of Cincinnati.

The Luca family was identified with Connecticut. As at first organized for professional purposes, it consisted of six persons—the father, the mother, and four sons. The father, born in Milford, Connecticut, in 1805, spent his early years on a farm but when twenty-one became apprentice to a shoemaker. While thus engaged he began to attend the village singing-school. Removing to New Haven, he became chorister in a Congregational church and married a young woman who was a singer. One of his sons, Simeon, "possessed a tenor voice of extraordinary compass, singing high C with the greatest ease" and delighting audiences with his selections from the great operas. Another son, Cleveland, was at the age of ten such a skillful pianist that he won the praise of noted musicians in New York. Often he created a furore by his brilliant playing. Sometimes an incredulous or prejudiced person would seek to embarrass him by a difficult test, but he always left the field with honor. Going to Liberia about 1860, he composed the national anthem for that country and died there in 1872.

In New Orleans Richard Lambert was well known as a teacher of music about 1850. There were two younger sons and two daughters, but distinction attaches to the work of the two older sons, Lucien and Sidney, both of whom became composers. Lucien

Lambert made it a rule to give six hours a day to practice on the piano, and in time excited the admiration and even the wonder of his audiences. Growing restless under the restraints of life in New Orleans, he went to Paris for further study, and finally to Brazil, where he became a manufacturer of pianos. Trotter lists among his compositions "La Juive," "Le Départ du Conscrit," "Les Ombres Aimées," "Le Brésiliana," "Paris Vienne," "Le Niagara," and "La Rose et le Bengali." Sidney Lambert, also a pianist, was decorated by the King of Portugal and later became a teacher in Paris. Among the pieces that he wrote or arranged are "Si j'étais Roi," "Murmures du Soir," "L'Africaine," "Transports Joyeux," and "Les Cloches."

Among the singers was at least one who evoked comparison with Jenny Lind, Parodi, and Malibran.

Elizabeth Taylor (1809-1876) was born in Natchez, Mississippi, but when hardly more than an an infant passed into the care of a Quaker lady of Philadelphia, who reared her attendant with as much care as she would have given a daughter. In course of time the young woman added the name of her benefactress, Greenfield, to her own. The story goes that the daughter of a friendly physician, having heard her sing, began to give her lessons. She was making rapid progress when someone informed Mrs. Greenfield about what was going on—maliciously, it seems, for it was thought that all such effort would be forbidden. "Elizabeth," asked the old lady, "is it true that thee is learning music and can play upon the guitar?" "It is true," was the trembling reply. "Go get thy guitar and let me hear thee sing." Elizabeth did so and when she had finished was thrilled to hear her friend say, "Elizabeth, whatever thee wants thee shall have."

Mrs. Greenfield died in 1844. By her will a substantial legacy was left for her attendant, but there was a contest and the money was not received. Thrown on her own resources, the young woman went to visit some friends in the western part of the state of New York. On the way to Buffalo she impressed the wife of an army officer by her singing, and that lady became her friend and patroness. In fact, for the next few years the city of Buffalo may almost be said to have adopted her. After a concert in 1851 before the Buffalo Musical Association a critic said: "Her voice has a full, round sound, and is of immense compass and depth. She strikes every note in a clear and well-defined manner, and reaches the highest capacity of the human voice with wonderful ease, and apparently an entire want of exertion. Beginning with G in the bass clef, she runs up the scale to E in the treble clef, and gives each note its full power and tone." The *Daily State Register,* of Albany, said (January 19, 1852): "Her singing more than met the expectation of her hearers, and elicited the heartiest applause and frequent encores. The compass of her marvelous voice embraces twenty-seven notes, reaching from the sonorous bass of a baritone to a few notes above even Jenny Lind's highest."

After appearing in nearly all of the free states, the singer decided to go to Europe in order to improve in technique. Learning of her intentions, the citizens of Buffalo tendered her a benefit concert. On her arrival in England, however, in April, 1853, she found the man with whom she had contracted unfaithful to his promises. Alone in a strange country, with little money and no prospects, she appealed to Lord Shaftesbury, who was known for his public spirit. That nobleman granted an interview and gave a letter to his lawyer. Harriet Beecher Stowe, who was then in London, and the Duchess of Sutherland also became interested. Mrs. Stowe described her at this time as dark in color, "of a pleasing and gentle face, though by no means handsome," saying further that she was "short and thick-set, with a chest of great amplitude, as one would think on hearing her tenor." At a concert in the hall of Stafford House after dinner, Sir George Smart, organist of the Chapel Royal, presided. With a touch of the informality of the occasion, he took Miss Greenfield to the piano between the parts of the program and tried her voice by striking notes at random, "from D in alto to A first space in bass clef." The singer followed with unerring precision and was greeted with rapturous applause. A little later she sang before Queen Victoria in Buckingham Palace. After a concert in Exeter Hall the *London Advertiser* (June 16, 1853) said: "Her voice is a contralto, of great clearness and mellow tone in the upper register, and full, resonant, and powerful in the lower, though slightly masculine in its *timbre*. It is peculiarly effective in ballad-songs of the pathetic cast." She remained in England a little more than a year and then the Duchess of Sutherland arranged for her passage home. Residing in Philadelphia in her later years, she occasionally appeared in concert but devoted most of her time to teaching.

One of her students was Thomas J. Bowers, who came of a musical family and was from all accounts a tenor of the first rank. This singer was a handsome man with fine stage presence. He was also a person with positive convictions. Sometimes he was asked to pose as an Indian, but declined. Moreover, if Negro people were discriminated against in the seating at his concerts, he would not sing until such injustice was rectified. He was opposed to the impression made by minstrel troupes, ever insisting on the highest ideals. He himself used such selections as "Spirito Gentil," from *La Favorita*, "Ah! I have sighed," from *Il Trovatore*, and "How so Fair," from *Martha;* and these he sang with a voice of extraordinary power, mellowness, and sweetness. He once made a tour of New York and Canada with Miss Greenfield, the two everywhere meeting with success.

IV

LITERATURE, 1865-1890

ALEXANDER CRUMMELL—GEORGE W. WILLIAMS—ALBERY A. WHITMAN—FRANCES E. W. HARPER

NEGRO literature in the generation after the Civil War was largely dominated by the political temper. It was the new day of freedom and men of the race sat in the National Congress. Before the period was over, the modern industrial development of the South had begun, and the Negro as an active political factor in the section declined.

Three of the men in Congress who were prominent as public speakers were Blanche K. Bruce, Robert B. Elliott, and later, John Mercer Langston. Bruce, of Mississippi, was the first man of Negro descent to serve a full term as United States senator. While he always remembered the people whom he represented, he also placed himself upon the broadest plane of statesmanship and won the respect of his colleagues accordingly. Elliott, a representative from South Carolina, had received much of his training in England. Highly intelligent, he knew well the arts of the orator and could be urbanely ironical. He is remembered chiefly by reason of a speech on the Civil Rights Bill in January, 1874, his opponent being

Alexander Stephens, formerly vice-president of the Confederacy. Langston, a congressman from Virginia in the winter of 1890-1891, was a graduate of Oberlin and a man of culture. Among the best of his occasional addresses were eulogies of Daniel O'Connell and Charles Sumner. On the Negro Exodus of 1879 he opposed Douglass, saying, "Let the freedman come to the North; let him go to the West, and his contact with new men, new things, a new order of life, new moral and educational influences will advance him in the scale of being in an incomparably short time, even beyond the expectations of the most sanguine."

A number of writers and speakers previously prominent continued their work far into or throughout the period, notably Douglass, Payne, and Brown; but the chief authors now to be considered are, in the occasional essay, Alexander Crummell; in history, George W. Williams; and in poetry, Albery A. Whitman and Frances E. W. Harper.

ALEXANDER CRUMMELL

Alexander Crummell (1819-1898) was one of Garnet's companions in the experience at the ill-fated academy in Canaan, New Hampshire, in 1835. While the two men were lifelong friends, they were years apart in the height of their influence. Garnet, four years the older, came into prominence early and is remembered chiefly by reason of his militant opposition to slavery. If he had passed as early as 1850, his reputation would not have been essentially changed. Crummell, a man of riper culture, seemed mainly concerned with the outlook for Africa and with moral and spiritual training. He spent years in England and Liberia before doing his best work in the United States. Surviving his friend by sixteen years, he was about 1890 one of the elder statesmen of the race.

Crummell underwent many trials in his endeavor to prepare himself for the Episcopal ministry. After early work at Oneida Institute, he at last succeeded in studying theology in Boston, and in 1847 went to England to solicit funds for a church he hoped to build in his native city, New York. After receiving the degree of Bachelor of Arts at the University of Cambridge in 1853, he was led by considerations of his health to seek a warmer climate. For most of the next twenty years he was in Liberia, and for the last twenty-two years of his life served as rector of St. Luke's Episcopal Church in Washington. Tall, erect, and noble in bearing, he was a marked man in any assemblage.

As early as 1847 Crummell published in New York a eulogy of Thomas Clarkson. Some of his later addresses were widely circulated. When the Reverend J. L. Tucker spoke in scurrilous terms about the Negro at the Church Congress in Richmond in 1882, he replied with "A Defence of the Negro Race in

America." "The Black Woman of the South: Her Neglects and her Needs" was a notable address before the Freedman's Aid Society of the Methodist Episcopal Church in 1882. There were three collections, each well indicated by its title, *The Future of Africa* (1862), *The Greatness of Christ, and Other Sermons* (1882), and *Africa and America* (1891). This last includes the three pamphlets or addresses first referred to, and others delivered over a period of more than forty years. All are in a style that in precision and elasticity is far above the average. While Crummell was largely concerned with the future of Liberia, "a rising Christian state" as he termed it in one address, he had a message infinitely more far-reaching, one closely connected with the subject of this book. He was perhaps the first man of the race who fully perceived the danger of emphasis on æsthetic rather than moral values. He irritated a number of people by a sermon in 1886 on "Common Sense in Common Schooling." Said he: "Everywhere I go throughout the country I discover two or three very disagreeable and unhealthy facts. I see, first of all, the vain ambition of very many mothers to over-educate their daughters, and to give them training and culture unfitted for their position in society and unadapted to their prospects in life. I see, likewise, too many men, forgetful of the occupations they held in society, anxious to shoot their sons suddenly, regardless of fitness, into literary characters and into professional life. This is the first evil. Next to this I have observed an ambition among the youth of both sexes for æsthetical culture; an inordinate desire for the ornamental and elegant in education to the neglect of the solid and practical. And thirdly, to a very large extent school children are educated in letters to a neglect of household industry. Scores of both boys and girls go to school. That is their life business and nothing else; but their parents neglect their training in housework, and so they live in the streets, and during the first twelve or fourteen years of their life are given to play and pleasure. And lastly, our boys and girls almost universally grow up without trades, looking forward, if they do look forward, many of them, to being servants and waiters; and many more, I am afraid, expecting to get a living by chance and hap-hazard."

This idea was further developed in an address of unusual cogency on "Rightmindedness," given to the young men of the Garnet Lyceum at Lincoln University. In this the speaker said: "We should put things in their proper order. All real success springs from that inward might which we exert upon society. . . . That training is the best which puts us in possession of our several capacities. The process by which this is effected is termed discipline. . . . We have various and diverse aptitudes. They are sign boards of duty. But don't be mastered by them; cultivate the very study you dislike. Bend your powers to the attainments to which you feel yourselves averse. . . . I have ventured to present this special train of thought because you are colored young men and, as such, allied to a people whose special need, for a long time, will be strength. You have got to organize a people who have been living nigh two hundred years under a system of the most destructive mental, moral, and physical disorganization the world has ever seen. . . . The youth of the present day are very many years in advance of their fathers. One marked and dangerous peculiarity, however, constantly betrays itself: the stream of tendency among cultivated colored Americans is too exclusively *æsthetical.* There is a universal inclination to that which is pleasing, polished, and adorning. There is much elegance and real taste in house decoration, and dress is everywhere and, in a true sense of the term, a Fine Art. The mind of our people seems to be a hot-bed of rich, precocious, gorgeous, and withal genuine plants. . . . At the same time, I must say that this love of the beautiful among our people shows all the signs of being but a mere possession. It looks like tendency and but little else. I see nowhere any counterbalance of the hardier studies and more tasking scholarship which serve to give vigor, hardihood, and robustness to a race. . . . If you are to be leaders, teachers, and guides among your people, you must have strength. No people can be fed, no people can be built up on flowers."

GEORGE W. WILLIAMS

George Washington Williams (1849-1891) lived for only forty-two years, but within that time he spent several years in the army, became ordained as a Baptist minister, and wrote the most thoroughgoing history of the Negro that had yet appeared in the United States. His career is almost bewildering in its frequent changes, but, as so often happens in such cases, through all that he did there ran a vein of consistent purpose.

Williams was born in Bedford Spring, Pennsylvania, his father being of Negro and Welsh and his mother of Negro and German descent. From his mother he inherited an interest in history and literature. When fourteen years of age he ran away and, against the advice of the examining surgeon, enlisted in the United States Army. He rose rapidly, was wounded and honorably discharged, then re-enlisted, and came to the end of the war with the rank of sergeant-major. He then entered the Mexican army, became a colonel, and, after the capture and death of Maximilian, returned to the United States and joined the regular cavalry, serving with bravery in the Comanche campaign. All this was before he was twenty years of age.

In February, 1868, while still in the far West, Williams was converted. He now decided to withdraw from the life of a warrior and to return to the East.

Applying himself to study, he was graduated in 1874 from the Newton Theological Institution, and ordained at a council called by the First Baptist Church in Watertown. Already for a year he had been pastor of the Twelfth Baptist Church in Boston. He served another year, then went to Washington to engage in newspaper work. Douglass and Langston gave their support to the *Commoner* that he started, but he soon abandoned his publishing venture and went to work in the post-office. There he remained for less than two months, for in February, 1876, he was called to the Union Baptist Church in Cincinnati. He served until near the close of the next year, by which time he was nominee for the legislature from Hamilton County. Aside from his term in the Ohio legislature, we hear of his being in the Internal Revenue, also of his serving as judge advocate of the Grand Army of the Republic of Ohio.

A Fourth of July address that he had to deliver in 1876 awoke in Williams an interest in the history of the Negro. For the next seven years he applied himself diligently and then produced his *History of the Negro Race in America from 1619 to 1880,* the work being issued in two large volumes by G. P. Putnam's Sons in 1883. Immediately thereafter he went again to Boston, and, working in poverty and loneliness, pressed forward with *A History of the Negro Troops in the War of the Rebellion,* published by Harper and Brothers in 1888. To the two works he had given twelve years of labor. We hear also of some poetry, three novels, and a tragedy that he wrote, but none of these were formally issued.

In the preparation of his *History of the Negro Race in America* Williams said that he consulted "over twelve thousand volumes,—about one thousand of which are referred to in the footnotes,—and thousands of pamphlets." The results reward his diligence. There are nine large sections or parts, each containing several chapters. As to the first section Williams defended himself as follows: "Two thoughts led me to prepare the chapters under the head of *Preliminary Considerations.* First, the defenders of slavery and the traducers of the Negro built their proslavery arguments upon biblical ethnology and the curse of Canaan. I am alive to the fact that, while I am a believer in the Holy Bible, it is not the best authority on ethnology. As far as it goes, it is agreeable to my head and heart. Whatever science has added I have gladly appropriated. I make no claim, however, to be a specialist. . . . Second, a growing desire among the enlightened Negroes in America to learn all that is possible from research concerning the antiquity of the race,—Africa, its inhabitants, and the development of the Negro governments of Sierra Leone and Liberia, led me to furnish something to meet a felt need."

As might be expected when the author was trained for the ministry, the style of the *History* is oratorical, with a fondness for biblical phrase. The quality of the work is uneven; some subjects are treated fully while others are passed over lightly. The prime emphasis is on military matters. Williams endeavors to write objectively, but sometimes his strong feeling overmasters him. No shortcoming, however, must be allowed to loom too large. The *History* is a painstaking performance and amply deserved the acclaim with which it was received. The following paragraph on the Negro Exodus may serve to show the oratorical style, the frequent employment of allusion, also an occasional inharmonious effect in the periods:

The story of the emigration of a people has often been repeated since the world began. The Israelites of old, with their wanderings of forty years, furnish the theme of an inspired poem as old as history itself. The dreadful tale of the Kalmuck Tartars, in 1770, fleeing from their enemies, the Russians, over the desolate steppes of Asia in midwinter; starting out six hundred thousand strong, men, women, and children, with their flocks and herds, and reaching the confines of China with only two hundred thousand left, formed an era in oriental annals, and made a combination from which new races of men have sprung. But still more appropriate to this occasion is the history of the Huguenots of France, driven by religious persecution to England and Ireland, where, under their influence, industries sprang up as the flowers of the field, and what was England's gain was irreparable loss to France. The expulsion of the Arcadians, a harmless and inoffensive people, from Nova Scotia, is another instance of the revenge that natural laws inflict upon tyranny and injustice. Next to the persecuted Pilgrims crossing a dreary ocean in mid-winter to the sterile coasts of a land of savages for freedom's sake, history hardly furnishes a more touching picture than that of the forty thousand homeless, friendless, starving Negroes going to a land already consecrated with the blood of the martyrs to the cause of free soil and unrestricted liberty. It was grandly strange that these poor people, persecuted, beaten with many stripes, hungry, friendless, and without clothing or shelter, should instinctively seek home in Kansas where John Brown had fought the first battle for liberty and the restriction of slavery! Some journeyed all the way from Texas to Kansas in teams, with great horned oxen, and little steers in front no larger than calves, bowing eagerly to the weary load. Worn and weary with the nine weeks' journey, the travellers strained their eyes toward the land of hope, blindly yet beautifully "trustin' de good Lord." Often they buried their dead as soon as they arrived, many dying on the hard floor of the hastily-built wooden barracks before beds could be provided, but praying all night long and saying touchingly: "Come, Lord Jesus. Come quickly. Come with dyin' grace in one hand and savin' love in the other."

ALBERY A. WHITMAN

One of those who were inspired by the zeal of Bishop Daniel A. Payne was Albery Allson Whitman (1851-1901), probably the ablest of the poets of the race before Dunbar.

Whitman was born in the Green River country, Hart County, Kentucky. His parents died early and

Emancipation found him still a boy. He improved the limited opportunity he had to get an education, and by the time he was twenty-six years of age was pastor of an African Methodist Episcopal Church in Springfield, Ohio, and financial agent of Wilberforce University. Thenceforth his life was one of ceaseless activity as a pastor, evangelist, and writer. He served in various places until in 1899 he went to St. Philip's A. M. E. Church in Savannah, Georgia. When the edifice was destroyed by a storm, he started rebuilding, but was soon sent by the bishop to Allen Temple in Atlanta, where he died before the completion of his fiftieth year.

Looking back when he was still not forty years of age Whitman said: "I was 'bred to the plow.' Amid the rugged hills, along the banks of Green River in Kentucky, I enjoyed the inestimable blessings of cabin life and hard work during the whole of my early days. I was in bondage,—*I never was a slave,*—the infamous laws of a savage despotism took my substance—what of that? Many a man has lost all he had, excepting his manhood. Adversity is the school of heroism, endurance the majesty of man, and hope the torch of high aspirations. Acquainted with adversity, I am flattered of hope and comforted by endurance." In the same connection he said: "Petition and complaint are the language of imbecility and cowardice—the evidences of that puerile fear which extinguishes the soul. The time has come when all 'Uncle Toms' and

'Topsies' ought to die. Goody goodness is a sort of man worship; ignorance is its inspiration, fear its ministering spirit, and beggary its inheritance. Genius, in a right good soul, is the highest impress of the Divine Image on clay. It alone can have the respect of God and man."

One of the reasons for the publishing of the poet's first book *Not a Man and Yet a Man* (1877), was the hope that being better known he might speak more effectively for Wilberforce. The work has running through it a fairly clear story but is a medley of imitative versification. There are echoes of the eighteenth century poets, also of Scott and Byron, Longfellow and Whittier. The hero is Rodney, a slave six feet three and "eighty-five per cent Saxon," who performs prodigies of valor. The story is set in Saville, a town in the Middle West in which the most prominent man is Sir Maxey, Rodney's master. Not far away is an Indian village, and so much attention is given to the maiden Nanawawa that one surmises that she was first intended as the central figure in an independent story on the order of *Hiawatha,* though Whitman's handling of the trochaic tetrameter shows as yet neither Longfellow's ear for metrical effect nor that poet's skillful use of repetition. Some huntsmen invade the Indian village and one wantonly shoots Nanawawa. There is a battle and many of the settlers are slain. Rodney, who scornfully reproaches the white men for their cowardice, is sent to Fort Dearborn for assistance. Though none can be sent, his bravery wins for him the friendly interest of Sir Maxey's daughter Dora. He returns to find Saville burned and Dora a captive. In an Indian encampment he rescues her single-handed, then takes her to Fort Dearborn. Her father has promised that whoever rescued her should have her hand, and gold besides; but when he finds that Rodney is the hero he has his slave sold down in Florida. There Rodney meets and loves the fair slave Leeona. The two escape and after many vicissitudes, including the loss of their little one, succeed in reaching Canada.

The poem is diffuse and discursive, but still interesting as Whitman's first long experiment in verse. There are many technical faults, the imagery being especially confused; but whenever one has about decided that the author is not worthy of consideration, he insists on a revision of judgment. The fact is that he shows a gift for brisk narrative, also a romantic lavishness of description with which one has to reckon.

> The tall forests swim in a crimson sea,
> Out of whose bright depths rising silently,
> Great golden spires shoot into the skies,
> Among the isles of cloudland high, that rise,
> Float, scatter, burst, drift off, and slowly fade,
> Deep in the twilight, shade succeeding shade.
>
> . . . . .

And now she turns upon a mossy seat,
Where sings a fern-bound stream beneath her feet,
And breathes the orange in the swooning air;
Where in her queenly pride the rose blooms fair,
And sweet geranium waves her scented hair;
There, gazing in the bright face of the stream,
Her thoughts swim onward in a gentle dream.

Great advance was indicated by *The Rape of Florida*, published in 1884 and reprinted the next year as *Twasinta's Seminoles; or, The Rape of Florida.* This production is notable as an attempt to use the Spenserian stanza throughout a long piece of work. The story is concerned with the capture of the Seminoles in Florida through perfidy and their removal to the West. It centers around three characters, Palmecho, an old chief, Ewald, his daughter, and Atlassa, Ewald's lover. This poem also is diffuse, nor is the characterization strong. Again and again, however, stanzas of merit strike the eye.

"Come now, my love, the moon is on the lake;
  Upon the water is my light canoe;
Come with me, love, and gladsome oars shall make
  A music on the parting wave for you,—
  Come o'er the waters deep and dark and blue;
Come where the lilies in the marge have sprung,
  Come with me, love, for Oh, my love is true!"
This is the song that on the lake was sung,
The boatman sang it over when his heart was young.

ALBERY A. WHITMAN

Twasinta's Seminoles; or, The Rape of Florida appeared in a third edition in 1890, and along with it *Not a Man and Yet a Man*, "second edition, carefully revised," and some miscellaneous poems under the general title, *Drifted Leaves*. In *Not a Man and Yet a Man* the sections on Nanawawa and the Indians have for the most part been done away with; many of the section headings have also disappeared; and there are numerous changes in the text. In this form the poem is much better co-ordinated.

Whitman continued to experiment and advance. In 1901 he published *An Idyl of the South*, "an epic poem in two parts." "The Octoroon" uses the tragic theme of the honest love of the son of a slaveholder for a beautiful slave. "The Southland's Charms and Freedom's Magnitude" moralizes about events connected with the Civil War, with tribute to Grant and Lee alike and a vision of a better day. There are some colloquialisms, but on the whole the *ottava rima* is competently handled.

The shorter pieces are mainly in the nature of youthful experiment, though "A Night among the Mountains of the Winding Tennessee," with its warning to a revenue officer not to be found in the section again, rises above triteness. "Custar's Last Ride" is reminiscent of both Drayton's "Ballad of Agincourt" and Tennyson's "The Charge of the Light Brigade." Among the poems printed as leaflets or pamphlets and not included in any of the volumes are "Bishop Allen" and "The Freedman's Triumphant Song," read at the World's Fair in Chicago September 22, 1893. It is to be regretted that Whitman did not have the training that comes from the best university education. He had the taste and the talent to benefit from such culture in the highest degree.

FRANCES E. W. HARPER

Frances E. W. Harper (1825-1911) was distinctly a minor poet, though sometimes her feeling flashed out in felicitous lines. To account for her reputation one must recall that she was more than a writer. For six years before the Civil War she was an anti-slavery agent in the East, and for more than three decades thereafter a lecturer in the South on temperance and home-building. Her prime concern was with moral and social reform.

Frances Ellen Watkins was born of free parents in Baltimore. When she was three years old her mother died, and at thirteen she had to earn her own living. When grown to womanhood she served for three years as a teacher in Ohio, but an incident of the year 1853 led her to devote herself to effort for freedom. Maryland passed an act forbidding free Negroes from the North to come to the state on penalty of being imprisoned and sold into slavery. A man who unwittingly violated this statute was sold into Georgia. Endeavoring to escape, he hid himself behind the wheel house of a boat bound for the North, but was discovered and remanded to slavery. He then died of exposure and hardship. "Upon that grave," said Miss Watkins, "I pledged myself to the anti-slavery cause." She became interested in the work of the "underground railroad" and in 1854 was engaged as a lecturer by the Anti-Slavery Society of Maine. In 1860, in Cincinnati, she married Fenton Harper, who died just four years later. After the war she worked under the auspices of the Woman's Christian Temperance Union. Her manner in her speeches was dignified; she made few gestures and was never theatrical.

Mrs. Harper's poems were the ornaments of her public addresses. Because she most frequently printed them in paper-back booklets that sold for a quarter or even less, it is now difficult to find copies of her work, while the rearrangements and the different editions offer the bibliographer a genuine problem. William Still, who wrote the Introduction to the novel, *Iola Leroy,* published in 1892, enumerated five previous publications—*Forest Leaves, Miscellaneous Poems, Moses: A Story of the Nile, Poems,* and *Sketches of Southern Life.* Of the first of these no copy is known to exist. *Poems on Miscellaneous Subjects* appeared in 1854 and by 1871 was in the twentieth edition. *Moses* was in the second edition in 1869, appeared in enlarged form in 1889, and was the chief piece in a collection entitled *Idylls of the Bible* (1901), though it must be said that this hardly lives up to its name. *Poems,* first appearing as a new collection in 1871, was enlarged more than once and by 1895 made a beautiful booklet of ninety pages, more firmly bound than usual. *Sketches of Southern Life,* first issued in twenty-four small pages in 1872, was enlarged in 1896.

With the exception of *Moses* and some shorter pieces on biblical subjects, Mrs. Harper's poems were mainly a reflection of the life of the Negro. In her loose, flowing meters she showed the influence of Longfellow and Felicia Dorothea Hemans. The secret of her popularity is to be seen in such lines as the following from "Bury Me in a Free Land":

> Make me a grave where'er you will,
> In a lowly plain or a lofty hill;
> Make it among earth's humblest graves,
> But not in a land where men are slaves.

Of the Emancipation Proclamation she wrote:

> It shall flash through coming ages,
>   It shall light the distant years;
> And eyes now dim with sorrow
>   Shall be brighter through their tears.

Of little children she said:

> I almost think the angels
>   Who tend life's garden fair,
> Drop down the sweet white blossoms
>   That bloom around us here.

In *Sketches of Southern Life* the speaker is Aunt Chloe, who recalls various experiences, among them the selling of her two boys away from their parents and the later happy reunion of the family. *Moses,* intended as a religious epic, records different incidents in the life of the lawgiver in what was an attempt at blank verse. Of the shorter pieces on biblical subjects "Vashti" stands out with something of distinction.

> She leaned her head upon her hand
> And heard the King's decree—
> "My lords are feasting in my halls;
> Bid Vashti come to me.
>
> "I've shown the treasures of my house,
> My costly jewels rare,
> But with the glory of her eyes
> No rubies can compare.
>
> "Adorn'd and crown'd I'd have her come,
> With all her queenly grace,
> And mid my lords and mighty men
> Unveil her lovely face.
>
> "Each gem that sparkles in my crown,
> Or glitters on my throne,
> Grows poor and pale when she appears,
> My beautiful, my own!"
>
> . . . . .
>
> She heard again the King's command,
> And left her high estate;

Strong in her earnest womanhood,
She calmly met her fate,

And left the palace of the King,
Proud of her spotless name—
A woman who could bend to grief
But would not bow to shame.

Iola Leroy is a story set mainly in North Carolina at the time of the Civil War. The heroine is an octoroon, the daughter of a wealthy planter and a beautiful woman of color who were supposed to be legally married. After she has had numerous adventures and trials, Negro friends help her to reach the Union lines. She becomes a nurse and is loved by a noble young officer, but at last marries a physician who might have denied his Negro descent but chooses not to do so. The book throbs with human interest, but lacks the smoothness of a well constructed piece of work, and especially toward the close assumes a didactic tone. Matter that in the hands of a finished novelist like Jane Austen would have been sufficient for a book is often rushed over in a page. The language is often stilted, chiefly so when Eugene Leroy, Iola's father, is speaking. As a whole the book is hardly more than an interesting experiment.

OTHER WRITERS

Many other Negroes were writing in the quarter of a century immediately after the Civil War, but for the most part their work was not creative. Several books were reminiscent of the struggle against slavery, and biography was accordingly prominent. This was the period of Langston's collection of addresses, *Freedom and Citizenship* (1883) and of Bishop Payne's *Recollections of Seventy Years* (1888). Frances E. Rollin Whipper, writing under the name Frank A. Rollin, produced the *Life and Public Services of Martin R. Delany* (1883), a book bright with fact and incident. Elizabeth Keckley, a modiste to Mary Todd Lincoln at the time of the war, published *Behind the Scenes; or, Thirty Years a Slave, and Four Years in the White House* (1868). The book was long neglected but has received much attention in recent years by reason of its vivid portrayal of the President's wife, especially when she was in straitened circumstances after the assassination of her husband. The author, who evidently had a mind of her own, also gave many sidelights on the striving of the Negro in the period. James M. Trotter, of Boston, produced *Music and Some Highly Musical People* (1879), a labor of love so well done that it is still our chief source of information for the earlier years. William J. Simmons, a dynamic and inspiring leader of the Baptists, interested in politics as well as religion and education, published *Men of Mark* (1887), a large biographical work that is not always accurate but that gives so much information not elsewhere obtainable that it is still valuable for reference. Joseph C. Price, the first president of Livingstone College, anticipated Booker T. Washington in cultivating friendly relations with the South and at the time of his early death (1893) had a name synonymous with eloquence, but unfortunately left little to give posterity an idea of his merit.

T. Thomas Fortune, one of the most intelligent and versatile Negroes of the era, long connected with the *New York Age*, produced even when a young man *Black and White: Land, Labor, and Politics in the South* (1884) and *The Negro in Politics* (1885), but was not so good when he turned to verse, as in *Dreams of Life: Miscellaneous Poems* (1905). The first of these books emphasized the need of elementary and industrial training, and Fortune later assisted Booker T. Washington in organizing the National Negro Business League. *The Negro in Politics* opposed the lack of independent thinking implied in the statement by Douglass that "for the Negro the Republican party is the deck; all else is the sea," and the author scored the tendency, "the outgrowth of ignorance, to brand as a traitor any man of us who has the intelligence and the courage to protest against the broken promises, the sugar-coated capsules, of political mountebanks." Another man of the period who wrote verse—verse better for its spirit than its technique—was George C. Rowe, pastor of the Plymouth Congregational Church, of Charleston, South Carolina, and author of *Thoughts in Verse* and *Patri-*

otic Poems. "A Noble Life," a poem of a dozen stanzas in memory of Joseph C. Price, was published independently in Charleston in 1894.

> A star arose at close of night:
> 'Tis dark before the dawn;
> A brilliant star, a righteous light,
> Foretoken of the morn—
> The day when the oppressor's hand
> Shall palsied be throughout the land.
>
> The tongue of fire is silent now;
> The loving heart is still;
> The mind surcharged with burning thought,
> Yet loyal to God's will,
> Has ceased to plan for mortals here,
> Is active in another sphere.

V

MUSIC AND ART, 1865-1895

"CENTENNIAL ARTISTS"—FISK JUBILEE SINGERS—"BLIND TOM"—THE HYERS SISTERS—MARIE SELIKA—FLORA BATSON BERGEN—SISSIERETTA JONES

The three decades just after the Civil War witnessed a flowering of effort in the field of music and, in only slightly less degree, in that of art. Some of the musicians who had become known before the war continued their work, and some of the greatest singers in the whole range of Negro history now appeared on the scene. It was as if the aspiration of a whole people, now emancipated, had found a voice in song.

The first organization of its kind to achieve any measure of success was "The Colored American Opera Company," formed in Washington in 1872 by a number of talented amateurs. In February, 1873, the troupe gave a total of seven performances of Julius Eichberg's *The Doctor of Alcantara* in Philadelphia and Washington, closing at Ford's Theatre in the latter city with much favorable comment in the press. Representative of those musicians who left the South for the freer air of foreign countries was

Edmund Dédé (1829-1903), a violinist, who was born of free parents in New Orleans and ultimately became director of the orchestra of L'Alcazar in Bordeaux, France. He composed numerous orchestral works, among them *Les Faux Mandarins* and *Le Palmier Overture.* José White (1833-1920), violinist and composer, won the commendation of some of the foremost musicians in the world by his masterly playing. Born in Cuba, he spent most of his life in France, but in 1876 visited the United States, appearing in New York at a Philharmonic Concert given by the Theodore Thomas Orchestra.

A beautiful and cultured singer who narrowly missed greatness was Nellie E. Brown (*c.* 1848-1924), of Dover, New Hampshire, who became the wife of Lieutenant Charles L. Mitchell, of the Fifty-fifth Massachusetts Regiment, and thus was best known as Nellie Brown Mitchell. She began as a singer in the Freewill Baptist Church, of Dover, a white congregation, later was engaged as soprano soloist by Grace Church, of Haverhill, Massachusetts, and then in turn by four of the leading white churches in Boston. Her voice was light and fine but of unusual compass, and her gracious presence assisted her singing. While her early reputation was largely based on her rendition of arias from French and Italian operas, she was especially good in ballads and sacred songs, and served as one of the soloists at the Sunday School Parliament on the island of Wellesley in the St. Lawrence River in 1876. In her later years she was a teacher and the inspiration of many younger workers.

"CENTENNIAL ARTISTS"

In the first decade after the Civil War several painters and sculptors became known to the public, and because of the fact that they exhibited at the Exposition of 1876, at least four have been termed by James A. Porter "Centennial Artists."

Edmonia Lewis, who was of mixed Negro and Indian descent, did work in sculpture which compared favorably with that produced by any other American woman of her day. In 1859, when sixteen years of age, she entered Oberlin, where she remained until 1863. Two years later, at a fair in Boston for the benefit of the Soldiers' Aid Fund, she exhibited a bust of Robert Gould Shaw, colonel of the Fifty-fourth Massachusetts, who died at Fort Wagner in 1863. In 1867 she completed a piece of work that is frequently referred to as "The Freedwoman" but that bears on its base the title "Forever Free," which is better. The marble statue, when last heard of, was in the possession of a family in Boston. It is not quite three feet in height. A man with left arm raised accepts freedom with a feeling of victory, while the woman beside him, resting on one knee and with hands clasped in prayer, receives it with conflicting emotions, overwhelmed by the precious gift. Miss Lewis went to Rome and thenceforth her work emphasized a neo-classical style. She produced, among other things, "Hagar in the Wilderness," "Madonna and the Infant Christ," "The Marriage of Hiawatha," busts of John Brown, Charles Sumner, Longfellow, and Lincoln, and two charming companion studies of child life, "Asleep" and "Awake." "The Death of Cleopatra" was exhibited at the Centennial Exposition.

Edward M. Bannister (1833-1903), whose home was in Providence, though little known to the younger generation, was very prominent sixty years ago. He gathered about him a coterie of artists and men of means who formed the nucleus of the Rhode Island School of Design. His paintings are mainly landscapes. Some are privately owned but others are in the Rhode Island Museum of Art. "Under the Oaks" received a first award medal at the Exposition.

William Simpson, a painter who lived in Buffalo and died in 1872, did not leave a great deal that we might study to-day, but what we have leads a critic to give him very high rating. William Wells Brown says that he painted whole families on a single canvas. Two of the portraits which have come down to us are those of Jeremiah and Caroline Loguen, known in connection with the anti-slavery agitation.

Another painter was J. G. Chaplin, who received his art education in Germany and seems to have attempted some work in grandiose vein, but who was best in his smaller pieces, such illustrations as those entitled "Macbeth Frightened by Banquo's Ghost," "Emancipation," and "The Fool."

FISK JUBILEE SINGERS

When the school that became Fisk University was opened in Nashville in January, 1866, it used some one-story frame buildings that had been erected as hospital barracks for the Union army. Year by year the problem of securing funds for a new site and new buildings became more acute. It was to this that the treasurer of the institution at length addressed himself.

George L. White, of Cadiz, New York, had seen service at Chancellorsville and Gettysburg and in the Freedmen's Bureau before being asked by the principal at Fisk to devote some of his leisure hours to the instruction of the students in vocal music. When the institution was chartered he became the treasurer, the "man-of-all-work in business matters." Within the next two years he presented his school chorus with success in Nashville, took a part of the choir to Memphis for a concert in the opera house, made a trip to Chattanooga, and then saw his students win special favor at the meeting of the National Teachers' Association in Nashville. The young people sang several classical selections but for the most part depended upon the religious songs that their fathers had sung—"Steal Away," "Swing Low, Sweet Chariot," "Nobody Knows the Trouble I See," "Deep River,"

"In Bright Mansions Above," "Roll, Jordan, Roll," and "The Rocks and the Mountains Shall All Flee Away." It was this music that George L. White now hoped to make known to the world at large. On October 6, 1871, with only infinite faith, he launched forth into the unknown—with eleven students, six young women and five young men, and a lady teacher who had oversight of the girls. Later there were changes and additions, so that twenty-four persons in all were said to belong to the company.

Progress was slow at first; at one point funds were so low that Mr. White had to borrow five dollars given to one of the young women in order to have enough for the purchase of overcoats for two of the men. However, on November 15 the group sang at Oberlin before the National Council of Congregational Churches, and two secretaries of the American Missionary Association advised the director to push on to the East. Henry Ward Beecher gave valiant assistance, and at length, at the Tabernacle Church in Jersey City, of which the Reverend G. B. Willcox was pastor, receipts from a single concert amounted to nearly seven hundred and forty dollars. At Waterbury, Connecticut, two men sent up a hundred dollars each. At New Haven, when two of the chief hotels declined to receive the singers, some families of the highest social standing opened their doors to them. Meanwhile throughout New England valuable presents—clocks, silverware, gas fixtures, books, and paintings—were made to the institution they represented. One firm asked them to take from its catalogue whatever goods the University might need. After a few months, having overcome the difficulty of securing passage, they embarked for England. The Earl of Shaftesbury, president of the Freedmen's Missions Aid Society, introduced them to the public; the Duke and Duchess of Argyll lent their good offices; and William E. Gladstone, then Prime Minister, received the group at his home. At the Tabernacle, presided over by Charles Haddon Spurgeon, the attendance was estimated at seven thousand. The singers worked with Moody and Sankey in the revival meetings conducted by the evangelists, declining all requests for concerts for several weeks in order to be free for the work. They returned to Fisk in time for commencement, but later made another trip abroad, this time spending eight months in Germany. J. B. T. Marsh, in words than can not be improved, thus summed up their effort: "They were at times without the money to buy needed clothing. Yet in less than three years they returned, bringing back with them nearly one hundred thousand dollars. They had been turned away from hotels, and driven out of railway waiting-rooms because of their color. But they had been received with honor by the President of the United States, they had sung their slave-songs before the Queen of Great Britain, and they had gathered as invited guests about the breakfast-table of her

Prime Minister. Their success was as remarkable as their mission was unique."

The appeal made by the Fisk Jubilee Singers was the same as has been made many times since, with the difference that to the spirituality of their songs was added novelty. Theodore F. Seward, a musician of Orange, New Jersey, said: "It is certain that the critic stands completely disarmed in their presence. He must not only recognize their immense power over audiences which include many people of the highest culture, but, if he be not entirely encased in prejudice, he must yield a tribute of admiration on his own part, and acknowledge that these songs touch a chord which the most consummate art fails to reach." A Highland girl in Scotland spoke for thousands when she said of the music: "It filled my whole heart."

"BLIND TOM"

Thomas Greene Bethune, "Blind Tom" (1849-1908), a Negro of unmixed blood and one of the prodigies of the century, was born near Columbus, Georgia. Although blind from his birth he was able to discern some objects, at least faintly, in later years. Blest with the gift of absolute pitch, in time he revealed also an astonishing memory. When four years of age, having heard some one play a piano, he developed a passion for the instrument, and when given opportunity would play for hours, not only such pieces as he had heard but also what the rain and the wind and the trees said to him. Thenceforth, having in one line the abnormal development of a genius, he was otherwise not well balanced. The ordinary plays of children made no appeal to him, but sometimes he would indulge in strange gymnastics in the course of a performance.

When Tom was sixteen years of age a number of prominent musicians in Philadelphia subjected him to a special examination, after which they said it was "impossible to account for these immense results upon any hypothesis growing out of the known laws of art and science." They continued: "In the numerous tests to which Tom was subjected in our presence, or by us, he invariably came off triumphant. Whether in deciding the pitch or component parts of chords the most difficult and dissonant; whether in repeating with correctness and precision any pieces, written or impromptu, played to him for the first and only time; whether in his improvisations, or performances of compositions by Thalberg, Gottschalk, Verdi, and others; in fact, under every form of musical examination,—and the experiments are too numerous to mention or enumerate,—he showed a power and capacity ranking him among the most wonderful phenomena recorded in musical history." The *Daily Herald*, of Glasgow, Scotland, said (January 2, 1867): "Mozart, when a mere child, was noted for the delicacy of his ear, and his ability to produce music on a first hearing; but Burney, in his *History of Music*, records no instance at all coming up to this Negro boy for his attainments in phonetics, and his power of retention and reproduction of sound. He plays first a number of difficult passages from the best composers; and then anyone is invited to come forward and perform any piece he likes, the more difficult the more acceptable, and, if original, still more preferable. Tom immediately sits down at the piano and produces *verbatim et literatim* the whole of what he has just heard."

At the height of his career "Blind Tom" would offer a list of eighty-two numbers from which the program for an evening might be selected. This included three sonatas by Beethoven, two fugues by Bach, and numerous selections from Chopin, Meyerbeer, Mendelssohn, and Donizetti, as well as fantasias, caprices, and original descriptions or imitations of the Rain Storm, the Battle of Manassas, and various musical instruments. The delicate shading of a Liszt or a Paderewski may have been lacking, but there was no question about rhythm, tempo, or harmony. Audiences were moved not only to enthusiasm but to wonder.

THE HYERS SISTERS

It was in 1871 that the Hyers Sisters of Sacramento, California, began their memorable tour of the continent. The older of the two, Anna Madah, was then seventeen years of age, and her sister, Emma Louise, a little more than a year younger; but already both had received careful training. After their parents had laid the foundation of their education, they worked with a German musician, Hugo Sank, then for some time with a former opera singer, Madame Josephine D'Ormy. Even then their parents were in no haste to have them appear before the public, and nearly two years more elapsed before they made their formal début at the Metropolitan Theatre in Sacramento, April 22, 1867, after which they appeared in San Francisco. Even then they were not more than children, but already the critics observed that Anna had a soprano voice of remarkable compass and smoothness, while Louise seemed equally good as an alto or tenor.

After this early success the sisters underwent another period of severe study, and then their father set out with them for the East. In Salt Lake City they made such a favorable impression that the citizens tendered them a complimentary benefit. Appearances in St. Joseph, Chicago, and Cleveland added to their reputation, the *Daily Herald* in the first of these cities saying, "We had read the most favorable reports of these sisters in the California papers, but confess that we were not prepared for such an exhibition of vocal powers as they gave us last night. Miss Anna Hyers, the eldest, is a musical phenomenon. When we tell musicians that she sings E flat above the staff as loud and clear as an organ, they will understand us when we say she is a prodigy. With the greatest ease in the world, as naturally and gracefully as she breathes she runs the scale from the low notes in the middle register to the highest notes ever reached by mortal singers."

The father, encouraged by the reception given his daughters, now determined to enlarge his troupe. He engaged the services of Wallace King, of Camden, New Jersey, a tenor, of John Luca, a baritone, and A. C. Taylor, of New York, pianist. In New York, Brooklyn, and Boston the singing of the sisters was a revelation to many; and the *Springfield Republican* said: "The voice of the soprano, Miss Anna Hyers, is beautifully pure and liquid in its higher range; and she sings notes far above the staff with the utmost ease, where most sopranos gasp and shriek. So easily, indeed, does she sing them that few persons are aware of the dizzy vocal heights which she scales. Mr. King possesses that great rarity, a *real* tenor voice, pure and sweet, and of great compass. But the charm of the concert consisted not so much in individual excellence as in the combination of the voices in some wonderfully fine four-part singing. . . . The shading was perfect; the modulations were absolutely pure and true; melody and harmony were alike beautiful."

The sisters remained in the East for three years; they sang at the Peace Jubilee in Boston and appeared at the Boston Theatre in a series of concerts with an orchestra of forty pieces. After these years of success, for some reason they ceased to be prominently before the public. Emma Louise died years before her sister, but Anna Madah became Mrs. Fletcher, the wife of a physician in Sacramento, and even in her old age kept up her interest in music, especially that of a religious nature.

MARIE SELIKA

Madame Marie Selika (1849-   ), in real life Mrs. Sampson Williams, has been thought by several competent critics to be the greatest Negro singer of her period. She adopted the name by which she became known from Meyerbeer's opera, *L'Africaine*. After three years of study in San Francisco under Signora G. Bianchi, and improvement in language in Boston, she entered upon a decade of triumphant success. In London on one occasion she appeared in a concert under the patronage of the Spanish minister, among the others on the program being Carlotta Patti and Percy Blandford. Some years later she and her husband settled in Philadelphia. When he died she became a teacher of voice at the Martin-Smith School of Music in New York. In that city she was still living in 1936, active and alert in spite of her advanced age, and keenly interested in the work of younger singers.

A coloratura soprano, Madame Selika often astonished audiences by her brilliant performance. The *Figaro*, of Paris, said after a concert in that city: "She has a strong voice of depth and compass, and trills like a feathered songster. Her range is marvelous, and her execution and style of rendition show perfect cultivation. Her 'Echo Song' can not be surpassed. It was beyond any criticism, an artistic triumph." The *Tageblatt* said after an appearance in Berlin: "The concert by Madame Selika was given before a well filled house, and this distinguished artist gave us genuine pleasure. She roused the audience to the highest pitch of enthusiasm. Of this wonderful singer we can only say that she is endowed with a voice of surpassing sweetness and extraordinary compass. With her pure tones, her trills and roulades, her correct rendering of the most difficult intervals, she not only gains the admiration of amateurs, but also that of professional musicians and critics. It is almost impossible to describe the effect of her voice. One must hear it to appreciate its thrilling beauty."

FLORA BATSON BERGEN

Flora Batson (1865-1906) was born in Washington, D. C. Her father having died, she was taken when three years of age by her mother to Providence, Rhode Island, where she attended school and began the study of music. While still a girl she sang for two years in connection with the work at Storer College, Harper's Ferry, West Virginia, then for three years at the (older) People's Church in Boston, and, after a year with Redpath's Lecture and Lyceum Bureau, spent two years in temperance work under the management of Thomas Doutney. It was at this time, during a series of great temperance meetings in the Masonic Temple in New York, that she sang for ninety successive nights "Six feet of earth make us all one size." By this time she was grown and ready for her larger career. J. G. Bergen, a white concert manager, who was entranced by her singing, succeeded in engaging her services for a year, during which time she was acclaimed at Music Hall in Boston and became popular in the South. The manager and the singer were married in New York December 13, 1887. There was much unfavorable comment at the time and the marriage later led to unhappiness, but just a week after it took place, before a vast audience in Philadelphia, Mrs. Bergen was crowned "Queen of Song" and presented with a diadem set with precious stones. A month later, at Steinway Hall in New York, she received a diamond necklace, a token of the esteem of many citizens. In the autumn of 1888 she embarked upon a three years' tour that took her to Europe, Australia, and New Zealand, greatly adding to her fame.

The voice that made Flora Batson known to the world was described by the conservative *News and Courier,* of Charleston, South Carolina, as "a highly cultivated mezzo-soprano, of great sweetness, power, and compass, and of dramatic quality." While she used numerous operatic selections, she was primarily

SISSIERETTA JONES

a ballad singer, and so thrilling was her work that audiences would be sent into the wildest enthusiasm. In San Diego one night, as on many other occasions, she showed the extraordinary range of her voice by singing a selection from *Il Trovatore* in baritone. The Pittsburgh *Commercial Gazette* said after a concert: "Flora Batson created such a furore in Old City Hall last evening that before the program was half through the excitement became so intense that cries of 'Bravo!' were heard from all parts of the house. Many people rose to their feet and the applause was uproarious and deafening in its intensity, and not only rounded out the conclusion of selections but broke in spontaneously at every interlude. The singer was certainly a marvel. Her voice showed a compass of three octaves, from the purest, clear-cut soprano, sweet and full, to the rich, round notes of the baritone register." Few singers have been so successful in reaching the heart of an audience.

SISSIERETTA JONES

Matilda S. Joyner, known after her marriage as Sissieretta Jones (1868-1933), was born in Portsmouth, Virginia, but was taken by her parents when very young to Providence, Rhode Island. When fifteen years of age she began her instrumental lessons in that city, and three years later became a student in voice at the New England Conservatory in Boston. Her advance was rapid, and in 1887 she was asked to sing at a concert in aid of the Parnell Defense Fund, on which occasion the audience numbered five thousand persons. The next year she began her professional career at Wallack's Theatre in Boston, and a musical director from New York who heard her telegraphed to Henry Abbey, of a prominent firm of managers, that he had found a "phenomenal singer." Mr. Abbey immediately sent an agent to secure her for a West Indian tour. Before leaving she sang in New York before the critics of the leading papers and they were a unit in declaring that she was destined to be one of the world's greatest singers.

The visit to the West Indies lasted eight months, and Mrs. Jones was constantly the recipient of medals and decorations. On her return to Providence she entered upon another season of study, and an Australian manager made her a flattering offer to go to his country. She declined because she had promised to return to the West Indies. In December, 1890, she was in Hayti, and the next month in St. Thomas. Pearls, rubies, and diamonds were showered upon her, and the citizens of Cape Haytien gave her a purse of five hundred dollars in gold, the presentation being made by the President of the republic.

Back in the United States Mrs. Jones entered upon her tours of the larger cities of the country. She also appeared in several private recitals before leaders of fashion in New York, her grand air and superb presence as usual assisting her voice. In April, 1892, she was the principal singer at the Madison Square Garden Jubilee. The *New York Clipper* in a glowing account called her the "Black Patti," a nickname that clung to her throughout her career. After three nights at the Jubilee her manager presented her at the Academy of Music, and so strong was the impression made that the management of the Metropolitan Opera House gave serious consideration to presenting her in *Aida* and *L'Africaine*. The plans did not materialize and she went forward with her work on the concert stage. In September, 1892, on invitation of President Harrison, she sang at a reception at the White House. A few days later she was for a week at the Pittsburgh Exposition as soloist with Levy's Band. Then followed with that organization a tour of the country, and the next year she appeared with Gilmore's Band. The *Chicago Tribune* (January 8, 1893) admirably described her performance in these years: "She has been endowed by nature with a voice that in any throat would be remarkable for its great range and volume, but which, with her, possesses even greater attractiveness by reason of its having also the wonderful richness and fullness and the peculiar timbre that lend the Negro singing voice its individuality. The tones in the lower and middle registers are of surpassing beauty, and those of the upper are remarkable for their clear, bell-like quality. Another striking element of the voice is its plantiveness. In every note Mrs. Jones sang in her concerts here that one quality was unfailingly present. In the arias, in ballads, comic or sentimental, it was noticeable, and it soon became evident that it was the most individualizing element in the voice, and that no amount of schooling or training could eradicate it. Not that one would desire to have it eradicated. It is the heritage the singer has received from her race, and it alone tells not only of the sorrows of a single life, but the cruelly sad story of a whole people. It lends to her singing of ballads an irresistible charm, making her work in this kind of music as artistically satisfactory as it is enjoyable."

Such success continued for most of the decade, in Europe as well as America. Just before the close of the century Mrs. Jones became the leader of a musical comedy company, "Black Patti's Troubadours." With this organization she remained for nineteen years, her work being primarily the singing of operatic airs near the close of the evening's entertainment. She was especially strong in her hold upon the South. In her retirement in Providence she lived quietly, devoted to church work and other good causes.

VI

THE MATURING OF NEGRO LITERATURE

CHARLES W. CHESNUTT—PAUL LAURENCE DUNBAR —BOOKER T. WASHINGTON—ARCHIBALD H. GRIMKÉ

ALREADY, says Holbrook Jackson, the eighteen nineties have become a legend; and legends, he reminds us, "live longer than history because they are more true." All the creative forces of the century seemed unleashed for a day of glorious experiment. There was abroad a new curiosity, a new spirit of daring, a tendency toward healthy controversy. Æstheticism was being worn thin, but the English public had yet to receive the audacious Aubrey Beardsley and the *Yellow Book.* Wilde, paraphrasing Pater, said: "Yes, there was to be a new Hedonism that was to recreate life, and to save it from that harsh, uncomely Puritanism that is having, in our own day, its curious revival. It was to have the service of the intellect, certainly; yet it was never to accept any theory or system that would involve the sacrifice of any mode of passionate experience. Its aim, indeed, was to be experience itself, and not the fruits of experience, sweet or bitter as they might be. Of the asceticism that deadens the senses, as of the vulgar profligacy that dulls them, it was to know nothing. But it was to teach man to concentrate himself upon the moments of a life that is itself but a moment."

Under this temper there was activity in all directions, and there were many new voices. Wilde himself wrote *Lady Windermere's Fan,* which Pinero matched with *The Second Mrs. Tanqueray;* and Shaw was already annoying the conservative with his *Plays Pleasant and Unpleasant* and *Plays for Puritans.* Kipling chanted his *Barrack Room Ballads,* and Richard Le Gallienne produced *The Book-Bills of Narcissus* and *English Poems,* even so early striking the note that, refined and exalted, was to give to the world *The Lonely Dancer.*

In America there was something of the same temper. *Trilby* appeared in *Harper's,* and *Ships that Pass in the Night* sold tens of thousands of copies. The most popular author, however, was not one of a gilded sophistication, but the poet of sentiment, James Whitcomb Riley; and the songs of Stephen Collins Foster were still to be heard on every hand.

Of the Negro writers of the period Paul Laurence Dunbar was most closely in touch with the dominant tendencies. He was influenced by Riley, also by the current hedonism. Yet he as well as others had special matters to consider. By 1890 the South had embarked upon a new era in industry, and the reaction from Reconstruction was complete. Disfranchisement had set in, peonage abounded, and lynching was nearing its height. Moral issues were no longer uppermost, and the Negro had to find in the new scheme such place as he could.

It was Booker T. Washington who perceived this better than others and strove to find a way out; but the first writer to gain high recognition was Charles W. Chesnutt, a novelist, whose work at its best has not yet been surpassed. Dunbar also wrote novels and stories, but is primarily remembered as a poet. Archibald H. Grimké, a man of great public spirit, was interested in biography and wrote numerous general articles. More brilliant than any stylist who preceded him was W. E. Burghardt DuBois, who placed studies in history and sociology on a new basis and was for years the chief critic of Washington. However, as he practically founded a school and has been active even in recent years, he is considered in another chapter.

CHARLES W. CHESNUTT

Charles Waddell Chesnutt (June 20, 1858—November 15, 1932) was born in Cleveland, Ohio. When sixteen years of age he began to teach in the public schools of North Carolina, from which state his parents had gone to Ohio, and at twenty-three became principal of the State Normal School in Fayetteville. In 1883 he left the South, engaging for a short while in newspaper work in New York City, but going soon to Cleveland, where he worked as a stenographer. He was admitted to the bar in 1887.

While in North Carolina Chesnutt studied to good purpose the traditions and superstitions of the Negro people of the state, and in August, 1887, his short story, "The Goophered Grapevine," appeared in the *Atlantic Monthly*. This was the beginning of a series later brought together in a volume entitled *The Conjure Woman* (1899). "The Wife of his Youth" also appeared in the *Atlantic* (July, 1898) and gave the title to the second volume, *The Wife of his Youth, and Other Stories of the Color-Line* (1899). Three novels were published later, *The House behind the Cedars* (1900), *The Marrow of Tradition* (1901), and *The Colonel's Dream* (1905). All of these books except the last were issued by the Houghton Mifflin Company. Chesnutt also contributed a compact little work, *Frederick Douglass* (1899), to the Beacon Biographies of Eminent Americans, and at least three stories not in any collection appeared later, "Baxter's Procrustes" in the *Atlantic* (June, 1904), and "The Doll" and "Mr. Taylor's Funeral" in the *Crisis* (April, 1912, and April-May, 1915).

The Conjure Woman naturally evoked comparison with *Uncle Remus*, and the chief story-teller, Uncle Julius, stands up well by the side of Harris's famous character. With his shrewdness, his kindness, and his ability to look out for himself, he is, if anything, more clearly individualized than Uncle Remus.

There are seven stories in the book. These are narrated by a man from Ohio who has gone to North Carolina to engage in grape culture, but in one after another the story of Julius that is interpolated becomes the center of interest. The Conjure Woman is Aunt Peggy, who happens to be free and is quite expert in meddling with other people's affairs. In "The Goophered Grapevine," when the master of the plantation was missing too many scuppernongs, she was engaged to call her arts into play, and "sa'ntered 'roun' 'mongs' de vimes, en tuk a leaf fum dis one, en a grape-hull fum dat one, en a grape-seed fum anudder one; en den a little twig fum here, en a little pinch er dirt fum dere,—en put it all in a big black bottle, en buried it under de root uv a red oak tree," and then remarked to one of the Negroes that anyone who ate the grapes would be dead within twelve months. Henry, one of her victims, found that as soon as the young grapes began to appear his hair "begun to quirl all up in little balls, des like dis yer reg'lar grapy ha'r, en by de time de grapes got ripe his head look des like a bunch er grapes." In telling his marvelous story so that a prospective owner would not feel inclined to purchase the vineyard, Julius remembered that he himself had been deriving a respectable revenue from the product of the neglected vines. So in "Po' Sandy," the sad story of a man who was turned into a tree and cut up as boards that went into a schoolhouse, it developed that Julius had in mind to use the old building for a church meeting. In "Hot-Foot Hannibal" he appears in a different light, helping to reconcile two young lovers higher in the world than himself. Chesnutt's dialect is not always above question, but, all told, *The Conjure Woman* showed that there had at last appeared among the Negro people a man who was able to write fiction with a firm sense of art.

"The Wife of his Youth" is the story of a very fair man of color who, just before the Civil War, with the aid of his Negro wife, made his way from slavery in Missouri to freedom in a Northern city, Groveland (Cleveland?). After the years have brought success and he has become the leader of his social circle and is about to marry an attractive young widow from Washington, his wife appears on the scene. "Perhaps," he says to the old woman who inquires about her husband, "he's outgrown you, and climbed up in the world where he wouldn't care to have you find him." "No, indeed, suh," she replies, "Sam ain't dat kin' er man. He wuz good ter me, Sam wuz, but he wuzn' much good ter nobody else, fer he wuz one er de triflin'es' han's on de plantation. I 'spec's ter haf ter suppo't 'im w'en I fin' 'im, fer he nebber would work 'less'n he had ter." The story ends with Mr. Ryder's acknowledging before a company of guests the wife of his youth. "The Bouquet" tells of the devotion of a little Negro girl to her white teacher and shows how the force of Southern prejudice might forbid the expression of simple love not only in a home but even in a church and at the cemetery. "The Sheriff's Children" is the tragic tale of the relations of a white father and his illegitimate colored son. The later story, "The Doll," is a powerful piece of work presenting the dilemma of a barber who has his own little daughter and other men's children to think of, but who also at last has in his power the man who dishonored his sister and murdered his father. Such stories as these, each setting forth a definite problem and working it out to a conclusion, reveal the skill of the author and also show his connection with Poe, De Maupassant, and Bret Harte. Of somewhat different quality was "Baxter's Procrustes," a gentle satire on curio and book collectors in which the Negro plays no part.

Chesnutt's novels are not quite as well done as his short stories and occasionally seem forced or unreal, but each has the vitality that comes from honest grappling with life. In *The House behind the Cedars* are treated some of the most searching questions raised by the color-line. The heroine, Rena Walden, is sought in love by three men, George Tryon, a white man, whose loyalty fails when put to the test, Jeff Wain, a coarse and brutal mulatto, and Frank Fowler, a young Negro, who makes every sacrifice demanded by love. In its last pages the novel moves with an intensity that leaves no doubt as to its power. In *The Marrow of Tradition* Wellington is evidently

Wilmington, North Carolina, and the book was suggested by the race troubles in that city in 1898. The main theme has to do with the relations of two women, one white and one colored, whose father, the same white man, had in time been married to the mother of each. The novel touches upon practically every social problem of the Negro and hardly satisfies the highest demands of art, but some of the single scenes are very vivid. One in the chapter "The Storm Breaks," reveals the difference between conservative Negro leaders and men of sterner mould in a crisis. *The Colonel's Dream* is a story of the failure of high ideals. Colonel Henry French, a Southerner who has achieved success in New York, returns to his old home for a vacation, only to find himself face to face with all the problems that one meets in a backward Southern town. "He dreamed of a regenerated South, filled with thriving industries, and thronged with a prosperous and happy people, where every man, having enough for his needs, was willing that every other man should have the same; where law and order should prevail unquestioned, and where every man could enter, through the golden door of hope, the field of opportunity, where lay the prizes of life, which all might have an equal chance to win or lose." Becoming interested in the injustice visited upon the Negroes in the courts, and in the employment of white children in the cotton-mills, Colonel French encounters opposition to his plans, opposition which finally sends him back to New York defeated. It thus appears that the method of the novelist was very largely naturalistic.

Chesnutt's more ambitious works are too full of propaganda to be ultimately satisfying. One constantly feels that if he could do so well he could have done better. At the same time he always knew what he was about; his main plots are well in hand; and his work as a whole shows notable advance. In 1928 he was awarded the Spingarn Medal for his "pioneer work as a literary artist depicting the life and struggle of Americans of Negro descent." This award was founded in 1914 by Dr. Joel E. Spingarn, formerly of Columbia University. It offered each year a gold medal of the value of one hundred dollars to be given to that Negro man or woman who, by his or her individual achievement as judged by a committee, shall have reflected most credit upon the race in any field of honorable endeavor.

PAUL LAURENCE DUNBAR

Near the close of the last century Paul Laurence Dunbar flashed like a meteor across the literary horizon. Within the next few years his success was so great that it became a vogue. On every hand he received the compliment of imitation, and schools, banks, and theatres have since been named in his honor. In very recent years there has been reaction, and other poets have been elevated at his expense. He has been found to have an excess of sentiment; his dialect has been belittled as mere entertainment; and he has been said to close an epoch rather than to point the way of the future. As yet, however, no one else has been able to duplicate his success or to approach his hold on the heart of the people.

Dunbar (June 27, 1872—February 9, 1906) has recently been the subject of a brief biography.* His parents, Joshua and Matilda Dunbar, of Dayton, Ohio, were uneducated but earnest, hard-working people. The father had a quaint mode of expressing himself, and the mother a keen sense of literary values. From his very early years the poet made little attempts at rhyming, but what he later regarded as his first achievement was the reciting of some original verses at a Sunday School Easter celebration when he was thirteen years old. He attended the Central High School in Dayton, where he was the only Negro student in his class, and by reason of his modest and yet magnetic personality became popular with his schoolmates. In his second year he became a member of the Philomathean Society, a literary organization, and he began to contribute to the *High School Times*. In his last year he was both president of the society and editor of the paper, and on the completion of his course in 1891 he composed the song for his class. After vainly seeking some work of a clerical nature,

---

* *Paul Laurence Dunbar*, by the author of this book. The University of North Carolina Press, Chapel Hill, 1936.

Dunbar accepted a position as elevator boy, working for four dollars a week. In 1893, at the World's Columbian Exposition in Chicago, he was given a position by Frederick Douglass, who was in charge of the exhibit from Hayti. *Oak and Ivy,* dated 1893, appeared just before Christmas, 1892; *Majors and Minors,* dated 1895, appeared early in 1896. Both of these books were privately printed, and the author, who had to assume responsibility for selling them, experienced many hours of discouragement. Gradually, however, with the assistance of friends, chief among whom was Dr. H. A. Tobey, of Toledo, the young poet came into notice as a reader of his verses. William Dean Howells wrote a full-page review of *Majors and Minors* in the issue of *Harper's Weekly* for June 27, 1896, Dunbar's twenty-fourth birthday, and the new author was launched upon his larger fame.

Dodd, Mead and Company now brought out *Lyrics of Lowly Life,* which included the best of the poems in the two privately issued volumes and a few more. This book is deservedly Dunbar's best known. It represented the fruitage of his young manhood and was never surpassed. In 1897 he went to England, and on his return to the country in October, through the influence of Robert G. Ingersoll, secured employment in the Library of Congress in Washington. This work he gave up after a year, for the confinement and his writing late at night were making rapid inroads upon his health. On March 6, 1898, he was married to Alice Ruth Moore, of New Orleans, who also had given promise as an author. Early in 1899 he went South, visiting Tuskegee and other institutions and giving many readings. Two months later he passed through a critical illness in New York. After that, as soon as he was able to travel, he went for a sojourn in Colorado. Books were now appearing in rapid succession, novels and short story collections as well as poems. *The Uncalled* (1898), written in London, reflected the author's thought of entering the ministry. It was followed by *The Love of Landry* (1900), a story of Colorado, then by *The Fanatics* (1901), set in an Ohio town at the close of the Civil War, and *The Sport of the Gods* (1902), which is the only one of the four novels primarily concerned with Negro characters. Collections of short stories were *Folks from Dixie* (1898), *The Strength of Gideon* (1900), *In Old Plantation Days* (1903), and *The Heart of Happy Hollow* (1904). Later volumes of verses were *Lyrics of the Hearthside* (1899), *Lyrics of Love and Laughter* (1903), and *Lyrics of Sunshine and Shadow* (1905). There were also six specially illustrated volumes of poems. In 1902, as Dunbar and his wife had begun to live apart, he went to the home he had bought for his mother in Dayton. His last years were a record of sincere friendships and a losing fight against disease. He

PAUL LAURENCE DUNBAR

was but a little more than thirty-three and a half years old when he died.

Dunbar's work naturally falls into four divisions: the poems in classic English, those in dialect, the short stories, and the novels. It was his work in the Negro dialect that was his distinctive contribution to American literature, but that it was not his desire to be known primarily for this may be seen from the eight lines entitled "The Poet," in which he longed for success in the singing of his "deeper notes" and spoke of his dialect as "a jingle in a broken tongue." Any criticism of Dunbar's verse in classic English will have to reckon with the following poems: "Ere Sleep Comes Down to Soothe the Weary Eyes," "The Poet and his Song," "Life," "Promise and Fulfilment," "Ships that Pass in the Night," and "October." In the pure flow of lyrical verse the poet rarely surpassed his early lines:*

> Ere sleep comes down to soothe the weary eyes,
> How questioneth the soul that other soul—
> The inner sense which neither cheats nor lies,
> But self exposes unto self, a scroll
> Full writ with all life's acts unwise and wise,
> In characters indelible and known;

* As we stated in the Preface, we are under obligation to Dodd, Mead and Company for permission to use the quotations from Dunbar. These are covered by copyright by this firm, as follows: "Ere Sleep Comes Down to Soothe the Weary Eyes," "The Poet and his Song," and "Life," 1896; "Lullaby," 1899; and "Compensation," 1905.

So, trembling with the shock of sad surprise,
The soul doth view its awful self alone,
Ere sleep comes down to soothe the weary eyes.

"The Poet and his Song" is notable for its simplicity as well as its lyric quality:

A song is but a little thing,
And yet what joy it is to sing!
In hours of toil it gives me zest,
And when at eve I long for rest;
When cows come home along the bars,
And in the fold I hear the bell,
As Night, the shepherd, herds his stars,
I sing my song, and all is well.

. . . . .

Sometimes the sun, unkindly hot,
My garden makes a desert spot;
Sometimes a blight upon the tree
Takes all the fruit away from me;
And then with throes of bitter pain
Rebellious passions rise and swell;
But life is more than fruit or grain,
And so I sing, and all is well.

The two stanzas entitled "Life" have probably been more quoted than any others written by the poet:

A crust of bread and a corner to sleep in,
A minute to smile and an hour to weep in,
A pint of joy to a peck of trouble,
And never a laugh but the moans come double;
And that is life.

A crust and a corner that love makes precious,
With a smile to warm and the tears to refresh us;
And joy seems sweeter when cares come after,
And a moan is the finest of foils for laughter;
And that is life.

"Promise and Fulfilment" was especially admired by Minnie Maddern Fiske," who frequently recited it. Other pieces, not more distinguished in poetic quality, are still of biographical interest. "To Louise" was addressed to the young daughter of Dr. Tobey, who cheered the poet on one occasion when he was depressed, by a rose given in the simple manner of a child. "The Monk's Walk" reflects his thought of being a preacher. "Robert Gould Shaw" was the expression of pessimism as to the Negro's future in America. Against it must be placed "When All is Done."

When all is done, say not my day is o'er,
And that thro' night I seek a dimmer shore;
Say rather that my morn has just begun,—
I greet the dawn and not a setting sun,
When all is done.

Finally there is the swan song, "Compensation," eight exquisite lines

Because I had loved so deeply,
Because I had loved so long,
God in his great compassion
Gave me the gift of song.

Because I have loved so vainly,
And sung with such faltering breath,
The Master in infinite mercy
Offers the boon of Death.

The dialect poems suffer by partial quotation, being artistic primarily as wholes. Of these, by common consent, the masterpiece is "When Malindy Sings." Other pieces in dialect that have proved successful as readings are "The Rivals," "A Coquette Conquered," "The Ol' Tunes," "A Corn-Song," "When de Co'n Pone's Hot," "How Lucy Backslid," "The Party," "At Candle-Lightin' Time," "Angelina," "Whistling Sam," "Two Little Boots," and "The Old Front Gate." Almost all of these poems represents a blending of humor and pathos, and all exemplify the delicate irony of which Dunbar was master. As representative of the dialect verse at its best, attention might be called to a little poem that was included in the illustrated volume, *Candle-Lightnin' Time,* but that, strangely enough, was omitted from both of the larger editions of the poems, probably because the title, "Lullaby," was used more than once by the poet.

Kiver up yo' haid, my little lady,
Hyeah de win' a-blowin' out o' do's;
Don' you kick, ner projick wid de comfo't,
Less'n fros 'll bite yo' little toes.
Shut yo' eyes an' snuggle up to mammy;
Gi' me bofe yo' han's, I hol' 'em tight;

Don' you be afeard an' 'mence to trimble
  Des ez soon ez I blows out de light.

Angels is a-mindin' you, my baby,
  Keepin' off de Bad Man in de night.
Whut de use o' bein' skeered o' nuffin'?
  You don' fink de da'kness gwine to bite?
Whut de crackin' soun' you hyeah erroun' you?—
  Lawsy, chile, you tickles me to def!—
Dat's de man what brings de fros', a-paintin'
  Picters on de winder wid his bref.

Mammy ain' afeard, you hyeah huh laughin'?
  Go 'way, Mistah Fros', you can't come in;
Baby ain' erceivin' folks dis evenin',
  Reckon dat you'll have to call ag'in.
Curl yo' little toes up so, my 'possum—
  Umph, but you's a cunnin' one fu' true!—
Go to sleep, de angels is a-watchin',
  An' yo' mammy's mindin' of you, too.

The short stories of Dunbar would have been sufficient to make his reputation even if he had not written his poems. One of the best technically is "Jimsella," in the *Folks from Dixie* volume. This reveals the pathos of the life of unskilled Negroes in the North, and the leading of a little child. "A Family Feud" shows the influence of an old servant in a wealthy Kentucky family. In similar vein is "Aunt Tempe's Triumph." "The Walls of Jericho" is an exposure of the methods of a sensational preacher. "The Ordeal of Mt. Hope" suggests the virtue of industrial education. Some other stories are much after conventional patterns but there is hardly one that does not show the sympathetic insight of the author.

Not quite so good are the novels. In *The Uncalled* the story of an orphan boy who was adopted by a prim maiden lady and by her prepared for the ministry against his will, is hardly convincing, and the English is decidedly mediocre. The author's lack of college training was more obvious when he attempted works in large form than when he wrote poems or short stories. *The Love of Landry* has the personal interest of reflecting the poet's stay in Colorado and his sympathy with all who grope for health, but it also fails to reach distinction. *The Fanatics* had much labor lavished upon it and deals with inflammable social and political questions, but was even less successful. Somewhat better is *The Sport of the Gods,* a realistic portrayal of the life of a Negro family transplanted from the South to New York, but even this is a work of promise rather than one of assured achievement. The author was primarily not a novelist but a lyric poet.

By his genius Paul Laurence Dunbar won the attention of the great, the wise, and the good. His bookcase contained many autographed works from his contemporaries, and there were other tokens of esteem. Upon his own people his influence was beyond all estimate. They gave him a place in their heart never accorded to any other man. Scores of young people tried to write verses like his. The difficulties he encountered no less than the acclaim he won, were theirs. In his success their fondest dreams came true.

BOOKER T. WASHINGTON

Booker T. Washington, like Dunbar, has suffered detraction in recent years. It has been observed that the technique of the trades which he advocated was becoming obsolete even while he spoke, and the style of *Up from Slavery* has been held to be so simple as to be childish. One must remember, however, the impression he made in his own day. At the turn of the century there was no question about his position as a leader; and if one is disposed to discount the style of the successive books, he must also keep in mind that of the public addresses. In firmness of organization, vividness of illustration, and sheer ability to tell a story, Booker T. Washington evokes comparison with Abraham Lincoln.

He was born at Hale's Ford, Franklin County, Virginia, April 5, 1856, being known in his early years simply as Booker. After the Civil War his mother and stepfather moved to Malden, West Virginia, where while still young he began to work in the salt furnaces and coal mines. It was not until he went to a little school at his home that he found that he needed a surname; then on the spur of the moment he adopted *Washington*. Later he learned that he was named Taliaferro, and thus we account for the middle initial. In 1872 he made his way to Hampton Institute, where he paid his expenses by assisting as a janitor. Graduating in 1875, he returned to Malden and taught for three years. He then attended for a year Wayland Seminary in Washington (now incorporated in Virginia Union University in Richmond), and in 1879 was appointed as an instructor at Hampton. In 1881 there came to General Samuel C. Armstrong, principal of Hampton Institute, a call from the little town of Tuskegee, Alabama, for someone to organize a school that the people wanted to start in that place. He recommended Mr. Washington, who opened school on the Fourth of July in an old church and a little shanty, with thirty students. In 1895 the principal of what had now become Tuskegee Institute came into national prominence by a speech at the Cotton States Exposition in Atlanta, and after that he interested educators and thinking people generally by his idea of practical training. In his later years only one or two other men in America could equal him in the power to attract and hold large audiences. Harvard University conferred the degree of Master of Arts in 1896, and Dartmouth that of Doctor of Laws in 1901. He died November 14, 1915.

In the course of his career Booker T. Washington delivered scores of addresses on important occasions. He was constantly in demand at colleges and universities, great educational meetings, and gatherings of a civic or public character. His Atlanta speech is famous for the so-called compromise with the white South: "In all things that are purely social we can be as separate as the fingers, yet one as the hand in all things essential to mutual progress." On receiving the degree at Harvard in 1896 he emphasized the fact that the welfare of the richest and most cultured person in New England was bound up with that of the humblest man in Alabama, each being his brother's keeper. Along the same line he spoke the next year at the unveiling of the Robert Gould Shaw Monument in Boston. At the Chicago Peace Jubilee in 1898 he reviewed the conduct of the Negro in the wars of the country, making a powerful plea for justice to a race that had always chosen the better part. The following paragraph from the Atlanta speech will represent his power of vivid and apt illustration:

A ship lost at sea for many days suddenly sighted a friendly vessel. From the mast of the unfortunate vessel was seen a signal: "Water, water; we die of thirst!" The answer from the friendly vessel at once came back: "Cast down your bucket where you are." A second time the signal, "Water, water; send us water!" ran up from the distressed vessel, and was answered: "Cast down your bucket where you are." And a third and a fourth signal for water was answered: "Cast down your bucket where you are." The captain of the distressed vessel, at last heeding the injunction, cast down the bucket, and it came up full of fresh, sparkling water from the mouth of the Amazon River. To those of my race who depend on bettering their condition in a foreign land, or who underestimate the importance of cultivating friendly relations with the Southern white man, who is their next door neighbor, I would say: "Cast down your bucket where you are"—cast it down in making friends in every manly way of the people of all races by whom we are surrounded.

The power to realize with fine feeling the possibilities of an occasion may be illustrated from the speech at Harvard:

> If through me, an humble representative, seven millions of my people in the South might be permitted to send a message to Harvard—Harvard that offered up on death's altar young Shaw, and Russell, and Lowell, and scores of others, that we might have a free and united country—that message would be, Tell them that the sacrifice was not in vain. Tell them that by habits of thrift and economy, by way of the industrial school and college, we are coming up. We are crawling up, working up, yea, bursting up—often through oppression, unjust discrimination and prejudice, but through them all we are coming up, and with proper habits, intelligence, and property, there is no power on earth that can permanently stay our progress.

The eloquence of Washington differed from that of Douglass as the power of a finished public speaker differs from that of an orator. One was objective, the other subjective. Douglass swayed his audience, and even himself, by the sweep of his passion and rhetoric; Washington weighed every word, keeping in mind the final impression to be made. Douglass was an idealist, impatient for the day of perfect fruition; Washington was a realist, making the most of each chance as it came. The one voiced the sorrows of the Old Testament; the other longed for the blessing of the New. Each in his own way worked as he could best see the light. By their sincerity both found a place in the oratory not only of the Negro but of the world.

ARCHIBALD H. GRIMKÉ

Archibald Henry Grimké (August 17, 1849—February 25, 1930) was one of two brothers well known for their public spirit, the other being the Reverend Francis J. Grimké, for nearly five decades pastor of the Fifteenth Street Presbyterian Church in Washington. He was born in Charleston, South Carolina, the son of Henry Grimké, a white man, and Nancy Weston, a beautiful slave. He with his brother was encouraged even while in college by two sisters of his father, Angelina and Sarah, who found the South uncongenial and the former of whom became the wife of the anti-slavery worker, Theodore D. Weld. After taking the usual degrees (A.B., Lincoln, 1870; A.M., *ibid.*, 1872; LL.B., Harvard, 1874) and spending some time in the office of William L. Bowditch, Grimké entered upon the practice of law in Boston, serving also as a special writer for the

Herald and the *Traveler*. *William Lloyd Garrison, the Abolitionist*, appeared in the American Reformers Series of biographies in 1891, and *The Life of Charles Sumner, the Scholar in Politics* the following year. From 1894 to 1898 Grimké was United States consul in Santo Domingo. On his return he became one of the leading spirits in the American Negro Academy in Washington, serving as president of the group from 1903 to 1916. In this connection he wrote several pamphlets, one of the best being "Right on the Scaffold, or the Martyrs of 1822," an account of the insurrection led by Denmark Vesey. Representative of his magazine articles in the period was "Why Disfranchisement is Bad," contributed to the *Atlantic* in 1904. In his later years he was prominently identified with the National Association for the Advancement of Colored People, and in 1919, for his public service, was awarded the Spingarn Medal.

Grimké was a journalist rather than a man of letters, and most of his work was colored by his own strong convictions. He did not excel in precision, yet in both his writing and his public addresses he was aglow with zeal for justice, and even in his old age could arouse young men to a high pitch of idealism. His lives of Garrison and Sumner are not essentially original, but they are readable and well represent the sweep of his style. He has a place in the literature of the Negro not only by reason of his own achievement but also because of the far-reaching influence exerted on others in his time.

OTHER WRITERS

Two of the many who felt the inspiration of the work of Dunbar were Daniel Webster Davis (1862-1913) and James David Corrothers (1869-1919). Davis was born on a farm in North Carolina but while still young was taken by his parents to Richmond, Virginia, which city was thenceforth his home. Beginning as a teacher, he soon turned toward the ministry and also became widely known for his wit and humor. His collection of verse, *'Weh Down Souf* (1897), has much of the spirit of Dunbar's work but is hardly so fine in taste. Corrothers, born in Michigan, was of mixed Negro, Indian, and Scotch Irish descent. He worked at various trades in his youth but later was able to attend Northwestern for three years. Then he became a minister and served in various places. He contributed poems to different periodicals; and chief among his prose works are a series of sketches, *The Black Cat Club* (1902), originally contributed to some daily newspapers in Chicago, and an autobiography, *In Spite of the Handicap* (1916). One or two of his pieces suggesting the harshness of the American attitude toward the Negro, appeared in the *Century*, but in general his dialect is not exact and an English poem is likely to be either too didactic in tone or marred by a bookish diction not in harmony with the subject.

Several other writers of fairly good verse were also on the scene. George Marion McClellan (1860-1934), a graduate of Fisk who was for years a financial agent of that institution and later a teacher and school principal in Louisville, in 1916 produced *The Path of Dreams,* a book containing several pleasant lyrics of nature though nothing of real distinction. Henrietta Cordelia Ray, daughter of the Reverend Charles Bennett Ray, an anti-slavery worker, was a writer with cultural contacts far beyond the average. A graduate in pedagogy of New York University and of the Sauveur School of Languages, she was for years before her death in 1916 a teacher in the public schools of New York. In 1910 she published a volume entitled simply *Poems,* with such section headings as "A Rosary of Fancies," "Meditation," "Champions of Freedom," "Ballads and Others Poems," and "Chansons D'Amour." The different pieces are fairly correct and show an interest in books, but none of the poems glow with irresistible emotion and the most ambitious of the ballads, "Rhyme of the Antique Forest," is hardly more than an echo of vigorous verse. Joseph Seamon Cotter, Sr. (1861-), after early experience in tobacco factories, distilleries, and brickyards, in time became an active teacher and school principal in Louisville. In the brisk verse of such a poem as "The Tragedy of Pete" he anticipated a later school of authors. J. Mord Allen, born in Montgomery, Alabama, in 1875, was taken in early life to Kansas, and in his mature years has resided in St. Louis. A boiler-maker by trade, he has also been interested in theatricals and poetry, and in 1906 published *Rhymes, Tales, and Rhymed Tales,* in which there are dialect pieces with a quiet kind of humor.

Three prose writers who produced articles in the vein of those of Crummell and Grimké were William Sanders Scarborough (1854-1926), Kelly Miller (1863-), and Mary Church Terrell. Scarborough was graduated at Oberlin in 1875 and soon thereafter entered upon his long connection with Wilberforce University, first as a professor, then as president from 1908 until his death. A classical scholar, he is remembered as the author of *First Lessons in Greek* (1881) and a treatise on *The Birds* of Aristophanes originally presented in 1886 before the American Philological Association; but he also wrote numerous general articles, some of which, like "Negro Folklore and Dialect" *(Arena,* January, 1897), dealt with the new subject of African origins. Others bore such titles as "The Educated Negro and Menial Pursuits" *(Forum,* November, 1898) and "The Negro and Our New Possessions" *(Forum,* May, 1901). With all of his good work there was in Scarborough as in several others of the day a certain temper that bordered on the sophomoric. Sometimes this took the form of pride in learning for its own sake; at other times it tended to give more attention to theory than to fact. It was this that led Booker T. Washington to feel that many political and educational leaders failed to come to grips with reality. Kelly Miller, a graduate of Howard in the class of 1886 (A.M., 1901; LL.D., 1903), wrote numerous articles and pamphlets on the questions of the day, the best being brought together in *Race Adjustment* (1908) and *Out of the House of Bondage* (1914). Mrs. Terrell (A.B., Oberlin, 1884) has also been a frequent contributor to periodicals, and a distinguished lecturer as well. Her article, "Lynching from a Negro's Point of View," appeared in the *North American Review* (June, 1904). The first president of the National Association of Colored Women's Clubs, she was twice re-elected and then, having declined to serve further, was made honorary president for life. She was one of the speakers at the International Congress of Women in Berlin in June, 1904. The *Washington Post* said: "The hit of the Congress on the part of the American delegates was made by Mrs. Mary Church Terrell, of Washington, who delivered one speech in German and another in equally good French." To this Ida Husted Harper added the comment: "It was more than a personal triumph; it was a triumph for her race."

VII

MUSIC AND ART, 1895-1920

HARRY T. BURLEIGH—MUSICAL COMEDY: WILL MARION COOK AND J. ROSAMOND JOHNSON—PAINTING: HENRY O. TANNER AND WILLIAM EDOUARD SCOTT—SCULPTURE: META WARRICK FULLER

WHEN we pass from literature to the fields of music and art, and consider those who were prominent in the early years of the century, we are immediately met by a man whose home was in England but who in so many ways identified himself with the Negro people of the United States that he deserves to be mentioned here. He visited America, found the inspiration for much of his work in African themes, and at once comes to mind in any review of the Negro in music.

Samuel Coleridge-Taylor (1875-1912) was born in London, the son of a physician who was a native of Sierra Leone, and an English mother. He began the study of the violin when not more than six years old, at the age of ten entered the choir of St. George's, at Croydon, and a little later became alto singer at St. Mary Magdalene's, Croydon. In 1890 he entered the Royal College of Music, continued his study of the violin, and worked with Stanford in composition, winning a scholarship in 1893. The next year he was graduated with honor. His earliest published work was the anthem, "In Thee, O Lord" (1892); but he gave frequent performances of chamber music at student concerts while at the Royal College and one of his symphonies was produced under Stanford's direction as early as 1896. His "Ballade in A Minor," produced at the Three Choirs Festival in Gloucester in 1898, showed something of his later quality, being distinctively Negro yet never going beyond recognized methods in harmonic, melodic, or orchestral structure. On November 11, 1898, Coleridge-Taylor became world-famous by the production at the Royal College of the first part of the "Hiawatha" trilogy, *Hiawatha's Wedding-Feast.* He at once took rank as one of the foremost of living English composers. The second part of the trilogy, *The Death of Minnehaha,* was given at the North Staffordshire Festival in the autumn of 1899; and the third, *Hiawatha's Departure,* by the Royal Choral Society, in Albert Hall, March 22, 1900. The success of the whole work was tremendous and such as the composer himself never duplicated. Requests for new compositions for festivals now became numerous, and in response to the demand were produced *The Blind Girl of Castél-Cuillé*" (Leeds, 1901), *Meg Blane* (Sheffield, 1902), *The Atonement* (Hereford, 1903), and *Kubla Khan* (Handel Society, 1906). Coleridge-Taylor also wrote the incidental music for the four plays by Stephen Phillips produced at His Majesty's Theatre, *Herod, Ulysses, Nero,* and *Faust;* incidental music for *Othello,* and that for *A Tale of Old Japan,* by Alfred Noyes. In 1904 he became conductor of the Handel Society. The composer's most distinctive work is probably that reflecting his interest in the Negro folk-song. Characteristic of the beauty, the color, and the passion of true Negro music are the pianoforte selections based on old melodies: *African Suite, African Romances* (to words by Dunbar), *Songs of Slavery, Three Choral Ballads,* and *African Dances.* Among numerous other works are *Dream-Lovers,* an operetta, *Five Choral Ballads* (to words by Longfellow), several vocal duets, and the anthems, "Now Late on the Sabbath Day," "By the Waters of Babylon," "The Lord is My Strength," "Lift Up Your Heads," "Break Forth into Joy," and "O Ye that Love the Lord."

HARRY T. BURLEIGH

Prominent among Negro composers in the United States for some years has been Harry T. Burleigh, who, while he has not given his time to symphonies or oratorios, has in the special field of the art-song won an international reputation. Mr. Burleigh first received recognition as a singer. As a young man he made his way from his home in Erie, Pennsylvania, to New York, where he spent four years in the National

Conservatory of Music, assisting for two years in the teaching of voice and solfeggio. In 1894, competing with sixty candidates, he won the position of baritone soloist at St. George's Episcopal Church, of which the Reverend Dr. William S. Rainsford was rector, and five years later he was also engaged at Temple Emanu-El. At the close of twenty-five years at St. George's he was given an engrossed testimonial expressing the appreciation of the congregation for his services. In May, 1936, he celebrated the close of his forty-second year as a member of the choir. His work in composition reveals a keen sense of melody and at the same time great technical excellence. Among the best known songs are "Jean," "One Year (1914-1915)," the "Saracen Songs," the "Five Songs" of Laurence Hope, and "The Young Warrior." This last, to words by James Weldon Johnson, was sung throughout the course of the war by Pasquale Amato, of the Metropolitan Opera, with tremendous effect; and the Italian version was popular in Italy. One notes also the strength of "The Grey Wolf," to words by Arthur Symons, "The Soldier," a setting of Rupert Brooke's famous sonnet, and "Ethiopia Saluting the Colors." A different phase of Mr. Burleigh's work, hardly less important than his songs, is that of his adaptations of Negro spirituals, especially for choral work, and he assisted Dvorak in his *New World Symphony,* based on the Negro folk-songs. In 1917 he was awarded the Spingarn Medal.

Asked one day by an interviewer how he felt toward the modern art-song and its development, Mr. Burleigh replied: "The text determines the character of the song. The kind of music one writes is governed by this solely, I believe. If the American composer will only remember that when he chooses he is to look for poems in which the spiritual forces of mercy, justice, and truth play a part, he will be adding to the literature things that have a big meaning. For me a poem must have more than just an ordinary sentimental reference before I can set it, or rather before it makes any impression on me. I read hundreds of perfectly good poems that I would never think of setting to music. There has been a neglect on the part of our composers, I think, of the kind of poems which in my estimation call out musical thought of real fibre."

MUSICAL COMEDY: WILL MARION COOK AND J. ROSAMOND JOHNSON

As the last century drew to a close a notable break with the old black-face minstrelsy came with the rise of a new and bright form of musical comedy. Important in the transition was the *Creole Show,* which featured a chorus of sixteen girls and appeared for five or six seasons in the decade. Opening in Chicago in 1891, it was in that city for the entire season of the World's Fair, and then created a sensation in New York. It was succeeded by *The Octoroons,* which made use of the "cake-walk" so popular at the time but also moved forward in that it gave several members of the chorus independent work to do. Then came *Oriental America,* a more ambitious production; although in the main it followed the old pattern, it made the innovation of presenting trained singers in operatic selections near the close of the evening's entertainment. This was the first colored show that formally won a place on Broadway.

An interesting group of men who had made their way to New York led in the new development. Outstanding among the comedians was an old minstrel man of great unctuousness and irresistible humor, Ernest Hogan. Another survivor of the elder day was Sam Lucas, who was born as early as 1840 and closed his career in January, 1916, after playing Uncle Tom in the first screen version of *Uncle Tom's Cabin.* Lucas was well educated, wore good clothes to advantage, and with his versatility and experience was an asset in the shows presented by younger men. Chief among the composers of lilting melodies were Will Marion Cook, who had studied in Berlin, and J. Rosamond Johnson, recently from the New England Conservatory in Boston. Paul Laurence Dunbar, who was for some time associated with the group, being especially attracted by Hogan's unique gifts, wrote lyrics for Mr. Cook, and James Weldon Johnson did the same for his brother. Bob Cole, who had been with the *Creole Show,* for three years (1898-

1901) teamed with Billy Johnson (not connected with the two brothers), then joined with J. Rosamond Johnson to form the better known Cole and Johnson vaudeville team. Later the company led by those two men presented some of the most popular shows of the period. Bert (Egbert Austin) Williams and George Walker came from the West to New York in 1896. Assisted by two young women, they led in making the cake-walk so popular that it became a fad. Later the Williams and Walker Company became the strongest Negro theatrical organization ever brought together. Walker, the smaller of the partners in stature, played the sleek, confident man of the world, while Williams was the thick-headed and shuffling but good-natured Negro who was always getting into trouble.

James Weldon Johnson in *Black Manhattan* has recorded once for all the shows and musical comedies presented by these and later organizations, but at least a few facts must be stated here. In 1898 Will Marion Cook, relying on the new syncopated music, composed *Clorindy,* a show that had sensational success. The lyrics were by Dunbar and the chief performer was Hogan. Cole and Johnson reached their height in 1906 with *The Shoofly Regiment,* which played at the Bijou Theatre on Broadway. Two years later they presented the tuneful operetta, *The Red Moon.* Meanwhile J. Rosamond Johnson was also writing songs for several white companies. Very recently

(1936) he has produced the book, *Rolling Along in Song*, and he collaborated with his brother on *The Book of American Negro Spirituals.* Williams and Walker, after three or four uncertain years, in 1902 arrived at the New York Theatre in Times Square with *In Dahomey.* The next year they had a successful season in London and received a royal command for a performance at Buckingham Palace in honor of the ninth birthday of the prince who became Edward VIII. In 1906 they presented *In Abyssinia* at the Majestic Theatre in New York, and the next year *Bandanna Land.* The chief composer was Will Marion Cook, and the leading woman was Ada Overton (Mrs. Walker), a singer and dancer of extraordinary magnetism.

With the year 1908 came change and disaster. The strength of George Walker failed during the run of *Bandanna Land.* Bob Cole also broke under the strain of heavy work. Ada Overton Walker died just a few years later. Bert Williams, one of the foremost comedians of his day, went over to the white companies and became a member of *The Follies.* He was just at the height of a new career when he too died in 1922.

PAINTING: HENRY O. TANNER AND WILLIAM EDOUARD SCOTT

Prominent among the painters of the world for four decades has been Henry Ossawa Tanner. This

HENRY O. TANNER

artist was born in Pittsburgh, Pennsylvania, June 21, 1859, his father being Bishop Benjamin T. Tanner, of the African Methodist Episcopal Church. When thirteen years of age, having seen a painter at work, he decided that he too would like to make pictures; and later he entered the Pennsylvania Academy of Fine Arts, where he studied under Thomas Eakins. While still a very young man he attempted drawings of all sorts and sent these to different publishers in New York, only to see most of them returned. A check for forty dollars for one that did not come back encouraged him, and a picture exhibited at the Academy of Design, "A Lion at Home," brought eighty dollars. Tanner now became a photographer in Atlanta, Georgia, and for two years was a teacher of drawing at Clark University. In this period came a summer of struggle in the mountains of North Carolina, and the knowledge that a picture that had originally sold for fifteen dollars had brought two hundred and fifty at an auction in Philadelphia. Desiring now to go to Europe, the young painter gave in Cincinnati an exhibition of his work. He sold not a single picture, but Bishop and Mrs. Joseph C. Hartzell, of the Methodist Episcopal Church, gave him a sum for the entire collection, and, thus equipped, he sailed for Rome January 4, 1891, going by way of Liverpool and Paris.

In the story of his career that he contributed to the *World's Work* some years ago, Mr. Tanner gave an interesting account of his early days in Paris. Acquaintance with the French capital led him to abandon all thought of going to Rome; but he had to live through five years of pitiless economy, broken only by a visit to Philadelphia, where he was able to sell a few pictures. He was encouraged, however, by Benjamin Constant, and studied at the Julien Academy. In his early years he had given attention to animals and landscapes, but now he was drawn more and more toward religious subjects. "Daniel in the Lions' Den" in the Salon of 1896 brought "honorable mention," his first official recognition. He was inspired and soon afterward made his first visit to Palestine. "The Resurrection of Lazarus" (1897) was bought by the French Government and now hangs in the Luxembourg. The enthusiasm awakened by it was so great that a friend wrote to the painter at Venice: "Come home, Tanner, to see the crowds behold your picture." After years of heartbreaking effort success had come at last. The artist's later career is a part of the history of the world's painting. He won medals at the Salon in 1897 and 1907, at the Paris Exposition in 1900, at the Pan-American Exposition in Buffalo in 1901, at the Louisiana Purchase Exposition in St. Louis in 1904, and at San Francisco in 1915; also the Walter Lippincott Prize in Philadelphia in 1900, and in 1906 the Harris Prize of five hundred dollars for the best picture in the annual exhibition of American paintings at the Art Institute in Chicago.

"Christ and Nicodemus" was purchased by the Pennsylvania Academy of Fine Arts. "The Bagpipe Lesson" and "The Banjo Lesson" are in the Collis P. Huntington Library of Hampton Institute. Other representative titles are "The Annunciation," "Moses and the Burning Bush," "Jews Wailing at the Wall of Solomon," "A Flight into Egypt," and "Christ and His Disciples on the Road to Bethany." "The Mothers of the Bible," a series of five paintings of Mary, Sarah, Hagar, Rachel, and the mother of Moses, marked the commencement of works emphasizing the portrayal of women. Others in the group are "The Five Virgins," "The Return of the Holy Women," and "Christ at the Home of Mary and Martha." Just which of these pictures excels the others is a question that might serve for long discussion. "The Resurrection of Lazarus" is in subdued coloring while "The Annunciation" is distinguished for its effects of light and shade. This latter painting must ever rank high in any consideration of the artist's work. Of "A Flight into Egypt" he himself said: "Never shall I forget two Persian Jews that I once saw at Rachel's Tomb; what a magnificent 'Abraham' either one of them would have made! Nor do I forget a ride one stormy Christmas night to Bethlehem. Dark clouds swept the moonlit skies, and it took little imagination to close one's eyes to the flight of time and see in those hurrying travelers the crowds that hurried toward Bethlehem on that memorable night of the

Nativity, or to transpose the scene and see in each hurrying group a 'Flight into Egypt.' "

Mr. Tanner's later life has been spent in Paris, with trips to the Far East, to Palestine, and the northern part of Africa. Some years ago he joined the colony of artists at Trepied, where he has built a commodious home and studio. Meanwhile he kept pace with some of the newer schools by brilliant experimentation in color and composition. Moonlight scenes appeal to him most, and he seldom uses other than biblical subjects. A landscape may attract him, but it is sure to be idealized. In spirit, if not in technique, there is much to connect him with the Pre-Raphaelite painter, Holman Hunt. Said he on one occasion: "It has very often seemed to me that many painters of religious subjects forget that their pictures should be as much works of art as are other paintings with less holy subjects. To suppose that the fact of the religious painter having a more elevated subject than his brother artist makes it unnecessary for him to consider his picture as an artistic production, or that he can be less thoughtful about a color harmony, for instance, than he who selects any other subject, simply proves that he is less of an artist than he who gives the subject his best attention."

In the early years of the century, when Tanner had become famous, hopes not always destined to be fulfilled were awakened by more than one young painter. William A. Harper, who died in 1910, was a product of the Art Institute in Chicago, at whose exhibitions his pictures received much favorable comment. After a season of study in Paris he took a prize of one hundred dollars at the Institute with his "Avenue of Poplars." Other subjects were "The Last Gleam," "The Hillside," and "The Gray Dawn." About 1912 Richard L. Brown interested the discerning with his landscapes, but he also died very early. However, it was just at this time that still another painter began to win recognition, one who has since passed on to assured achievement and fame.

William Edouard Scott, now best known for his mural and portrait work, was born in Indianapolis in 1884. After some years at the Art Institute in Chicago, where he took various prizes, he journeyed to Paris to continue his studies. There he encountered difficulties innumerable, but he made progress in different academies, worked for a while in the studio of Tanner, and at last, in 1912, saw one of his paintings, "La Pauvre Voisine," accepted at the autumn Salon. For this achievement he received praise in the French newspapers, and the Argentine Government, having heard about the picture, purchased it for six hundred dollars. "La Misère," exhibited in 1913, was reproduced in the French catalogue, and the next year took first prize at the Indiana State Fair. In 1913 also "La Connoisseure" was exhibited at the Royal Academy in London. In 1918 the city of Indianapolis purchased "A Rainy Night in Étaples." By this time the artist was concentrating more and more on mural work. For a bank in Edwardsville, Illinois, he executed a commission for a painting illustrating the signing of the treaty between the Indians and Governor Edwards in 1819. A series for the City Hospital in Indianapolis made necessary the treatment of not less than three hundred life-size figures. Other murals include those for the State House at Springfield, Illinois, the Court House at Fort Wayne, Indiana, a large Catholic church and the First Presbyterian Church in Chicago, and many for public schools throughout the country. In 1931, under the auspices of the Julius Rosenwald Fund, Mr. Scott studied Negro types in Hayti. Before returning to the United States he gave in Port-au-Prince a special exhibition from which the President of the republic purchased twelve paintings. In 1927 he received from the Harmon Foundation the award of a gold medal aside from the regular competition, this being given on the basis of "the finished and excellent character of his paintings and the recognition already received."

SCULPTURE: META WARRICK FULLER

When Tanner and Burleigh and Paul Laurence Dunbar had just risen to the height of their achievement a young woman from Philadelphia who had made her way to Paris began to attract attention by the distinctive note in her sculpture.

Meta Vaux Warrick (born June 9, 1877) first

compelled recognition of her talent by her work in the Pennsylvania School of Industrial Art, which she attended for four years. In her graduating year, 1898, she won a prize for metal work by a crucifix upon which hung the figure of Christ torn by anguish, also honorable mention for her work in modeling. In a post-graduate year she won the George K. Crozier first prize for the best modeling throughout the year, her particular piece being "Procession of Arts and Crafts." The young student now went to Paris, where she worked and studied for three years, chiefly at Colarossi's Academy. She met St. Gaudens and other artists, and finally there came a day when the great Rodin himself, thrilled by the figure in "Secret Sorrow," beamed upon her with the attitude of a father and said, "Mademoiselle, you are a sculptor; you have the sense of form." "The Wretched" was exhibited in the Salon in 1903, and along with it went "The Impenitent Thief." At one of Byng's exhibits in L'Art Nouveau gallery it was said of the sculptor that "under her strong and supple hands the clay has leaped into form: a whole turbulent world seems to have forced itself into the cold and dead material." On her return to America Miss Warrick resumed her studies at the School of Industrial Art, winning in 1904 the Battles first prize for pottery. In 1907 she was called on for a series of tableaux representing the advance of the Negro, for the Jamestown Tercentennial Exposition, and in 1913 for a group for the New York State Emancipation Proclamation Commission. Meanwhile, in 1909, she had become the wife of Dr. Solomon C. Fuller, of Framingham, Massachusetts. A disastrous fire in 1910 destroyed some of her most valuable pieces while they were in storage in Philadelphia, but by May, 1914, she had recovered from the blow sufficiently to be able to hold a public exhibition of her work. Between her studio and her home she leads a busy life; at present (1937) the oldest of her three sons has completed his college work and is taking a professional course, and the youngest is in high school. Mrs. Fuller was one of the first women invited to join the Boston Art Club, and she is also a member of the Wellesley Society of Artists, the Women's Club, the Civic League and the Players. In 1917, in a competition under the auspices of the Massachusetts Branch of the Women's Peace Party, she took second prize with "Peace Halting the Ruthlessness of War."

The early work of the sculptor is not delicate or pretty, but there can be no doubt as to its power. In "The Wretched" seven figures representing as many forms of human anguish greet the eye. Above the others is that of the philosopher, who, realizing his powerlessness, sinks into the stoniness of despair. "Man Carrying Dead Body" portrays a scene on a battlefield. A soldier bears upon his back the body of a comrade that has lain on the field for days; though the thing is horrible, he continues to bear his burden,

META WARRICK FULLER

tottering under the weight until he can find a place for decent burial. "Secret Sorrow" and "Œdipus," two of the pieces destroyed in the fire, had the same characteristics. The first represented a man, worn and gaunt, as bending his head and eating out his own heart. The figure was the personification of lost ambition and despair. For "Œdipus" the sculptor chose the hero of the old Greek legend at the moment when, realizing that he has killed his father and married his mother, he tears his eyes out. "Three Gray Women," from the legend of Persues, portrayed the Grææ, the three sisters who had but one eye and one tooth among them.

Perhaps the most haunting creation of Mrs. Fuller is "John the Baptist." With head upraised and eyes looking into the eternal, the prophet rises above all things earthly and soars into the divine. The second model of the group for the New York State Emancipation Proclamation Commission shows a recently emancipated Negro youth and maiden standing beneath a gnarled, decapitated tree that has the semblance of a human hand stretched over them. Humanity is pushing them out into the world, while at the same time the hand of Fate, with obstacles and drawbacks, is restraining them in the exercise of their freedom. More and more after this production the sculptor seemed to turn from her early interest in the gruesome and *macabre* to themes of social interest.

"Immigrant in America" was inspired by two lines from Robert Haven Schauffler's "Scum of the Earth":

> Children in whose frail arms shall rest
> Prophets and singers and saints of the West.

An American mother, the parent of one strong healthy child, is seen welcoming the immigrant mother of many children to the land of plenty. In "The Silent Appeal" a mother capable of caring for three children is making a voiceless plea for the suffrage (or peace, or justice). "The Awakening of Ethiopia," which was enlarged to life size for the Making of America Exposition, later went to the 135th Street Branch of the New York Public Library; and a relief portrait of Moorfield Storey, done in bronze, was presented to the distinguished publicist by the National Association for the Advancement of Colored People on his eightieth birthday. Recent work includes a number of statuettes, among them "Richard B. Harrison as 'De Lawd,' " "Swing Along, Chillun," "Lazy Bones," "Bacchante," and "Water Boy." Of the last a student remarked, "He looks as if he would come when he got around to it." A group of special importance on which the sculptor has been at work is "Exodus," this including seven or eight figures and representing Negroes leaving the South for the North at the time of the World War.

Mrs. Fuller's work has steadily broadened in social significance and some of the smaller pieces of recent years show her technique at its highest point; yet there are many who hope that she will not utterly forsake the field in which she first became known. Such productions as "The Wretched" and "Secret Sorrow" are grim and terrible, but they are also vital, and from them speaks the very tragedy of the Negro race in the New World.

Another sculptor who was on the scene about 1920 was Mrs. May Howard Jackson, of Washington, who produced several busts, among her subjects being the Reverend Francis J. Grimké, Dean Kelly Miller, and Dr. W. E. B. DuBois. Prominent among her other studies was "Mother and Child." Mrs. Jackson was represented in several notable exhibitions and was in 1928 the recipient of a Harmon award.

VIII

PROTEST AND VINDICATION

W. E. BURGHARDT DUBOIS—WILLIAM STANLEY BRAITHWAITE—JAMES WELDON JOHNSON—LESLIE PINCKNEY HILL—ALICE DUNBAR NELSON—GEORGIA DOUGLAS JOHNSON—WALTER WHITE—JESSIE FAUSET—COUNTEE CULLEN—ALAIN LOCKE

ONE day in August, 1905, there assembled at Niagara Falls a company of men whose influence on the literature of the Negro has been beyond all estimate. Forty years after the Civil War the reaction against Reconstruction was so complete, disfranchisement had been so successful, and lynching was so atrocious that to many earnest thinkers it seemed necessary to make a simple declaration of human rights. The twenty-nine men who now came together were representative of a far larger number of Negro people who were not only concerned about the immediate future but who also had misgivings about the larger import of the program of Booker T. Washington. They were not wealthy, and to more than one even the trip to Niagara meant a financial problem; but, bound by a noble zeal, they were embarked in what to them was a holy cause.

Their manifesto declared their aims to be freedom of speech and criticism, an unlettered and unsubsidized press, manhood suffrage, the abolition of caste distinctions based on race and color, the recognition of the principle of human brotherhood as a practical present creed, the recognition of the highest and best training as the monopoly of no race or class, a belief in the dignity of labor, and united effort to realize these ideals under wise and courageous leadership.

The meeting at Harper's Ferry the next year, amid scenes reminiscent of John Brown, took on the solemnity of a crusade. Already, however, lines of cleavage were appearing in the organization, and to some observers there seemed to be something a little too ingenuous about high-sounding pronouncements that pointed no way to realization. In the meeting in Boston in 1907 the lack of coherence was apparent, and the Niagara movement as such declined. Yet it had not failed. For one thing it had paved the way for a larger and stronger organization, the National Association for the Advancement of Colored People. In addition it had fixed attention upon a teacher and scholar in Atlanta about whom it was felt more and more that he was needed on the national scene.

Already, in 1903, two years before the meeting at Niagara, W. E. Burghardt DuBois had published the book that made him famous, *The Souls of Black Folk.* This included a straightforward criticism of the leader at Tuskegee. The author said that in Negro thought Mr. Washington represented the old attitude of adjustment and submission, his propaganda giving the impression that the South was justified in its attitude toward the Negro and that the prime cause of the Negro's failure to rise more quickly was his wrong education in the past. It was maintained that Mr. Washington had accepted even if he had not directly favored the disfranchisement of the Negro, the legal creation of a status of civil inferiority, and the withdrawal of aid from institutions of higher learning. It was necessary accordingly to get at the facts, to study Negro housing and schooling and crime, to see what justification, if any, the South had for its position, and, not least, to see that facts favorable to the black man but previously suppressed were brought to the light of day.

This led to study of the history of the Negro and to interest in sociology, in both of which fields Dr. DuBois had become distinguished. Already he was editing from year to year the Atlanta University Studies of Negro Problems, and he was soon to become editor of the *Crisis,* the organ of the National Association for the Advancement of Colored People. He may not have intended it, but in taking the position that he did he practically founded a school of writers, one given to protest against the discrimination practiced upon the Negro, and to vindication of the black man's right to the full heritage of American citizenship. This is not to say that everyone mentioned in this chapter was directly under his influence; five or six years previously Alice Dunbar Nelson had published a volume of Creole stories, and Mr. Braithwaite was already making a reputation in another field. At the same time it is worthy of note that several of those now under consideration have had official connection either with the *Crisis* or the National Association, and that all have either contributed to the *Crisis* or otherwise had close touch with it.

The matter may be stated differently. It will be observed as we proceed that those now under consideration have moved in the more favored walks of life. They are the editors, the teachers, the school officials, the executive secretaries. Some have done excellent work in creative vein, but for the most part there is an air of propaganda about their work, and they are generally self-conscious. As for the Negro, they are the defenders, the apologists. The writers studied in the chapter to follow, the realists, those closer to the proletariat, would say that these represent the bourgeoisie. Yet let no one discount their achievement. At its best it reaches the highest point attained by the literature of the Negro in America and is a contribution to that of the nation.

Here too, if we were considering literature in the large, we should have to include the work of some other men known for the distinctive quality of their effort, especially Robert R. Moton, Carter G. Woodson, and Charles S. Johnson. Dr. Moton, who has now retired after twenty years as president of Tuskegee Institute, is the author of an autobiography, *Finding a Way Out*, and *What the Negro Thinks*. Dr. Woodson, editor of the *Journal of Negro History*, has written *The Negro Church*, *The Education of the Negro Prior to 1861*, and numerous other works. Mr. Johnson, after several years as editor of *Opportunity*, is now a professor in Fisk University and the author of *The Negro in American Civilization* and the forthcoming *The Negro College Graduate*.

Distinguished also are some speakers on the public platform. Just now we might note Reverdy C. Ransom, Mordecai Wyatt Johnson, and Mary McLeod Bethune, each of whom in some way eminently represents the Negro Genius. Dr. Ransom, a bishop of the A. M. E. Church, has exhibited at times an exalted eloquence that reminds one of the old orators. Among his addresses are eulogies of William Lloyd Garrison, Wendell Phillips, and John Brown. "What kind of Negroes do the American people want?" he asks in the first of these. "Do they want a voteless Negro in a republic founded upon universal suffrage? Do they want a Negro who shall not be permitted to participate in the government which he must support with his treasure and defend with his blood? Do they want a Negro who shall consent to be set apart as forming a distinct industrial class, permitted to rise no higher than the level of serfs or peasants? Do they want a Negro who shall accept an inferior social

Photograph by A. N. Scurlock

W. E. BURGHARDT DU BOIS

position, not as a degradation, but as the just operation of the laws of caste based on color? What kind of Negro do the American people want? Taught by the Declaration of Independence, sustained by the Constitution of the United States, this nation can no more resist the advancing tread of the hosts of the oncoming blacks than it can bind the stars or halt the resistless motion of the tide." Dr. Johnson, who in 1926 became president of Howard University, attracted national attention by a speech at the Harvard Commencement in 1922 on "The Faith of the American Negro." Since then on numberless occasions he has seemed almost to weave a spell over his audience, his speaking being practical but ever directed toward a spiritual end. Mrs. Bethune has served as president of Bethune-Cookman College, as president of the National Association of Colored Women's Clubs, and very recently as director of work for the Negro in the National Youth Administration. There is a warm human appeal in her addresses, something that keeps in mind the destiny of her people and the country, and that awakens in all who listen the angels of their better nature.

W. E. BURGHARDT DUBOIS

William Edward Burghardt DuBois was born at Great Barrington, Massachusetts, February 23, 1868. He received the degree of Bachelor of Arts at Fisk University in 1888, the same degree at Harvard in

1890, that of Master of Arts at Harvard in 1891, and, after a season of study at the University of Berlin, that of Doctor of Philosophy at Harvard in 1895, his thesis being *The Suppression of the African Slave-Trade to the United States of America.* Dr. DuBois taught for a brief period at Wilberforce University, and for a time was an assistant and fellow in sociology at the University of Pennsylvania, producing in 1899 his study, *The Philadelphia Negro.* In 1896 he accepted the professorship of history and economics at the old Atlanta University. For a number of years he was the moving spirit of the Atlanta Conference, and by the Studies of Negro Problems which he edited in this connection became known as one of the foremost sociologists of the day. In 1910 he left Atlanta to go to New York as director of publicity and research for the National Association for the Advancement of Colored People. At the close of the World War he organized the Pan-African Congress, the first meeting being held in Paris. After twenty-four years of service in New York, he went in 1934 to the reorganized Atlanta University to assist in placing that institution on a graduate basis. About the same time he became chairman of the board of editors of a proposed *Encyclopedia of the Negro.* In 1920 he was awarded the Spingarn Medal.

Aside from his more technical studies Dr. DuBois has written seven books that must be considered in a review of Negro literature. Of these one is a biography, two are novels, two are collections of essays and sketches, and two are in the nature of apologetics, each defending a definite thesis. In 1909 appeared *John Brown,* a contribution to the series of American Crisis Biographies. The subject was one well adapted to treatment at the hands of the author, and in the last chapter, "The Legacy of John Brown," he showed that his hero had a message for twentieth century America as well as for his own day, this: "The cost of liberty is less than the price of repression."

The two novels not unnaturally reflect the public work of the writer. *The Quest of the Silver Fleece* (1911) has three main themes: the economic position of the Negro agricultural laborer, the subsidizing of a certain kind of school, and Negro life and society in the city of Washington. The tone is frequently one of satire, the chief characters are hardly plausibly developed, and in general the work offered little that could add to the reputation of the author. Nearly two decades later appeared *Dark Princess* (1928), a production more intense even if not better organized. In this the real theme is the furious conflict in the hearts of Negro men. The book is episodic and kaleidoscopic, but certain characters stand out clearly. Matthew Towns passes through tragedy to a deeper understanding of his people. "We come out of the depths," he says, "the blood and mud of battle. And from just those depths, I take it, came most of the things worth while in this old world." Then there is

Perigua, the revolutionist, who blows himself up with the dynamite intended for others; also Sara Andrews, the woman of the world, who cares nothing for those less fortunate, satisfied if she alone is smug and comfortable.

The two collections of essays give the author's reaction to the seething cauldron in which he has lived most of his life. In 1903 fourteen papers, some of which had appeared in such magazines as the *Atlantic* and the *World's Work*, were brought together in a volume entitled *The Souls of Black Folk*. The style of the book as well as its content at once commanded attention. "The Dawn of Freedom" is a study of the Freedmen's Bureau; "The Meaning of Progress" is a story of life in Tennessee, told by one who has been the country schoolmaster; "The Training of Black Men" is a plea for liberally educated leadership, while "The Quest of the Golden Fleece," like one or two related essays, portrays conditions in the "black belt." The production as a whole is a powerful plea for justice; nor can a note of pessimism running through it detract from its literary quality. Not quite so successful was the later collection, *Darkwater* (1920). This was written at white heat just at the close of the war and the tone is somewhat too strident for the most felicitous effect. The book has the interest, however, of including a introductory autobiographical sketch.

Different was *The Gift of Black Folk* (1924), projected as a contribution to a series advanced by the Knights of Columbus largely to offset the propaganda of the KuKlux Klan. The book was hastily done, but in its optimistic temper, its catholicity of interest, and its constructive spirit, it was a pleasant surprise. The central chapter, "The Reconstruction of Freedom," shows "how the black fugitive, soldier, and freedman after the Civil War helped to restore the Union, establish public schools, enfranchise the poor white, and initiate industrial democracy in America." "The North, being unable to free the slave, let him try to free himself. And he did, and this was his greatest gift to the nation." The main idea of the book was carried further in *Black Reconstruction* (1935). This large work attempted nothing less than the changing of the conventional view of the period with which it dealt, and, in spite of some shortcomings in method, was in the main successful. It showed that the decade immediately after the Civil War had been given such distorted treatment by supposedly reputable universities and so exploited by men of journalistic temper, that truth cried aloud for a hearing. "The chief witness in Reconstruction, the emancipated slave himself, has been almost barred from court. His written Reconstruction record has been largely destroyed and nearly always neglected." Many of the chapters in the book are repetitious and might have been more firmly organized, but the last one, "The Propaganda of History," is brilliant in its exposure of the fallacies of popular authors. In general it is made clear that "we have been cajoling and flattering the South and slurring the North, because the South is determined to re-write the history of slavery and the North is not interested in history but wealth."

This book has its interest and the merit of a trail-blazer. Even after the lapse of years, however, it appears that, from the strictly literary standpoint, *The Souls of Black Folk* remains the author's best work. This it is that shows his style at its best. That style is marked by all the arts of rhetoric—strong antithesis, frequent allusion, liquid and alliterative effects, and poetic suggestiveness. The color-line is the "Veil," the familiar melodies the "Sorrow Songs." The following paragraphs may be considered representative:

> I have seen a land right merry with the sun, where children sing, and rolling hills lie like passioned women wanton with harvest. And there in the King's Highway sat and sits a figure veiled and bowed, by which the traveler's footsteps hasten as they go. On the tainted air broods fear. Three centuries' thought has been the raising and unveiling of that bowed human heart, and now behold a century new for the duty and the deed. The problem of the Twentieth Century is the problem of the color-line.
>
> . . . . .
>
> I sit with Shakespeare and he winces not. Across the color-line I move arm in arm with Balzac and Dumas, where smiling men and welcoming women glide in gilded

halls. From out the caves of evening that swing between the strong-limbed earth and the tracery of the stars, I summon Aristotle and Aurelius and what soul I will, and they all come graciously with no scorn nor condescension. So, wed with Truth, I dwell above the Veil. Is this the life you grudge us, O knightly America? Is this the life you long to change into the dull red hideousness of Georgia? Are you so afraid lest peering from this high Pisgah, between Philistine and Amalekite, we sight the Promised Land?

. . . . .

My journey was done, and behind me lay hill and dale, and Life and Death. How shall man measure Progress there where the dark-faced Josie lies? How many heartfuls of sorrow shall balance a bushel of wheat? How hard a thing is life to the lowly, and yet how human and real! And all this life and love and strife and failure—is it the twilight of nightfall or the flush of some faint-dawning day?

Thus sadly musing, I rode to Nashville in the Jim Crow car.

W. E. Burghardt DuBois combines in unusual degree the temper of the scholar and the romanticism of the Negro race. Forced by the pressure of circumstance, gradually he was led from the retreat of the scholar into the arena of social struggle. He has passed through storms; a "Close Ranks" editorial in the *Crisis* at the time of the war aroused protest in some quarters, and some years later a seeming willingness to accept the principle of segregation, in part at least, led to new discussion. Yet for more than three decades now he has striven to interpret the desires and aspirations of his people. He gave to them a new sense of literary values and scholarly achievement, and, so doing, he became an inspiration to many younger men.

WILLIAM STANLEY BRAITHWAITE

The work of William Stanley Braithwaite belongs not so much to Negro literature as to American literature in the large. With singleness of purpose he has given himself to books and the book world, and it is by this devotion that he has won the success he has achieved.

Born in Boston December 6, 1878, Mr. Braithwaite was largely self-educated. In 1904 he published a small volume of poems entitled *Lyrics of Life and Love*. This was followed four years later by *The House of Falling Leaves*. Thereafter he gave little time to his own verse, becoming more and more distinguished as a critic of American poetry. For several years he was a valued contributor to the *Boston Evening Transcript*, and he has had verse or critical essays in the *Forum*, the *Century*, *Scribner's*, and the *Atlantic*. He published the *Anthology of Magazine Verse* for each year from 1913 to 1929, and also collected and edited *The Golden Treasury of Magazine Verse*, *The Book of Elizabethan Verse*, *The Book of Georgian Verse*, and *The Book of Restoration Verse*.

In 1917 he brought together in a volume, *The Poetic Year,* a special series of articles which he had contributed to the *Transcript.* The aim of this was, in the form of conversations among a small group of friends, to whom fanciful and suggestive Greek names had been given, to discuss the poetry that had appeared in 1916. After the war appeared *Victory: Celebrated by Thirty-eight American Poets* and *The Story of the Great War* for young people. There were also other anthologies. In 1934 Mr. Braithwaite was called to the new Atlanta University, his special field being that of writing in creative vein. Already, in 1918, he had received the Spingarn Medal.

Lyrics of Life and Love brought together the best of the poet's early work. The little book contains eighty pages, and no one of the lyrics takes up more than two pages, twenty being just eight lines in length. This appearance of fragility, however, is a little deceptive. While Keats and Shelley are constantly present as the models in technique, the yearning of more than one lyric reflects the deeper romantic temper. The bravado and the tenderness of the old poets are in the two Christmas pieces, "Holly Berry and Mistletoe" and "Yule-Song: A Memory."

December comes, snows come,
  Comes the wintry weather;
Faces from away come—
  Hearts must be together.

Down the stair-steps of the hours
Yule leaps the hills and towers—
Fill the bowl and hang the holly,
Let the times be jolly.

"The Watchers" and the lines "To Dante Gabriel Rossetti" show the influence of the Pre-Raphaelites, the former also suggesting Kingsley; and the poet's handling of the sonnet may be seen from the following:

My thoughts go marching like an armed host
Out of the city of silence, guns and cars;
Troop after troop across my dreams they post
To the invasion of the wind and stars.
O brave array of youth's untamed desire!
With thy bold, dauntless captain Hope to lead
His raw recruits to Fate's opposing fire,
And up the walls of Circumstance to bleed.
How fares the expedition in the end?
When this my heart shall have old age for king
And to the wars no further troop can send,
What final message will the arm'stice bring?
The host gone forth in youth the world to meet,
In age returns—in victory or defeat?

After a year or two Mr. Braithwaite began to strike a new note of mysticism in his verse, and through this to influence the poetry of his day. It was first observed in "Sandy Star," that appeared in the *Atlantic* (July, 1909). It was also in "The Mystery" (or

"The Way," as the poet prefers to call it) in *Scribner's* (October, 1915):

> He could not tell the way he came
> Because his chart was lost:
> Yet all his way was paved with flame
> From the bourne he crossed.
>
> He did not know the way to go,
> Because he had no map:
> He followed where the winds blow,—
> And the April sap.
>
> He never knew upon his brow
> The secret that he bore—
> And laughs away the mystery now
> The dark's at his door.

It would take an independent study to do justice to the critical introductions placed by Mr. Braithwaite in the successive issues of the *Anthology of Magazine Verse*. The books increased in size from the thin collection of eighty-seven pages for 1913 to the stout Sesqui-Centennial volume for 1926 running to nearly a thousand pages and containing a number of special articles. Clement Wood, writing in *Hunters of Heaven*, said of the editor: "He may be over-catholic in his inclusions, but he has shifted his emphasis from echoes to real poetry. He is an admirable anthologist, and his books are indispensable to a grasp of modern poetry." The *Transcript* said

(November 30, 1915), after a special reception had been accorded the critic in New York by the authors of America: "He has helped poetry to readers as well as to poets. One is guilty of no extravagance in saying that the poets we have—and they may take their place with their peers in any country—and the gathering deference we pay them, are created largely out of the stubborn, self-effacing enthusiasm of this one man. In a sense their distinction is his own."

The method of the critic has been to find out about any author's work that quality which is original or enduring, and so he has endeavored to do in occasional articles about Negro writers in the *Crisis* or *Opportunity*. So generous has he been and so catholic his taste that a reader once told him there was too much perfume in his ink. He holds, however, that few are likely to be injured by a little praise, while it would be fatal not to recognize even one deserving spirit. Thus one young writer after another he has encouraged rather than chastened, and all he has beckoned to the nobler heights of song.

JAMES WELDON JOHNSON

With a varied career as teacher, author, and publicist, James Weldon Johnson has been increasingly prominent in the life of the country. Born in Jacksonville, Florida, June 17, 1871, he was educated in the public schools of that city and at the old Atlanta University; later he studied for three years at Columbia; and Talladega and Howard have since conferred upon him the degree of Doctor of Letters. For seven years after his graduation in Atlanta (1894) Mr. Johnson was principal of the Stanton Public School in Jacksonville, and, with the tact that was later to prove one of his outstanding qualities, gradually raised the status of an institution doing only grammar grade work to that of a full-fledged high school. Meanwhile he studied law, being admitted to the bar in Florida in 1897. While still in Jacksonville also, he began with his brother, Rosamond Johnson, that collaboration in song-making which within the next few years was to prove so successful. In 1900 one wrote the words and the other the music for "Lift Ev'ry Voice and Sing," now widely known as the Negro National Anthem. This was originally composed for a group of school-children preparing for a Lincoln's birthday exercise, but its noble words and swelling music made it deservedly popular, and it is now regularly sung in Negro schools and colleges throughout the country. In 1901 the brothers launched forth upon the great adventure of their lives, and removed to New York. It was the day of Ernest Hogan, and Williams and Walker in musical comedy; and the Cole and Johnson company became one of the best known of the decade. The writing of the words for popular songs was fairly lucrative, but after a while it palled upon a man with aspirations for higher things, and in 1906 Mr. Johnson accepted the post of United States consul to Puerto Cabello in Venezuela. Here he remained until 1909, when he was transferred to Corinto, Nicaragua, where he served until 1912. As a consul he saw three revolutions, one in Venezuela and two in Nicaragua, and in general his work for the Government gave him valuable experience. Returning home he found a new life awaiting him, first as field secretary and then as secretary of the National Association for the Advancement of Colored People. In 1915 he made for the Metropolitan Opera the English translation of the Spanish opera *Goyescas,* by Granados and Periquet; and the next year, while connected with the *New York Age,* won a third prize of two hundred dollars in a competition opened by the *Public Ledger,* of Philadelphia, to editorial writers throughout the country. The success of the poem, "The Young Warrior," has been mentioned in connection with the work of Mr. Burleigh, who wrote the music. In 1920 Mr. Johnson went to Hayti to investigate conditions under the American occupation; in 1925 he was awarded the Spingarn Medal; and five years later he became Adam K. Spence professor of creative literature at Fisk University. Since 1934 he has also given each year a series of lectures at New York University.

Mr. Johnson's first formal publication, *Autobiography of an Ex-Colored Man,* was published anonymously in 1912, but in 1927 was given new issue over the author's name. The method of the book is primarily that of fiction, but the writer draws upon his own experience as freely as he chooses. So doing he is able to interpret without any restriction the life of which he has been a part. In the career of the central figure the book touches upon practically every phase of the race question. While it is as fresh to-day as when it was written, it also shows that it anticipated the temper we have had in literature and music since the war. At the close the character of whom we have spoken decides, after many misgivings, to remain beyond the color-line. He is not satisfied, however. Attending a meeting in Carnegie Hall, he hears Booker T. Washington speak and the Hampton students sing, and feels that he too, had he not been small and selfish, might have made his life great, and been part of the making of a people's history.

In 1917 appeared *Fifty Years and Other Poems,* which also came out some years later in a new edition and with a new publisher. The title piece in noble stanzas celebrates the anniversary of freedom, with a call to courage for the future; and there is a section of "Jingles and Croons" including the threnody, "Sence You Went Away." Chief distinction attaches to such pieces as had appeared in the *Century Magazine,* one of the best being that in which the poet praises the unknown makers of the Negro melodies.

O black and unknown bards of long ago,
  How came your lips to touch the sacred fire?
How, in your darkness, did you come to know
  The power and beauty of the minstrel's lyre?
Who first from 'midst his bonds lifted his eyes?
  Who first from out the still watch, lone and long,
Feeling the ancient faith of prophets rise
  Within his dark-kept soul, burst into song?

There is a wide, wide wonder in it all,
  That from degraded rest and servile toil,
The fiery spirit of the seer should call
  These simple children of the sun and soil.
O black singers, gone, forgot, unfamed,
  You—you alone, of all the long, long line
Of those who've sung untaught, unknown, unnamed,
  Have stretched out upward, seeking the divine.

You sang not deeds of heroes or of kings:
  No chant of bloody war, nor exulting pæan
Of arms-won triumphs; but your humble strings
  You touched in chords with music empyrean.
You sang far better than you knew, the songs
  That for your listeners' hungry hearts sufficed
Still live—but more than this to you belongs:
  You sang a race from wood and stone to Christ.

In 1922 Mr. Johnson brought out an anthology, *The Book of American Negro Poetry*, with an Introduction that was a notable contribution to the literature of the subject; and a revised edition appeared in

JAMES WELDON JOHNSON

1931. In *God's Trombones: Seven Negro Sermons in Verse* (1927) the author endeavored to catch something of the rhythm and imagery of the older Negro preachers; and such subjects as "The Creation," "Noah Built the Ark," and "The Judgment Day" were singularly adapted to the purpose. About the same time appeared *The Book of American Negro Spirituals* and *The Second Book of American Negro Spirituals*, with scholarly introductions by James Weldon Johnson and with the music transcribed or arranged by Rosamond Johnson.

> Then God raised His arm and He waved His hand*
> Over the sea and over the land,
> And He said: Bring forth! Bring forth!
> And quicker than God could drop His hand,
> Fishes and fowls
> And beasts and birds
> Swam the rivers and the seas,
> Roamed the forests and the woods,
> And split the air with their wings.
> And God said: That's good!
>
> Then God walked around,
> And God looked around
> On all that He had made.
> He looked at His sun,
> And He looked at His moon,
> And He looked at His little stars;

* From *God's Trombones*, by James Weldon Johnson. Copyright, 1927, by The Viking Press, Inc., New York, N. Y.

He looked on His world
With all its living things,
And God said: I'm lonely still.

Then God sat down—
On the side of a hill where He could think;
By a deep, wide river He sat down;
With His head in His hands,
God thought and thought,
Till He thought: I'll make me a man!

Up from the bed of the river
God scooped the clay;
And by the bank of the river
He kneeled Him down;
And there the great God Almighty
Who lit the sun and fixed it in the sky,
Who flung the stars to the most far corner of the night,
Who rounded the earth in the middle of His hand;
This Great God,
Like a mammy bending over her baby,
Kneeled down in the dust
Toiling over a lump of clay
Till He shaped it in His own image;

Then into it He blew the breath of life,
And man became a living soul.
Amen. Amen.

Black Manhattan (1930) had as its prime purpose the writing of "the record of the Negro's progress on the New York stage, from the attempted classical performances of the African Company, at the corner of Bleecker and Mercer Streets in 1821, down to *The Green Pastures* in 1930," but reaches even beyond the metropolis to a consideration of some of the tides in the life of the country at large. *Saint Peter Relates an Incident of the Resurrection Day* (1930), an ironic poem on the Unknown Soldier, was written, as the author says, "while meditating upon Heaven and Hell and Democracy and War and America and the Negro Gold Star Mothers." It was first published in a limited edition for private distribution only, but later there was a larger issue with some other poems. A formal autobiographical work, *Along this Way* (1933), had much attention lavished upon it, yet somehow failed to impress the discerning as one of the author's best books. Perhaps the reason, as some suggested, is that the writer is unduly self-conscious, with a glance too frequently directed at the reader; perhaps it is that at times there seems to be even a suggestion of condescension. Not even these points, however, can alter the fact that the book is the record of a full and varied life, crowded with matter not to be found elsewhere. One comes upon a first-hand sketch of Paul Laurence Dunbar, upon an account of the meeting of kindred spirits at the Marshall in New York, and even of clashes between some of those of sensitive temper. There are sidelights on Woodrow Wilson, Warren G. Harding, Florenz Ziegfeld, H. L. Mencken, Marie Dressler, Madame Schumann-Heink, and a host of other notables. On page after page there is a glimpse of a fresh scene or the thrill of a new adventure.

Yet, when all is said, one remembers best the early song of aspiration,

Lift ev'ry voice and sing
Till earth and heaven ring,
Ring with the harmonies of Liberty;
Let our rejoicing rise
High as the list'ning skies,
Let it resound loud as the rolling sea.
Sing a song full of the faith that the dark past has
taught us;
Sing a song full of the hope that the present has brought us;
Facing the rising sun of our new day begun,
Let us march on till victory is won.

LESLIE PINCKNEY HILL

Leslie Pinckney Hill, born in Lynchburg, Virginia, May 14, 1880, attended a high school in East Orange, New Jersey, and was graduated at Harvard in 1903, receiving the Master's degree the next year. He taught for three years at Tuskegee, was then for six years principal of the Manassas Industrial School, Manassas, Virginia, and in 1913 entered upon his career as head of the Cheyney Training School for Teachers, which under his administration has ceased to be a private institution and become one of the standard normal schools of the state of Pennsylvania. Mr. Hill is the author of a collection of poems, *The*

Wings of Oppression (1921), and *Toussaint L'Ouverture* (1928), a play in five acts, in blank verse with occasional prose and lyrical passages. In his writing he is almost always conscious of his mission as a schoolmaster and mindful of the uncertain destiny of those before him. His verse may not reveal the greatest inspiration or flexibility, but sometimes, as in the sonnet below, his earnest feeling is embodied in memorable expression.

"*So Quietly*"

(News item from the *New York Times* on the lynching of a Negro at Smithville, Ga., December 21, 1919: "The train was boarded so quietly . . . members of the train crew did not know that the mob had seized the Negro until informed by the prisoner's guard after the train had left the town. . . . A coroner's inquest held immediately returned the verdict that West came to his death at the hands of unidentified men.")

So quietly they stole upon their prey
And dragged him out to death, so without flaw
Their black design, that they to whom the law
Gave him in keeping, in the broad, bright day,
Were not aware when he was snatched away;
And when the people, with a shrinking awe,
The horror of that mangled body saw,
"By unknown hands!" was all that they could say.
So, too, my country, stealeth on apace
The soul-blight of a nation. Not with drums
Or trumpet blare is that corruption sown,
But quietly—now in the open face
Of day, now in the dark—and when it comes,
Stern truth will never write, "By hands unknown."

ALICE DUNBAR NELSON

Alice Ruth Moore (1875-1935) was born in New Orleans and educated in the schools of that city, with later courses at Columbia, Cornell, the University of Pennsylvania, and the School of Industrial Art in Philadelphia. In 1898 she was married to Paul Laurence Dunbar, and ten years after his death in 1906, to Robert J. Nelson, of Philadelphia.

The mature life of this writer was that of a busy teacher and lecturer as well as author. She served for three years in New Orleans and for a term in Brooklyn before her first marriage, and in 1914 began her work at the Howard High School in Wilmington, Delaware. For several summers also she taught at the State College in Dover and other institutions. She was one of the founders of the White Rose Industrial Home in New York, and the Industrial School for Colored Girls in Delaware. Aside from her stories and poems she edited *Masterpieces of Negro Eloquence* (1913) and *The Dunbar Speaker and Entertainer* (1920), this last containing "the best prose and poetic selections by and about the Negro race."

An early collection, *Violets, and Other Tales,* was privately issued in 1895, but was completely superseded by *The Goodness of St. Rocque, and Other Stories,* published by Dodd, Mead and Company in 1899. About this book, with its quaint charm and gentle sentiment, there is something of the air of yesterday. The style is that of a writer still young—high-flown and generous in its use of adjectives. In one place we read: "There was no moon to-night, but the sky glittered and scintillated with myriad stars, brighter than you can ever see farther North, and the great waves that the Gulf breeze tossed up in restless profusion gleamed with the white fire of phosphorescent flame." Yet even such writing as this seems not wholly unadapated to the Creole life described and the little stories of love and pique and jealousy. The title-piece shows that St. Rocque is a good saint who will grant one's wishes if one will but be sure not to fail to make his novenas with a clean heart. "The Fisherman of Pass Christian" has as its central figure one who was not really a fisherman after all. Perhaps better than the other stories, certainly more tender, is "M'sieu Fortier's Violin," which tells of an old musician fallen on evil days to whom the would-be purchaser of his beloved instrument is generous in the end. " 'Minesse,' he said one day to the white cat,—he told all his troubles to her; it was of no use to talk to Ma'am Jeanne, she was too deaf to understand,—'Minesse, we are gettin' po'. You' père git h'old, an' hees han's dey go no mo' rapidement, an' dere be no mo' soirées dese day. Minesse, eef la saison don' hurry up, we shall eat ver' lil' meat."

The poems of Alice Dunbar Nelson have never been collected but they appeared in various magazines and frequently reached distinction. One of the best is an early sonnet:

> I had not thought of violets of late,
> The wild, shy kind that spring beneath your feet
> In wistful April days, when lovers mate
> And wander through the fields in raptures sweet.
> The thoughts of violets meant florists' shops,
> And bows and pins, and perfumed papers fine;
> And garish lights, and mincing little fops,
> And cabarets and songs, and deadening wine.
> So far from sweet real things my thoughts had strayed,
> I had forget wide fields and clear brown streams;
> The perfect loveliness that God has made—
> Wild violets shy and Heaven-mounting dreams
> And now unwittingly, you've made me dream
> Of violets, and my soul's forgotten gleam.

In very different temper is such a poem as "I Sit and Sew," suggested by the war.

> I sit and sew—a useless task it seems,
> My hands grown tired, my head weighed down with dreams—
> The panoply of war, the martial tread of men,
> Grim-faced, stern-eyed, gazing beyond the ken
> Of lesser souls, whose eyes have not seen Death,
> Nor learned to hold their lives but as a breath—
> But—I must sit and sew.
>
> I sit and sew—my heart aches with desire—
> That pageant terrible, that fiercely pouring fire

On wasted fields, and writhing grotesque things
Once men. My soul in pity flings
Appealing cries, yearning only to go
There in that holocaust of hell, those fields of woe—
But—I must sit and sew.

The little useless seam, the idle patch;
Why dream I here beneath my homely thatch,
When there they lie in sodden mud and rain,
Pitifully calling me, the quick ones and the slain?
You need me, Christ! It is no roseate dream
That beckons me—this pretty futile seam,
It stifles me—God, must I sit and sew?

GEORGIA DOUGLAS JOHNSON

Georgia Douglas was a teacher in Atlanta before becoming, in 1903, the wife of Henry Lincoln Johnson, later recorder of deeds in the District of Columbia. She is the author of three small volumes, *The Heart of a Woman* (1918), *Bronze* (1922), and *An Autumn Love Cycle* (1928). While much of her work transcends the bounds of race, her second booklet was dominated by the striving of the Negro; and her sympathy may also be seen in such a later poem as "Old Black Men."

They have dreamed as young men dream
  Of glory, love and power;
They have hoped as youth will hope
  Of life's sun-minted hour.

They have seen as others saw
Their bubbles burst in air,
And they have learned to live it down
As though they did not care.

In her earlier work Mrs. Johnson cultivated especially the poignant, sharply chiselled lyric that became so popular with Sara Teasdale and some other writers a decade or two ago. Later, however, there came into her verse a deeper, a more mellow note, as in "I Closed My Shutters Fast Last Night."

I closed my shutters fast last night,
Reluctantly and slow,
So pleading was the purple sky
With all the lights hung low;
I left my lagging heart outside
Within the dark alone,
I heard it singing through the gloom
A wordless, anguished tone.

Upon my sleepless couch I lay
Until the tranquil morn
Came through the silver silences
To bring my heart forlorn,
Restoring it with calm caress
Unto its sheltered bower,
While whispering, "Await, await
Your golden, perfect hour."

WALTER WHITE

Walter (Francis) White, born in Atlanta in 1893, was graduated at Atlanta University in 1916, and later studied at the College of the City of New York. In 1918 he began his connection with the National Association for the Advancement of Colored People, first as assistant and eleven years later as acting secretary, then after March, 1931, as secretary of the organization. In this capacity he has been alert to the interests of the Negro throughout the country. A notable victory was scored in 1931 when he led in persuading the United States Senate not to confirm for the Supreme Court a man some of whose utterances had not been friendly to the race.

Mr. White's first novel, *The Fire in the Flint* (1925), contains an abundance of philosophizing, and the workmanship, especially near the beginning, is uncertain; but before the book is finished it presents a situation that grips the reader with its power, and so close do we come to the life of a family in a South Georgia town that the double tragedy near the close seems to come to our own friends. *Flight* (1926) was on the whole not so successful, the latter portion showing signs of haste; but the book attempts something finer than *The Fire in the Flint*, and the struggle of the heroine back to respectability holds the interest firmly. *Rope and Faggot: A Biography of Judge Lynch* (1929) presents graphically the result of ten years of investigation of America's most disgraceful institution. In his addresses and magazine articles as well as his books Mr. White has cultivated a vigorous, elastic style that is admirably adapted to its purpose.

JESSIE FAUSET

Jessie Fauset was born in Philadelphia and spent her early years in that city. In school she was for several terms the only student in her class identified with the Negro, and this fact may partly account for the self-conscious air in her work. After a brilliant career in college at Cornell, Miss Fauset went to the University of Pennsylvania for her Master's degree, and then taught Latin and French in the Dunbar High School in Washington. For some years she served as literary editor of the *Crisis,* and more recently has been a teacher in the DeWitt Clinton High School in New York. Her activities have included study in France, travel in other countries on the Continent, and the writing of considerable poetry, but she is best known for the novels of which she has been the author.

Of these there are four, and to some extent they originated in protest against the unfaithful portrayal of the educated Negro in T. S. Stribling's *Birthright.* In each there is a woman of color whose racial identity might be in doubt and who struggles in the toils of fate. In *There is Confusion* (1924) Joanna Marshall, with something of the artist's desire to realize her ambitions in the larger world of achievement, comes face to face with more than one difficulty and confesses to the intelligent but sensitive Peter Bye that after all she cares more for happiness than greatness. In *Plum Bun* (1928), which showed more maturity, Angela Murray experiences not only the pleasure but also the pain of those who pass beyond the color line. In *The Chinaberry Tree* (1931) Laurentine Strange, the daughter of a white father and an ostracized mother, "awful high and mighty when she was a girl," after disillusion and sorrow at last finds peace. In *Comedy: American Style* (1933), the title being ironic, is the terrific Olivia Cary, one of the most vivid and devastating characters in the whole range of American fiction. Some critics have been disposed to regard *Plum Bun*, with its description of old Philadelphia, as the best of these books; but such an opinion hardly takes note of the human interest in *The Chinaberry Tree* or of the relentlessness with which *Comedy: American Style* drives to its conclusion. There is something very appealing about the family group gathered at last under the tree that came from Alabama to New Jersey, "like spent swimmers who had given up the hope of rescue and then had suddenly met with it, sensing with all their being the feel of the solid ground beneath their feet . . . and everywhere about them the immanence of God." Olivia Cary is moved by the desire to divorce herself from anything pertaining to or suggestive of the

Negro, and in having her way ruins her husband, forces her daughter into marriage with a worthless Frenchman, and drives her youngest son to suicide. At the last she sits a lonely figure amid the havoc she has wrought, far from the happiness she dreamed of and hoped might be hers.

No one of these books is a great novel, and one might especially find fault with the earlier productions. The plotting is not perfect; the style is sometimes overloaded; and perhaps too frequently there is a didactic note. There are also, however, some strong situations, and much of tenderness and beauty. The books not only contributed some memorable characters to the literature of the Negro but also directed attention to a phase of life that, except for the work of Chesnutt, had been almost untouched in American fiction.

COUNTEE CULLEN

No account of Negro poets of the present day can fail to include Countee Cullen. If we may judge by the volumes issued and the prizes received, he has been the most successful of all. One might suppose that he would be treated in the following chapter with McKay and Hughes, but his sympathies, unlike theirs, are with tradition and convention. In some lines he has proclaimed that he is a Negro poet, but again he has said that he wishes his work to be judged on its merit, "with no racial consideration to bolster it up"; and when he wrote a long poem on lynching, he dated it from Paris. Something of this cleavage runs through all that he has written and gives to it an artificiality, a thinness of substance, of which one is not conscious with his two compeers. Yet, in spite of its obvious faults and sometimes its lapses in taste, his work shows much delicate perception and a keen instinct for beauty.

Countee Cullen was born in New York City in 1903 and reared in the atmosphere of a Methodist parsonage. One of his problems has been "that of reconciling a Christian upbringing with a pagan inclination." Even before graduating from high school he began to take prizes in poetry contests. In 1925 he received the degree of Bachelor of Arts at New York University, a year later that of Master of Arts at Harvard; for two years he served as associate editor of *Opportunity,* and there has since been experience as a teacher. In the year of his graduation from college Mr. Cullen brought out his first collection of poems, *Color;* and this has been succeeded by *Copper Sun* (1927), *Caroling Dusk: An Anthology of Verse by Negro Poets* (1927), *The Ballad of the Brown Girl* (1928), *The Black Christ and Other Poems* (1929), *One Way to Heaven,* a novel (1931), and *The Medea and Some Poems* (1935). In 1926, on the basis of his first book, he received the Harmon gold award for literature.

Color, that appeared when the author was but

twenty-three years of age, was a work of promise. The details of color conflict suggest a struggle that is more than racial and common to all mankind. Such poems as "Yet Do I Marvel," "The Shroud of Color," and "Heritage" challenged the attention of any reader. *Copper Sun* hardly indicated the advance that was expected. The book was thinner than its predecessor in both form and content; and when all due credit was given to the lyric impulse of the author, one could hardly fail to note the awkward lines and the faulty rhythms that were all too frequently in evidence. The fact is that there is a sophomoric note in the work of Mr. Cullen that he finds it hard to outgrow. He is seen at his worst in such a stanza as

> I come to no flower but I pluck,
> I raise no cup but I sip,
> For a mouth is the best of sweets to suck;
> The oldest wine's on the lip.

He appears to better advantage in these lines from *Ballad of the Brown Girl:*

> O lovers, never barter love
>   For gold or fertile lands,
> For love is meat and love is drink,
>   And love heeds love's commands.
>
> And love is shelter from the rain,
>   And scowling stormy skies;
> Who casts off love must break his heart
>   And rue it till he dies.

The Black Christ deals with a lynching in a mystical rather than a realistic vein. The victim of the mob returns to those he had known in a form suggesting the Christ. The poem has the importance of showing the author in a sustained effort and is free from much of the earlier affectation. *The Medea* is a translation from Euripides originally made for Rose McClendon. Prose is the medium except for the choruses. The poems included in the book were the result of a pleasure trip to Europe, and once more the author seemed hardly to come face to face with reality. *Caroling Dusk,* the anthology, included the verse of several of the older writers but is distinctly modern in tone. *One Way to Heaven* is a story of life in Harlem in a vein popular for some years. It deals with two phases of life. One is concerned with Mattie, a simple-hearted young serving woman, and Sam Lucas, a rascal who uses revivals to his advantage by feigning conversion but who also has his good qualities. The other has to do with a sophisticated circle of which Constantia Brandon is the center. The story is bright but not wholly convincing and in general had little to add to the reputation of the author.

ALAIN LOCKE

Alain Locke (A.B., Harvard, 1907; Ph.D., *ibid.*, 1918; Rhodes scholar at Oxford, 1907-10), professor of philosophy at Howard University, has been so interested in the work of other writers and artists that one may easily overlook the significance of his own achievement. If the authors in the chapter succeeding and a certain school of sculptors were conceived of as an orchestra, he might well be considered the *maestro* of the performance. Yet he himself belongs in the present chapter, for he has been the critic, the apologist, the teacher. In 1925 he edited *The New Negro,* and two years later, with Montgomery Gregory, *Plays of Negro Life.* In more recent years he has taken as his special province the presentation and enhancement of native African art. On this subject he has written more than a score of articles, but these have been half-hidden in esoteric or scholarly magazines, so that it is not to be wondered at that they are not fully known to the public. Each year also for several years past there has appeared in *Opportunity* a stimulating review of Negro literature. Dr. Locke has a fine sense of the value of words, but with all that he has written he has not yet produced the book of which he is capable, one that will formally organize the content of his numerous articles and give final presentation to his point of view. That book might well be the great work of his life, but for it we have still to wait.*

* Very recently announcement has been made of the Bronze Booklet Series, issued by Associates in Negro Folk Education, Washington, D. C. To the series Dr. Locke has contributed *The Negro and His Music* and *Negro Art: Past and Present.*

OTHER WRITERS

Somewhat in the vein of *Plum Bun* are two books by Nella Larsen (Mrs. Imes), *Quicksand* (1928) and *Passing* (1929). These have as their main theme the lot of the woman of unusual attractiveness face to face with the ways of the world. *Passing* is the story of Clare Kendry, white "with a touch of the tar-brush," who marries away from her people only to be brought back to them by a yearning that ends in tragedy.

Three other writers who by their distinctive gifts have won the attention of the discerning are Angelina W. Grimké, Anne Spencer, and Effie Lee Newsome. Miss Grimké, after excellent early training in the North, was graduated from the Boston Normal School of Gymnastics, and then served for some years as a teacher in the Armstrong and Dunbar high schools in Washington. She is the author of *Rachel* (1921), a three-act prose drama, and numerous poems that show a high degree of finish. Among these is a noble sonnet, "To the Dunbar High School." Mrs. Spencer, whose home is in Lynchburg, Virginia, has an independent and compressed style of writing that makes special appeal to the intelligent. There is hardly any reference to race at all in her poems; instead there is sometimes an exotic note, as in "Before the Feast of Shushan." She shows a preference for modern verse-forms and never leaves one in doubt as to her command of her medium. Mrs. Newsome, of Wilberforce, Ohio, has mastered the difficult art of writing verses for children that keep a sense of literary values and that do not offend by too much of a juvenile air. A typical piece is "Sky Pictures":

> Sometimes a right white mountain
> Or great soft polar bear,
> Or lazy little flocks of sheep
> Move on in the blue air.
> The mountains tear themselves like floss,
> The bears all melt away;
> The little sheep will drift apart
> In such a sudden way.
> And then new sheep and mountains come,
> New polar bears appear
> And roll and tumble on again
> Up in the skies so clear.
> The polar bears would like to get
> Where polar bears belong;
> The mountains try so hard to stand
> In one place firm and strong.
> The little sheep all want to stop
> And pasture in the sky,
> But never can these things be done,
> Although they try and try.

IX

THE NEW REALISTS

THE FORERUNNERS—CLAUDE MCKAY—LANGSTON HUGHES—ERIC WALROND—RUDOLPH FISHER—STERLING BROWN—ZORA NEALE HURSTON—ARNA BONTEMPS

ONE day toward the close of the war a man from Jamaica, Marcus Garvey, rode through the streets of New York in gay apparel as president of the Provisional Republic of Africa, head of the Universal Negro Improvement Association and African Communities League of the World, and president of the Black Star Line of steamships and the Negro Factories Corporation. The central thought that appealed to hosts of people was that of freedom for the race in every sense of the word. Such freedom, it was maintained, transcended the mere demand for political and social rights, and could only be realized under a vast supergovernment controlling the destiny of the race in Africa and throughout the world. It was asserted that the time had come for the Negro to cease depending upon favors grudgingly wrested from the white man and to rely solely on his own resources and the might of his own right arm. Conservative men stood aloof from Mr. Garvey's grandiose schemes, and after a while his career went into eclipse; nevertheless, as no other man of the era, he had given to the Negro a new sense of freedom. His influence on the literature we are now to consider was beyond all estimate.

That literature, like most produced in America in recent years, has been realistic and to some extent analytical. In subject-matter there was influence from some writers who were not of the race and who were disposed to exploit it. Harlem began to be attractive, also anything suggesting the primitive. The popular demand for the exotic and exciting was met by a strident form of music originating in Negro slums and known as jazz. Along with this was a mood that was of the essence of hedonism and paganism. Introspection and self-pity ran riot, and the result was a kind of song known as the "blues," very sad but offered for amusement, the spirit of which may be seen from the following:

> Everybody in Hoboken town—everybody an' me
> Hopped upon a warehouse that was swinging around
> An' went to sea;
> Oh, all day long I's looking for trees—
> Lookin' for sand, lookin' for land,
> 'Cause I've got dose awful, weepin', sleepin',
> Got dose awful sailin', wailin',
> Got dose awful deep sea blues.

Such influences as have been described received strong re-enforcement from the band conducted by

James Reese Europe in the course of the war. This organization was connected with the 369th United States Infantry Regiment (the old 15th New York); it made a specialty of jazz; and about the close of the war it was exceedingly popular with the American Expeditionary Forces and throughout France.

On its more serious side the new temper was represented by such collections as *The New Negro,* edited by Alain Locke, and *Ebony and Topaz,* edited by Charles S. Johnson. These were of immense help in freeing the genius of the Negro. At the same time in the new day there were some deterrent factors. The first was a lack of regard for any accepted standards whatsoever. Young writers were led to believe that they did not need any training in technique, and the popular form of poetizing known as "free verse" was most acceptable because most unrestrained. In prose the desired outlet was found in a sharp staccato form of writing that some well known authors used as a medium but that attacked the very foundations of grammar. A second result of the dominant mood was a preference for sordid, unpleasant, or forbidden themes; and close to this was a certain blatant quality, a striving for effect, that gave an impression of artificiality. In general the writers were closer to the heart of the folk than those considered in the last chapter, but while Uncle Tom and Uncle Remus were outmoded, there was now a fondness for the vagabond or roustabout, so that one might ask if after all the new types were an improvement on the old.

In large measure there was influence from a number of Southern writers who were concerned with Negro folkways in the deep South. The treatment of the black man by Southern authors has undergone considerable change within the last few years. This has been due to a disposition on the part of some to deal fearlessly with phases of life not always brought to the fore, or to a Marxist approach that put considerations of labor above those of race. Accordingly we have had such unusual books as *Amber Satyr*, by Roy Flannagan, *Portrait of Eden*, by Margaret Sperry, and *Stars Fell on Alabama*, by Carl Carmer. John L. Spivak's *Georgia Nigger* is a vivid exposure of the evils of peonage and the chain-gang. There are also at least a few novels that deal with lowly life but endeavor to be above prejudice; such are *Mamba's Daughters*, by DuBose Heyward, and *Glory*, by Nan Bagby Stephens, a recasting of the play *Roseanne*. At the same time there has been the plea of the old South in Stark Young's *So Red the Rose*, and the justification of the section at the expense of both the North and the Negro, as in Margaret Mitchell's *Gone with the Wind*. So far as the Negro is concerned, the typical novels are still such as *Black April* and *Scarlet Sister Mary*, by Julia Peterkin, and *Candy*, by L. M. Alexander. The first of these books has as its central figure a man and the second a woman on the Blue Brook plantation in South Carolina, both of whom are very light in their love affairs. In a later book, *Roll, Jordan, Roll,* the same author's complacency leads her to say, "Negro self-respect demands that since they are destined to be servants, they have a right to be servants of worthy people." Over all such literature is an atmosphere of futility or fatalism. The upstanding and industrious black man who succeeds in the battle of life, is not mentioned; instead the Negro is set before us as a picturesque and simple child that one can afford to humor, or occasionally as a furious animal that one may wish to watch. He must be a genuine artist, white or black, who can deal with the folk material of the Negro and not be overwhelmed or swayed by the social implications of his task.

When we pass from the South to the North, we are immediately met by *Nigger Heaven* (1926), by Carl Van Vechten, which for the present purpose may be regarded as the work of most significance in its decade. This is the perfect illustration of a book that gives facts but that does not tell the truth. Nothing is set down about Harlem for which the author might not be able to cite the evidence; at the same time the work as a whole gives a distorted impression. Even so the book was in some ways well written; it went through several editions; and as no other it influenced the effort of young Negro authors in New York City.

THE FORERUNNERS

Even before the beginning of the so-called Negro literary renaissance there were poets in different parts of the country who threw strong emphasis on the racial idea. Not all reached fulfilment, but there is hardly one who does not have some significance, and collectively they are of the highest importance. Just now we may note George Reginald Margetson, Fenton Johnson, Walter Everette Hawkins, Lucien B. Watkins, Roscoe Conkling Jamison, and Joseph S. Cotter, Jr.

George Reginald Margetson was born at St. Kitts in the British West Indies in 1877 but came to the United States when twenty years of age. While still a young man he produced three small books of poetry, *England in the West Indies* (1906), *Ethiopia's Flight* (1907), and *Songs of Life* (1910), but is best known for a remarkable production, *The Fledgling Bard and the Poetry Society* (1916). In this the young poet sets out to find the Poetry Society and on his way he comments on the politics of the day, questions of interest to the Negro, and anything else that comes to mind, all being in a vein that might well be cultivated more. The seven-line stanza closing with an Alexandrine is suggestive of Byron, and the work as a whole is in the mood of *Don Juan*, but interpolated are various lyrical passages that give free rein to the author's humor. The satire is not always effective, but sometimes, as when directed toward President Woodrow Wilson, it hits the mark.

I'm out to find the new, the modern school
Where Science trains the fledgling bard to fly,
Where critics teach the ignorant, the fool,
To write the stuff the editors would buy;
It matters not e'en though it be a lie—
Just so it aims to smash tradition's crown
And build up one instead decked with a new renown.

I hope I'll be an eligible student,
E'en though I am no poet in a sense,
But just a hot-head youth with ways imprudent—
A rustic ranting rhymer like by chance
Who thinks that he can make the muses dance
By beating on some poet's borrowed lyre,
To win some fool's applause and please his own desire.

. . . . .

Come, Woody, quit your honeymooning;
The Austrians have sunk a boat;
Cut out your wooing and your spooning,
Get busy, write another note!

Fenton Johnson, one of the first of the Negro revolutionary poets, was born in Chicago in 1888 and educated in the public schools of that city and at the University of Chicago. In some of his work he has used free verse and at times has even struck a fatalistic note. He is the author of *A Little Dreaming* (1912), *Visions of Dusk* (1915), and *Songs of the*

Soil (1916), also of a little book of prose sketches entitled *Tales of Darkest America* (1920). The first sketch is entitled "The Story of Myself" and recounts among other things Mr. Johnson's experience with the *Favorite Magazine*. Few poets have struck a more passionate note. In "Tired" the speaker has had enough of "building up somebody else's civilization"; he "will go down to the Last Chance Saloon, drink a gallon or two of gin . . . and sleep the rest of the night on one of Mike's barrels." Of very different temper is "Children of the Sun."

> We are children of the sun,
> Rising sun!
> Weaving Southern destiny,
> Waiting for the mighty hour
> When our Shiloh shall appear
> With the flaming sword of right,
> With the steel of brotherhood,
> And emboss in crimson die
> Liberty! Fraternity!

Walter Everette Hawkins, born in Warrenton, North Carolina, in 1886, went while still in his youth to the city of Washington, where he was employed in the post-office. In more recent years he has lived and worked in Brooklyn. In 1909 he brought out *Chords and Discords,* reissued in Boston in 1920. The strong racial note in his work may be seen from some lines from the poem entitled "A Festival in Christendom."

And so this Christian mob did turn
From prayer to rob, to lynch and burn.
A victim helplessly he fell
To tortures truly kin to hell;
They bound him fast and strung him high,
They cut him down lest he should die
Before their energy was spent
In torturing to their heart's content.
They tore his flesh and broke his bones,
And laughed in triumph at his groans;
They chopped his fingers, clipped his ears
And passed them round as souvenirs.
They bored hot irons in his side
And reveled in their zeal and pride;
They cut his quivering flesh away
And danced and sang as Christians may . . .
And then they raised a Sabbath song;
The echo sounded wild and strong,
A benediction to the skies
That crowned the human sacrifice.

Lucien B. Watkins (1879-1921), born in Chesterfield, Virginia, was educated in the public schools near his home and at the institution in Petersburg now known as the Virginia State College. He became a teacher, but lost his health in the World War and died in Fort McHenry Hospital. Some of his verse is trite and in conventional vein, but his significance may be seen from such a sonnet as "The New Negro," in which he speaks of one who "thinks in black."

Roscoe Conkling Jamison (1888-1918), born in

Winchester, Tennessee, and partly educated at Fisk University, was like Watkins distinctly a minor poet. However, at least once, in "The Negro Soldiers," his muse took wing. This and other pieces were brought together in a booklet, *Negro Soldiers and Other Poems,* published soon after his death by his friend, Charles Bertram Johnson.

These truly are the Brave,
These men who cast aside
Old memories, to walk the blood-stained pave
Of sacrifice, joining the solemn tide
That moves away, to suffer and to die
For Freedom—when their own is yet denied!
O Pride! O Prejudice! when they pass by,
Hail them, the Brave, for you now crucified!

These truly are the Free,
These souls that grandly rise
Above base dreams of vengeance for their wrongs,
Who march to war with visions in their eyes
Of Peace through Brotherhood, lifting glad songs,
Aforetime, while they front the firing line.
Stand and behold! They take the field to-day,
Shedding their blood like Him now held divine,
That those who mock might find a better way!

Joseph S. Cotter, Jr. (1895-1919), the son of a father who has been mentioned in these pages, was graduated from the Central High School in Louisville and had studied just a year and a half at Fisk University when his health broke. He is remembered for the title-piece in *The Band of Gideon and Other Lyrics* (1918).

> The band of Gideon roam the sky,
> The howling wind is their war-cry,
> The thunder's roll is their trump's peal,
> And the lightning's flash their vengeful steel.
> Each black cloud
> Is a fiery steed;
> And they cry aloud
> With each strong deed,
> "The sword of the Lord and Gideon."
>
> . . . . .
>
> The lightnings flash and the thunders roll,
> And "Lord have mercy on my soul,"
> Cry men as they fall on the stricken sod,
> In agony searching for their God.
> Each black cloud
> Is a fiery steed;
> And they cry aloud
> With each strong deed,
> "The sword of the Lord and Gideon."

CLAUDE MCKAY

Most vigorous of Negro poets in the years immediately after the World War was Claude McKay. This author was born in the parish of Clarendon in Jamaica in 1889. His father was a peasant proprietor and his early schoolmaster an older brother who was a freethinker. When nineteen years of age he joined the

Kingston Constabulary, but served for only ten months. In 1911 an English friend who had become interested in his dialect verse helped him to publish *Songs of Jamaica,* six poems with music. Coming to the United States the next year, he spent a brief season at Tuskegee and then went to the Kansas State University, where he remained two years. A legacy of a thousand dollars he has said he lost in "high living and bad business." His daring sonnet, "The Harlem Dancer," attracted attention, and in the course of the war the militant poem, "If We Must Die," was much quoted. For a while Mr. McKay was associate editor of *The Liberator* and *The Masses,* and since then he has traveled much in Europe, especially in Russia and France. In the early days in England he arranged for the publication of *Spring in New Hampshire and Other Poems* (1920); and *Harlem Shadows,* his best known collection, appeared in New York in 1922, the introduction being by Max Eastman, of the *Liberator.* Later publications, all fiction, include *Home to Harlem* (1928), *Banjo,* "a story without a plot" (1929), *Gingertown,* a collection of stories (1932), and *Banana Bottom* (1933). In 1928 Mr. McKay received the Harmon first award for literature.

Spring in New Hampshire, a booklet of forty pages, contains a number of poems on subjects suggested by nature, also several in more dynamic vein. Among the best pieces are not only such as "Flame-Heart" and "The Tropics in New York" but also

Photograph by James Latimer Allen

CLAUDE MC KAY

"The Lynching," "The Harlem Dancer," and "Harlem Shadows." "Flame-Heart" came very near to greatness.

So much have I forgotten in ten years,
  So much in ten brief years! I have forgot
What time the purple apples come to juice,
  And what month brings the shy forget-me-not.
I have forgot the special, startling season
  Of the pimento's flowering and fruiting,
What time of year the ground doves brown the fields
  And fill the noonday with their curious fluting.
I have forgotten much, but still remember
The poinsettia's red, blood-red in warm December.*

Harlem Shadows included the best known poems in the earlier volume and many more.

Through the long night until the silver break
  Of day the little gray feet know no rest,
Through the lone night until the last snow-flake
  Has dropped from heaven upon the earth's white breast,
The dusky, half-clad girls of tired feet
Are trudging, thinly shod, from street to street.

It was not, however, the poem of tenderness or yearning that made most appeal to the public in the decade immediately after the war. The year 1919

---

* This quotation and the next are from *Harlem Shadows*, by Claude McKay. Copyright, 1922, by Harcourt, Brace & Co., New York.

was marked by racial conflicts in Washington, Chicago, Knoxville, and Omaha, while in Elaine, Arkansas, there were prolonged disorders growing out of the system of farm tenancy. The indignation and the forced restraint of the poet were expressed in "White Houses."

> Your door is shut against my tightened face,
> And I am sharp as steel with discontent;
> But I possess the courage and the grace
> To bear my anger proudly and unbent.
> The pavement slabs burn loose beneath my feet,
> A chafing savage, down the decent street;
> And passion rends my vitals as I pass,
> Where boldly shines your shuttered door of glass.
> Oh, I must search for wisdom every hour,
> Deep in my wrathful bosom sore and raw,
> And find it in the superhuman power
> To hold me to the letter of your law!
> Oh, I must keep my heart inviolate
> Against the potent poison of your hate.

To turn from the poems of Claude McKay to the novels he has written is to be aware of something very close to a tragedy. For years he had been writing exquisite or dynamic verse, and the favor of the public, judged at least by commercial standards, was but luke-warm. Now there was a change of tone and emphasis. It is impossible for him to write incompetently; on everything he puts the stamp of virility. After the success of Mr. Van Vechten's *Nigger*

Heaven, however, he and some other authors seemed to realize that it was not the poem or story of fine touch that the public desired, but metal of a baser hue; and he decided to give what was wanted. The result was a novel, *Home to Harlem,* that sold thousands of copies but that with its emphasis on certain degraded aspects of life hardly did justice to the gifts of the writer. Jake Brown, on his first night home from France, meets in a cabaret the little girl Felice, and the book is largely concerned with his search until he finds her again. There is not much of a story, but the realism is stark, the color vivid, and there is an impressionistic view of the crowds in the Harlem streets. Importance attaches to Ray, a character of superior intellect who might be taken for the novelist himself. He overlooks the scene and makes shrewd comment, reappearing in *Banjo,* a longer but more formless work dealing with a group of adventurers left in the wake of the war. This book is not without its deeper notes; the didactic strain in fact may even seem to be overdone. "You're a lost crowd, you educated Negroes," Ray says to a student of lighter hue; "and you will only find yourself in the roots of your own people." He himself was conscious of a deep kinship with the Senegalese and other Africans whom he met. "They made him feel that he was not merely an unfortunate accident of birth, but that he belonged definitely to a race weighed, tested, and poised in the universal scheme. They inspired him with confidence in them. Short of extermination by the Europeans, they were a safe people, protected by their own indigenous culture. Even though they stood bewildered before the imposing bigness of white things, apparently unaware of the invaluable worth of their own, they were naturally defended by the richness of their fundamental racial values."

Gingertown is a collection of twelve stories, six of which are set in Harlem and the others in the West Indies. The author shows that he is best when he is on his native heath, but all of the stories are marked by robustness, though again and again the characters are wanton or gross. *Banana Bottom* goes back to Jamaica and in telling of the career of Bita Plant gives a fine satire on the ways of benevolent folk. An exceptional character is Squire Gensir, an Englishman interested in studying folk-ways but without any semblance of patronage. This book like the others has elements of strength, but one can not help thinking what Mr. McKay might do if he would take a little vacation from slums and water-fronts, see life somewhat more as a whole, and conceive the really great novel of which he is undoubtedly capable.

LANGSTON HUGHES

The significance of Langston Hughes grows out of the fact that, whatever may be his shortcomings, he has been singularly honest in adhering to his point of view and in emphasizing the racial idea. Far more than most men he has rebelled against conventional patterns and lived his life as to himself seemed best. The freedom he has sought for himself he has also insisted upon for others. Born in Joplin, Missouri, in 1902, he spent several of his early years with a grandmother in Lawrence, Kansas, then went to Cleveland, Ohio, where he attended the Central High School and graduated as class poet. His later career has seen travel in many countries and broad acquaintance with life. He went to be with his father, who was in Mexico City, but broke with this parent a year later while he was studying at Columbia. Thrown on his own resources, he worked on a truck farm on Staten Island, next as delivery boy for a florist in New York, and then for two years on a freight steamer that made trips to the Azores and Africa. When twenty-two years of age he found himself in Paris, almost penniless, but jobs as a doorman and as a cook tided him over his difficulty; and at Genoa there was a tramp steamer that permitted him to work his way home. He arrived in New York in November, 1924. In Washington he worked for some months in the office of the *Journal of Negro History,* then as a bus boy at the Wardman Park Hotel. Meanwhile he drew upon his varied experience for a number of poems and became acquainted with Vachel Lindsay and Carl Van Vechten, who helped to introduce him to the wider public.

In 1925, in a contest conducted by *Opportunity*, Mr. Hughes took first prize with his poem "The Weary Blues." The next year he published his first collection, a volume of the same title. Having determined to complete his education, he entered Lincoln University and had been there only a year when he took the Witter Bynner poetry prize for undergraduates. He completed his course in 1929.

The notable thing about *The Weary Blues*, popular in its hour, was that it brought over into literature the jazz and swing of the cabaret, "droning a drowsy syncopated tune" and finding joy in the jungle mood at night. At the same time there are in the book some pieces of very different temper, such as "The Negro Speaks of Rivers" and the noble "Mother to Son."

Fine Clothes to the Jew (1927), the second collection, exaggerated the faults without having the merits of its predecessor. It passes from jazz to the "blues," which, we are reminded, have "a strict poetic pattern—one long line repeated and a third line to rhyme with the first two"; but it would have been just as well, perhaps better, if the book had never been published. No other ever issued reflects more fully the abandon and the vulgarity of its age.

In 1930 Mr. Hughes struck out in a new field, that of the novel, and with *Not Without Laughter* scored a success. He makes very real the story of little Sandy and his grandmother in a town in the Middle West.

We leave the boy in high school in Chicago and can not help hoping that he will prove valiant and that the future will be good to him. Incidentally there is sharp satire on a certain sort of educated person in the character Tempy, the aunt at whose home Sandy sojourns awhile. "At Aunt Hager's house there had been no books except the Bible and the few fairy-tales that he had been given at Christmas; but Tempy had a case full of dusty volumes that were used to give dignity to her sitting-room: a row of English classics bound in red, an *Encyclopedia of World Knowledge* in twelve volumes, a book on household medicine full of queer drawings, and some modern novels—*The Rosary, The Little Shepherd of Kingdom Come*, the newest Harold Bell Wright, and all that had ever been written by Gene Stratton Porter, Tempy's favorite author. The Negro was represented by Chesnutt's *House Behind the Cedars*, and the *Complete Poems* of Paul Laurence Dunbar, whom Tempy tolerated on account of his fame, but condemned because he had written so much in dialect and so often of the lower classes of colored people." The satire is otherwise directed in *The Ways of White Folks* (1934). There is hardly any phase of insincerity that is not exposed, but in "Slave on the Block," "Poor Little Black Fellow," and "The Blues I'm Playing," the book is especially caustic on those who adopt toward the Negro a patronizing attitude. Not all of the stories are equally good, but the best leave an indelible impress;

and if the author had been willing to let his work reveal itself simply as art, without too much complication from the subjective element, the book might have risen to an even higher plane.

Some other productions of Mr. Hughes have special, sometimes limited, social or literary interest. *Dear Lovely Death* (1931) is a collection of a dozen poems of which only a hundred copies were privately printed at the Troutbeck Press in Amenia, New York. *Scottsboro Limited* (1932) consists of four poems and a play on a subject that became of national interest. *Mulatto*, with a title that had already been used for a poem, is a play that opened in New York in the autumn of 1935 and ran throughout the winter. *Popo and Fifina, Children of Haiti* (1932) is a book for young people written in collaboration with Arna Bontemps and illustrated by E. Simms Campbell. *The Dream Keeper and Other Poems* (1932), also a collection for children, is in every way one of the best things Mr. Hughes has done. There are rollicking songs and some typical "blues," but also stanzas in serious vein and lyrics of mystery and beauty. To some extent the book is indebted to the author's previous collections, but it shows far more faith in humanity than either of the earlier works.

> Hold fast to dreams
> For when dreams go
> Life is a barren field
> Frozen with snow.

RUDOLPH FISHER

Rudolph Fisher (1897-1934) was a brilliant figure in the literature of the Negro whose career seemed too soon cut short. He was born in Washington, the son of a minister, the Reverend John Wesley Fisher, but, his father having accepted a pastorate in Providence, Rhode Island, he grew up in that city and in time attended Brown University. Giving attention first to English literature and then to biology, he received the Bachelor of Arts degree in 1919 and the Master's degree the following year. He won Phi Beta Kappa honors, and in his junior year was elected to two other national scholastic fraternities, Sigma Psi for scientific work and Delta Sigma Rho for forensics. Having entered the Medical School at Howard University, he received his degree in 1924 with honors in all subjects, and served for a year as interne in the Freedmen's Hospital in Washington. He then registered at Columbia University to do research work in biology, and a little later became connected with the X-ray division of the New York Department of Health. Already his scientific articles and stories were attracting attention. Interested also in music, he arranged a number of spirituals and was for a while associated with Paul Robeson in giving concerts in and around New York.

Dr. Fisher differed from other writers in giving a light touch to the novel of Negro life. With keen perception and a fine sense of irony he had also the detachment of the artist, and could employ humor when he pleased or be serious without being heavy. *The Walls of Jericho* (1928) is the story of Shine, a young piano mover of marvelous strength. It gives a view of every stratum of society in Harlem. The professional "uplifter" that the writers of the period liked to satirize appears in the person of Miss Cramp. *The Conjure-Man Dies* (1932) is largely concerned with the exploits of "N. Frimbo, Psychist," and shows further ripening of the talent revealed in the earlier work. It may be asked, however, if even these productions take precedence over the short stories for which the author became known. Several of these appeared in the *Atlantic Monthly*, among them "The City of Refuge" (February, 1925) and "Blades of Steel" (August, 1927). They give vivid transcriptions of life in Harlem and show what might have been possible for ability that had just come to full maturity.

ERIC WALROND

Eric Walrond was born in British Guiana in 1898 and in his youth gained wide acquaintance with the West Indies. Coming to New York in 1918, he studied at the College of the City of New York and at Columbia, and a little later was on the staff of *Opportunity*. In 1926 he brought forth *Tropic Death*, a collection of ten stories or sketches dealing with the tragedy in the lives of the poorer people in the West Indies. Sometimes death comes to the Negro peasant through starvation, sometimes through lingering and loathsome disease; or it may be that a drunken marine pulls a trigger to uphold the established order. The book is not always a pleasant one, nor is it a perfect one. Some of the stories are episodic, and frequently the suggestion is so veiled that even the diligent reader is puzzled. "Drought" and "Subjection," however, leave no doubt as to their power. In general Mr. Walrond excelled in the freshness of his material, in his clear perception of what has value, and in the strength of his style. One can only regret that he has not produced more within recent years.

STERLING BROWN

Of the poets now at work Sterling Brown is in the front rank. He differs from some other writers in the impression of maturity he gives and in his firm handling of any material he chooses to use. Never does he suggest the need of apology or patronage. While he is capable in classic English verse, his chief contribution to the literature of the Negro and the country has been the road-song—the voice of the humble worker, the bad man, the roustabout. For this he has discarded the dialect of a previous generation and employed a racy idiom that is the very speech of the folk. He has been quite as good in his critical articles, one of his chief objectives being the building up of an audience that will not be deterred by puritanical inhibitions or any question of social implication. Thus he said in *Opportunity* (February, 1930): "I submit for consideration this statement, probably no startling discovery: that those who might be, who should be a fit audience for the Negro artist are, taken by and large, fundamentally out of sympathy with his aims and his genuine development. I am holding no brief for any writer, or any coterie of writers, or any racial credo. I have as yet no logs to roll, and no brickbats to heave. I have, however, a deep concern with the development of a literature worthy of our past, and of our destiny; without which literature certainly we can never come to much. I have deep concern with the development of an audience worthy of such a literature."

Sterling Brown, born in Washington in 1901, after completing his secondary education in the schools of that city entered Williams College in 1918. He was elected to Phi Beta Kappa in his junior year, duly graduated in 1922, and the next year received the Master of Arts degree at Harvard. After some work as a teacher at other institutions, he entered in 1929 upon his period of service at Howard University. There he is now a member of the department of English, being chiefly responsible for the courses in American literature, especially those having to do with the literature of the Negro.

In 1932 Mr. Brown brought out his first collection of poems, *Southern Road*, and the strong portrayal of Negro folk characters made an immediate impression. Here are road songs, chants of the "onrestless river," "tin roof blues," and poems in more personal vein. One may not always have the preference of the author but can at least respect his obedience to his vision. A prominent characteristic of his work, one linking him with the bards of old, is that several poems almost read themselves aloud. Among the most notable pieces is "Strong Men." *

They cooped you in their kitchens,
They penned you in their factories,
They gave you the jobs that they were too good for,
They tried to guarantee happiness to themselves
By shunting dirt and misery to you.

You sang:
Me an' muh baby gonna shine, shine,
Me an' muh baby gonna shine.
The strong men keep a-comin' on
The strong men git stronger. . . .

They bought off some of your leaders
You stumbled, as blind men will . . .
They coaxed you, unwontedly soft-voiced. . . .
You followed a way,
Then laughed as usual.

---

* The quotation is the second half of the poem. This and "Salutamus" are from *Southern Road*, by Sterling Brown. Copyright, 1932, by Harcourt, Brace & Co., New York, N. Y.

They heard the laugh and wondered;
Uncomfortable;
Unadmitting a deeper terror. . . .
The strong men keep a-comin' on
Gittin' stronger. . . .

What, from the slums
Where they have hemmed you,
What, from the tiny huts
They could not keep from you—
What reaches them
Making them ill at ease, fearful?
Today they shout prohibition at you
"Thou shalt not this"
"Thou shalt not that"
"Reserved for whites only"
You laugh.

One thing they cannot prohibit—
The strong men . . . coming on
The strong men gittin' stronger.
Strong men . . . .
Stronger. . . .

Not wholly different in spirit even if in form is the sonnet "Salutamus," which takes as a keynote the line from *Henry IV*, "O Gentlemen, the time of life is short."

The bitterness of days like these we know;
Much, much we know, yet cannot understand
What was our crime that such a searing brand
Not of our choosing, keeps us hated so.

Despair and disappointment only grow,
Whatever seeds are planted from our hand,
What though some roads wind through a gladsome land?
It is a gloomy path that we must go.

And yet we know relief will come some day
For these seared breasts; and lads as brave again
Will plant and find a fairer crop than ours.
It must be due our hearts, our minds, our powers;
These are the beacons to blaze out the way.
We must plunge onward; onward, gentlemen. . . .

ZORA NEALE HURSTON

Zora Neale Hurston, born in Eatonville, Florida, went for her preparatory school training to Morgan College in Baltimore, later studied at Howard, and in 1927 received a degree at Columbia. Since then she has lived mainly in New York. Her story "Spunk" took a prize in the *Opportunity* contest in 1925, and by that time her work was appearing in other periodicals also. In 1932 some of her folk sketches were presented for a brief run at the John Golden Theatre, and more recently she has been connected with the Federal Theatre Project.

Miss Hurston early began to go back to her old home to collect the tales heard in childhood and to inveigle people into telling her "big old lies." She would get together a group of men in a railroad or turpentine camp or in a phosphate mining village, talk informally until they were no longer self-conscious, and then see which could outdo the other with his yarn. Similarly she studied voodooism in New Orleans. With such a background she produced the novel, *Jonah's Gourd Vine* (1934). This is largely concerned with John Buddy Pearson, the offspring of a white tenant farmer and a Negro woman who leaves the sordid home of his stepfather to make his way in the world. Capable and magnetic, he prospers and rises in social position, eventually becoming moderator of a Baptist association; but he is far too amorous and at the end of a long lane meets his fate. The story is not well integrated, and any merit the book possesses is largely in such a detached episode as Pearson's sermon on the creation. The author struck her true vein with *Mules and Men* (1935), the first part of which brings together a number of folk tales, the latter portion describing voodoo practices in the South. There are animal tales, stories of race relations, and spontaneous and original creations, in all of which may be seen the lively imagination of the Negro. Like some others who have dealt in folk-lore, Miss Hurston has not escaped criticism at the hands of those who frowned upon her broad humor and the lowly nature of her material. Her interest, however, is not in solving problems, the chief concern being with individuals. As for the untutored Negro, she presents him without apology, a character as good as other characters but different. Taking a bright story wherever it may be found, she passes it on, leaving to others the duty and the pleasure of philosophizing.

ARNA BONTEMPS

One of the recent Negro authors who will best bear watching is Arna Bontemps. This writer was born in Alexandria, Louisiana, in 1902, but while still very young was taken by his parents to California. He spent his boyhood in Los Angeles, studied for a while at the University of Southern California, and in 1923 was graduated with honor at Pacific Union in Angwin. Since then he has had a varied career as a teacher, has spent much time in New York, and more recently has lived in Chicago.

Mr. Bontemps has been alert to later styles of writing but is in no sense to be identified with the Harlem school. Better balanced than most of his contemporaries, he has lived above the fads of the moment, and had full respect for standard literary forms. However, the poem that first gave the public some idea of his ability, "Golgotha is a Mountain," was in free verse. It was in 1926 that this won the Alexander Pushkin poetry prize of one hundred dollars in a contest conducted under the auspices of *Opportunity* and made possible by the donation of a thousand dollars by Mr. Casper Holstein, of New York, for several awards in literature and music. Yet ultimately it is likely that all of the verse of Mr. Bontemps will be regarded simply as a means of developing his sensitive and elastic prose. His first novel, *God Sends Sunday* (1931), goes to the race track, giving a brisk account of the career of Augie, a jockey "no bigger than a minute," who basks in the light of success until his "luck done change" and wanders to California to dream of his vanished glory. While the book is perhaps stronger in incident than in character, it had the merit of opening a new field and contains some scenes not easily forgotten. Of different temper was *Black Thunder* (1936), a story based on the attempted insurrection of Gabriel Prosser in Richmond, Virginia, in 1800. In spite of the detachment and restraint of Mr. Bontemps, in all that he has written there seems to be an undertone of tragedy. In this new novel the tragedy rises to the dignity and sweep of an oratorio. The characters also show a ripening art. Aside from the stalwart Gabriel himself, there is Juba, his well beloved, a young woman beaten with many stripes but of spirit still unbroken; and Melody, who is in touch with the white friends of Liberty, Equality, Fraternity. One remembers also Mingo, the free Negro, to whom "anything would be better than the sight of his own woman stripped and bleeding at a whipping post"; and Pharaoh and old Ben, slaves not only in body but in soul. In spite of an occasional blemish, one is led to ask if in the whole range of Negro fiction there is a book to equal this in quality. Some smaller things have been written by the author

—*Popo and Fifina, Children of Haiti* (1932), mentioned in connection with Mr. Hughes, and *You Can't Pet a Possum* (1934); but in all that Mr. Bontemps may do or attempt in the future it is the standard of this work that he will have to keep in mind. *Black Thunder* is not only an achievement but a challenge.

OTHER WRITERS

Among the writers from whom much may be expected in the future is Arthur Huff Fauset, a graduate of the University of Pennsylvania (A.B., 1921; A.M., 1924) and now principal of the Joseph Singerly Public School in Philadelphia. In 1926, in the Holstein contest conducted by *Opportunity*, Mr. Fauset won the first prize of one hundred dollars in the short story section with "Symphonesque," a beautiful piece of work that found its way into the anthologies. He has studied folk-lore in Nova Scotia and the lower South, has written *For Freedom*, a book on Negro achievement primarily for children, and is the author of a forthcoming life of Sojourner Truth. His ambition, we have been told, is "to tell the story of the Negro in America and the working class, wherever we find it, from the worker's point of view and in his behalf"; but he has also an appreciation of the classic and writes ever with a firm sense of style.

George S. Schuyler, born in Providence, Rhode Island, received his early training in the schools of

Syracuse, New York, and later entered the army of the United States, becoming a lieutenant. He served for some years on the editorial board of the *Messenger*, and more recently has been on the staff of the *Pittsburgh Courier*, writing the column "Views and Reviews." He is the author of *Slaves To-Day: A Story of Liberia* (1931), also of *Black No More* (1931), this being "an account of the strange and wonderful workings of science in the land of the free, A. D., 1933-40." Mr. Schuyler is a free lance and has contributed numerous articles to the *Nation* and other periodicals. He delights in puncturing smugness, but he often has something vital to say and his point of view is always worth considering.

John Frederick Matheus, an honor graduate of Western Reserve (A.B., 1910; A.M., Columbia, 1921), was for twelve years a teacher of the Romance languages at the Florida Agricultural and Mechanical College in Tallahassee, and since 1922 has been a professor at the West Virginia State College in Institute. He has won several prizes, taking the first award with his story "Fog" in the contest conducted by *Opportunity* in 1925, and winning first place the next year in the Personal Experience section with a sketch entitled "Sand." In 1926 also his story "Swamp Moccasin" took first place in the contest conducted by the *Crisis*. Mr. Matheus has been interested in the drama as well as the short story and some of his one-act plays have found their way into the collections. One wonders why he has not published more in book form, for his work is vivid and powerful, reaching a high grade of excellence.

Of the poets several of the more capable and promising are represented in Countee Cullen's *Caroling Dusk*, among them Gwendolyn B. Bennett, Helene Johnson, Lucy Ariel Williams, George Leonard Allen, Lewis Alexander, and Jonathan Henderson Brooks. Gwendolyn Bennett was born in Texas but educated in the East. She spent two years in the Fine Arts department of Teachers College at Columbia, and was graduated from Pratt Institute in Brooklyn in 1924. She had been teaching just a few months at Howard University when she was awarded the foreign study scholarship of the Delta Sigma Theta Sorority. Later she became connected with *Opportunity*. Her own work shows respect for established forms, but much of it has also strong racial emphasis. Helene Johnson's home was in Boston, but she has studied largely in New York, at Columbia, and has contributed to *Vanity Fair* and several metropolitan dailies. Her "Sonnet to a Negro in Harlem" is especially effective in its sensuousness. Lucy Ariel Williams was born in Alabama, studied at Talladega College and Fisk University, then went to the Conservatory of Music at Oberlin. Her poem "Northboun' " received first prize in the *Opportunity* contest of 1926. George Leonard Allen, of North Carolina, has adhered mainly to standard forms of writing but also strikes the racial note in his work. His poem "To Melody" was awarded the prize for the best sonnet in a contest conducted within the state by the North Carolina division of the United Daughters of the Confederacy. Lewis Alexander, orginally of Washington, studied in the public schools of that city and at Howard and the University of Pennsylvania. He has cultivated Japanese forms of writing, has been connected with several Little Theatre movements, and edited the Negro number of the *Carolina Magazine* (May, 1927). His work shows a vein of genuine ability. Among the titles of individual poems are "Africa," "The Dark Brother," and "Negro Woman." Jonathan Henderson Brooks, of Mississippi, after a youth of hardship finally attended Tougaloo College and entered the ministry. He has been alert to new tendencies and much of his work has been moved by the racial impulse; at the same time the religious note is prominent in his poems.

Several magazines representing literary groups here and there have appeared within recent years. *Black Opals* ran for several numbers in Philadelphia, beginning in 1927; and the *Saturday Evening Quill* was brought out annually in Boston for some years, beginning in 1928. *Fire,* "a quarterly devoted to the younger Negro artists," was issued in November, 1926, under the editorship of Wallace Thurman, and its flame was so intense that it burnt itself up immediately. More recently *Challenge* has been issued occasionally from offices in New York or Boston. There are also the college magazines or annuals. At Howard is the *Stylus,* with at least one special number each spring. *The Brown Thrush,* an interesting collection of the verse of students at Talladega and Tougaloo, appeared in book form in 1932, featuring the work of Lucy Ariel Williams and Jonathan Henderson Brooks. A second number of the anthology appeared in 1935, with contributions from students in six other institutions.

Two young women of Philadelphia have recently published collections of their poems. "Eve Lynn" (Evelyn Reynolds) and Mae V. Cowdery are respectively the authors of *No Alabaster Box* (1936) and *We Lift Our Voices* (1936). Both books contain verse of beauty, the latter perhaps burning with the more intense glow. Miss Cowdery won the *Crisis* poetry prize in 1927 with "Longings" and "Lamps," but for the moment we may pass even these by for the short piece entitled "Feast" and the latter portion of "Having Had You."

> I am drunk with beauty
> For
> I have had a feast
> Of gold and scarlet leaves
> And the deep blue wine
> Of autumn wind.

. . . . .

Were you anything
But what you are . . .
A dream come true
And now a dream again . . .
I might have you back!

But having had you once
And lost you,
It is too much
To want you back again!

Also now of Philadelphia is a young man, Theodore Anthony Stanford, recently the author of a thin but beautiful volume, *Dark Harvest* (1936). Mr. Stanford's work is without special racial emphasis and may be open to improvement in technique, but such lines as "A silver echo flung against the dawn" and "The shape and hue of their impermanence" show that we have to reckon with a genuine poet. Of different quality is the vigorous and lusty verse of Willard Wright contributed to *The American Caravan: 1936*. This perhaps could be more articulate, but at least in its vein it gives promise for the future.

Finally there are those two obstreperous poets, Frank Marshall Davis, of Chicago, and J. Harvey L. Baxter, of Roanoke, Virginia. They are different but each has such assurance as could hardly be equalled in this world or in the world to come. Mr. Davis is the author of *Black Man's Verse* (1935), a book in an extremely modernistic vein. He describes himself as "a Duskymerican born December 31, 1905, in

Arkansas City, Kansas, and exposed to what is termed education at the public schools there, at Friends University in Wichita and at Kansas State College." He says that if his book is condemned he has "enough ego to blame it upon the innate stupidity of the human species," and then proceeds to give us some brisk free verse, representative pieces being "Chicago's Congo," "sonata for an orchestra," and "Love Notes at Night," "melody for a zither." The last section, "Ebony under Granite," gives a series of striking vignettes. Mr. Baxter is the author of *That Which Concerneth Me* (1934) and *Sonnets for the Ethiopians and Other Poems* (1936). His diction is sometimes strange, especially in his first book, and he often begins a poem better than he ends it, but he certainly has flashes with which one has to reckon. In the second book the sonnets on the Ethiopians show strong and natural feeling but are especially lacking in finish. Among the other sonnets, however, is "Blackmail," beginning, "Call me not daddy of your new-born son." "To a Common Question" has a clear conception but like many other pieces is weakest at the close.

What school did you attend? Name your degrees,
  And were you bred at Harvard or at Yale?
How many years abroad, across the seas
  To gulp at Bonn, or sup old Oxford's ale?
What alphabets of Greek do you possess,
  And what about your class, fraternity?

Talk of the badge you wear upon your breast,
  And other boons of your divinity.

I did not come the way of classic halls,
  My keys were won from hard begrudging earth,
I go as scholar of the cabin walls,
  As student of the common heath and hearth.
Each page into the book of life I turn,
I view as ashes of a cankered urn.

X

DRAMA AND STAGE, 1916-1936

EFFORT IN THE DRAMA: WILLIS RICHARDSON AND RANDOLPH EDMONDS—CHARLES GILPIN—RICHARD B. HARRISON—ROSE MCCLENDON—PAUL ROBESON

THE decade immediately after the World War witnessed a great awakening of interest in the portrayal of Negro life in the drama. Within a decade and a half more was accomplished than in all the years preceding. In large measure the new temper was due to the forces mentioned in the last chapter. The American people were willing as never before to attend to anything pertaining to the Negro in the arts, and lovers of the theatre were alert to any fresh development. Meanwhile among the Negro people themselves there was a new consciousness, with an increasing regard for all forms of racial achievement.

The attention now given to the Negro in the drama was not as sudden a development as it seemed. As early as 1909 Edward Sheldon, already known for *Salvation Nell*, brought forth a play, *The Nigger*, in which the central figure was the lieutenant-governor of a Southern state who proved to be of

Negro descent. The title was unfortunate, the treatment of much of the material superficial, and the cast was made up wholly of white performers; but the drama in its brief career at least suggested the serious treatment of themes relating to the Negro. In the first decade of the century also an aspiring little group of players at the Pekin Theatre in Chicago gained some measure of success in the legitimate drama, and within a few years the Lafayette Players in New York worked with similar effect. Through these and other agencies such capable performers as Charles Gilpin, Andrew Bishop, Frank Wilson, Carlotta Freeman, Anita Bush, Cleo Desmond, and Inez Clough became known to the public. In the spring of 1914 a one-act tragedy of Negro life, *Granny Maumee,* by Ridgely Torrence, was produced by the Stage Society of New York, the part of the central figure being taken by Dorothy Donnelly, one of the most sincere of American actresses. On April 5, 1917, Mrs. Norman Hapgood and Robert Edmond Jones presented the Hapgood Players—all Negroes—in *Granny Maumee* and two other dramas by Mr. Torrence, *The Rider of Dreams* and *Simon the Cyrenian.* Prominent in the casts were Andrew Bishop, Opal Cooper, Blanche Deas, and Inez Clough; and in general the performances betokened a new day in the Negro theatre. After the war several colleges that had been giving standard English plays began also to be interested in those employing racial themes. The

Howard (University) Players, originally organized a decade before, in 1921 struck out in the new vein; the Hampton Players began work in 1926; and at Tougaloo was formed the Robeson Dramatic Club. The Gilpin Players, organized in Cleveland in 1920, in course of time were able to give for a week at a commercial theatre such a work as *Roseanne*. Early in 1923, under the direction of Raymond O'Neil, the Ethiopian Art Players began to appear in Chicago, the first production being Wilde's *Salomé*, with Evelyn Preer in the title-part and Laura Bowman as Herodias. Late in the spring the aggregation was shifted to New York, and for at least brief periods there were performances at the Frazee and Lafayette Theatres, included in the repertoire being a one-act play, *The Chip Woman's Fortune*, by a Negro writer, Willis Richardson.

As we proceed we shall have to note at one time or another the effort of Negroes in plays having nothing to do with race; second, that in plays of Negro life written by white authors; and finally, that in plays, chiefly of Negro life, written by Negroes. The second of these three spheres has so far been the most important, and one notes also that it is here that old patterns have been most persistent. A typical production was *Goin' Home*, by Ransom Rideout, presented at the Masque Theatre in New York in the early autumn of 1928. In this a New Orleans Negro marries a mercenary young French woman; a white

American major whom the Negro had served in the United States is too friendly with the wife; and the Negro, letting old fidelity rise above all other considerations, kills his best friend, a majestic Senegalese, to save the major's life, and is last seen going home with the man who had betrayed him. George Sklar, writing in the *New Theatre Magazine* (July, 1935), said: "The American theatre has never given up its minstrel-show conception of the Negro. The fiction of that conception has continued from the first burnt-cork end man down to Amos and Andy to-day. It was the fiction which played up the mythical idiosyncrasies of color and made those idiosyncrasies a butt for the white man's laughter." What has held with reference to the drama has been even more true of the moving picture. That form of entertainment must be adapted to all the people and all the sections of the country, so that, as James Weldon Johnson has observed, it must be "built on the greatest common denominator of public opinion and public sentiment." It thus happens that Negro actors for the screen have in general not been permitted to portray even so high a type of character as is occasionally presented on the stage. Quite in line with convention were *Hallelujah* and *Hearts in Dixie*, and the more recent *Imitation of Life*.

With the new emphasis on the drama, and the increasing popularity of moving pictures, there was a decline in the old form of musical comedy; but, even so, early in the period three or four shows were exceedingly successful. In the summer of 1921, after various vicissitudes in getting started, *Shuffle Along* came by way of Washington and Philadelphia to the Sixty-third Street Theatre in New York, and immediately became a sensation. The production included many catchy songs, mainly in the new "jazz" or "blues" vein; it gave Florence Mills her first appearance on Broadway; and it featured the comedians, F. E. Miller and Aubrey Lyles. One of the mirth-provoking scenes was that in which these two men offered a burlesque of going into "big business," the result of their exploit being a small grocery-store. Two years later Miller and Lyles brought out a new show, *Runnin' Wild*, while some of their former colleagues presented still another offering. Meanwhile Florence Mills found other opportunity for the exercise of her talent.

This remarkable performer, small in stature but with a genius for light entertainment, was born in Washington in 1895. As a child six years of age she appeared in private recitals for members of the diplomatic corps, amazing people even then by her skill in singing and dancing. Later she was with two sisters in vaudeville or with small troupes touring the country, and was employed in a cabaret in Harlem when the call came to succeed one of the principals in *Shuffle Along*. In course of time she left that show to become the star of Lew Leslie's *Plantation Revue*, and going to London was acclaimed as one of the most gifted entertainers that great city had ever seen. The vehicle, known in England as *Dixie to Dover,* became *Dixie to Broadway* on the return to New York, and gave still further proof of the ability of the star. In the spring of 1926 Florence Mills appeared in a new revue called *Blackbirds,* first at the Alhambra in New York, later for some months in Paris, and then for most of the next winter in London. Her success was unbounded. Petite and piquant, she knew how to make the most of a small birdlike voice, and was especially appealing in the song, "I'm a Little Blackbird Looking for a Bluebird." After a tour of Europe she returned to New York in October, 1927, and was making extensive plans for the future when she died after an operation on the first of November.

Harlem was stunned, and throughout the great city the blow was felt. Thousands who had never met the artist felt that they had lost a friend. The service at Mother Zion A. M. E. Church was set for one o'clock, but the crowd was there at half-past ten; and tens of thousands were in the streets. Melville Charlton played; Jules Bledsoe, Jessie Zackary, and other friends from the stage sang solos; and one, overcome, fell to the floor, screaming. The audience was deeply moved. Outside an aeroplane, circling low, released a flock of blackbirds.

For the *Boston Evening Transcript* W. A. Macdonald wrote a story whose movement impressed

CHARLES S. GILPIN AS "THE EMPEROR JONES"

every reader. The *Evening Journal* and the *Evening Graphic* gave the life of the young woman in serial form. The *New York Times* said in an editorial: "Her fame in the international theatre is more than a sign of the advancement of Negroes. She was one of the leaders whose accomplishment sets the whole racial movement a notch or two forward. No special plea for lenient judgment was suggested in her work. None was needed. The quality of her performance, the very timbre of her voice, cut the ground from under the critic who might have liked to patronize. [She did her work] with an air of childlike enjoyment, knowing how good it was, certain of delighting her audience, performing always with a relish and assurance as far removed as possible from conceit."

When we turn from shows and revues to the standard drama we find that there have never ceased to be those who aimed at the highest achievement; thus in the spring of 1916 the Edward Sterling Wright Players made a favorable impression in *Othello* in some of the larger cities of the East. In the new day, however, chief importance attached to the fresh interpretation of Negro life, and in work in this vein for the stage some writers who were not of the race led the way.

We have already mentioned in passing the three short plays by Ridgely Torrence. On October 31, 1919, the rising dramatist, Eugene O'Neill, offered at the Provincetown Playhouse *The Dreamy Kid*, a one-act tragedy set in the underworld of Harlem with a cast made up wholly of Negroes. A year later he produced *The Emperor Jones,* the vehicle in which Charles Gilpin became famous. In May, 1924, appeared *All God's Chillun Got Wings,* a play in which the leading characters are a Negro student and a young white woman not of the best character; and it was in this production that Paul Robeson first became known to the larger public. Although some of the sensational papers in New York endeavored to make capital out of the theme and to have the performance forbidden, the play held the boards for several weeks. Yet it can not be considered satisfactory, for it fundamentally violates the truth of life, and the Negro people were quite as strong as others in registering their objections. *The Emperor Jones* accordingly remains the author's strongest contribution to the racial drama of the period, and indeed one of the most distinctive works he has yet produced.

The play is a highly dramatic study of panic and fear. The Emperor Jones is a Negro who has broken out of jail in the United States and escaped to what is termed "a West Indian island not yet self-determined by white marines." Here he is sufficiently bold and ingenious to make himself ruler within two years. He moves unharmed among his sullen subjects by virtue of a legend of his invention that only a silver bullet can harm him; but at length, when he has seized all the riches in sight, he deems it advisable to flee. As the play begins, the measured sound of a tom-tom beating in the hills gives warning that the natives are in conclave, using all kinds of incantations to work themselves up to the point of rebellion. Nightfall finds the Emperor at the edge of a forest where he has food hidden and through whose trackless waste he knows a way to safety. His revolver carries five bullets for his pursuers and a silver one for himself in case of need. Bold and adventurous, he plunges into the jungle at sunset; but at dawn, half-crazed, naked, and broken, he stumbles back to the starting-place, only to find the natives quietly waiting for him. Now follows a vivid succession of strange sounds and shadows, with terrible visions from the past. As the Emperor's fear quickens, the forest seems alive with threatening people who stare at and bid for him. Finally, shrieking at the worst vision of all, he is driven back to the clearing and to his death, the tom-tom beating ever faster as the fatal moment nears.

In the closing days of 1926 was presented at the Provincetown Playhouse *In Abraham's Bosom*, a drama of frustration in which the central figure cries out at the climax to the ghosts of his parents that they should never have conceived him. The leading parts were taken by Jules Bledsoe (later Frank Wilson) and Rose McClendon, and in the spring of 1927 the production was awarded the Pulitzer Prize. The author was Paul Green, of the faculty of the University of North Carolina, who has also written *The No 'Count*

Boy and in his book, *Lonesome Road,* brought together several other plays of Negro life. Meanwhile, in 1923, Nan Bagby Stephens had offered *Roseanne,* a play set in the South in which the chief character is a magnetic but erring Negro preacher. Very different and with more emphasis on mass effects was *Lulu Belle* (1926), a melodrama by Edward Sheldon and Charles MacArthur that had extraordinary success. The story is that of a little colored adventuress who goes from Harlem to an apartment in Paris provided for her by a nobleman. The leading woman was Lenore Ulric, but Evelyn Preer also had an important part, and the great majority of those in the large mixed cast were Negroes. Several of the scenes were very vivid. Then in 1927 came *Porgy,* by DuBose and Dorothy Heyward, an adaptation from the novel by the former. The play was well staged and proved to be one of great emotional power, the singing at some points being exceedingly effective. Rose McClendon took the part of Serena, whose husband is murdered in the first act and in whose room a company gathers for the wake.

On February 26, 1930, at the Mansfield Theatre, was presented *The Green Pastures,* a work by Marc Connelly adapted from Roark Bradford's *Ol' Man Adam and His Chillun.* Nothing could have been further from the usual dramatic offering. Instead of following the standard pattern, the play used a succession of eighteen scenes, these portraying Biblical events as they might be imagined by a group of untutored Negroes in the bayou country of the deep South. To these unlettered but devout folk heaven was a place where there would be one long holiday, where fish-frys were plentiful, and where "de Lawd" had a box of thunderbolts ready for any who incurred his displeasure. In the course of the action the chief figure appeared in all but two scenes, creating Adam and Eve, driving Cain "clean out o' de county," reproving his "chillun" for breaking the Sabbath with jazz music and crap games, and helping Joshua to win the battle of Jericho. Many people felt that the whole thing was sacrilegious; others found it singularly moving, with the laughter that is close to tears.

Other plays of Negro life followed, but not one of three now to be mentioned was for people of delicate taste. *Bloodstream* (1932), presented at the Times Square Theatre, was the work of a young playwright from Montana, Frederick Schlick. Four Negroes and one white convict work out their destinies in the gloom of the Black Top Mine Prison, over them being a brutal warden. The drama was well acted but proved to be too violent and gruesome even for a public inured to shocks. *They Shall Not Die* (1934), a work in three acts by John Wexley produced by the Theatre Guild at the Royale Theatre, was a vivid presentation of the well known Scottsboro Case. Again the acting was good, as might be supposed, but the strong realism of the scenes made but limited appeal to the public. *Stevedore,* however, presented in the same season by the Theatre Union at the Civic Repertory Theatre, was, by reason of its dramatic values, surprisingly successful. This play, the work of Paul Peters and George Sklar, struck a new note in its revelation of the economic and spiritual struggle of the black laboring man. Florrie Reynolds, a young white woman beaten by the man with whom she has been secretly in love, in the endeavor to deceive her husband says that she has been attacked by a Negro. To this theme is added that of unrest among the stevedores, who at last are protesting against starvation wages and inhuman hours of work. Lonnie Thompson, their stalwart leader, girds them for the contest. He himself is arrested in connection with the crime suggested by Florrie Reynolds, but escapes. A mob forms, and he is finally killed; but the lynch-gang is routed and it is indicated that those who stood with the hero will continue the fight until victory and justice are won.

When one turns to original Negro effort in the drama he finds that most of the work that has been produced has not yet gone beyond the range of experiment and that there is great room for advance in technique. He notes immediately *Appearances* (1925), by Garland Anderson; *Harlem* (1929), by Wallace Thurman in collaboration with William Jordan Rapp; *Run Little Chillun* (1933), by Hall Johnson; and *Mulatto* (1935), by Langston Hughes.

There are also the productions of the Federal Projects Theatre under the auspices of the Works Progress Administration.

Appearances had Negro actors in three of the seventeen parts and included a court scene in which the hero was charged with assault; yet it was not really a racial drama, being dominated by the idea that all things are possible to him that believeth and who will make the best use of his powers. The author was a bellboy and switchboard operator in San Francisco who made many friends by the good cheer which he radiated. His simple moralizing offering was given much publicity and was politely received, but had hardly the strength to hold the public interest for any length of time. *Harlem* included scenes that were authentic in locol color, but did not rise above the plane of routine racketeering melodrama. *Run Little Chillun* was not so much a play as sublimated vaudeville. It depended for success on two of its four scenes, one being the gathering of a primitive religious cult at night, the rites and dances developing into an orgy, and the other being a church scene that gave opportunity for the singing of a number of spirituals. *Mulatto* dealt with the old theme of the plight of children born to white planters by the Negro women dependent upon them, though a new twist was given when Colonel Norwood, running for the legislature, was rejected by his neighbors because of his intimacy with his housekeeper. The play was more than once said to be special pleading, and it was caustically criticised for its technical faults, but, to the surprise of many, it remained on the stage for months, for the reason that, as one critic said, it was "not without its theatrical punches." The WPA Negro Theatre project in New York rendered the double benefit of encouraging the legitimate drama and of enlisting the services of about three hundred Negro actors, some of them performers with rich experience. There was opportunity not only in interpretation but also in stage hand technique, play direction, and other fields in which formerly there had been little or none. The success attending the early productions at the New Lafayette, *Walk Together Chillun*, *The Conjure-Man Dies*, adapted from the novel by Rudolph Fisher, and a modernistic version of *Macbeth*, fully justified the hopes that had been held for the venture.

WILLIS RICHARDSON AND RANDOLPH EDMONDS

Quite as significant as such efforts as those just considered was the work of some writers farther South, representative of whom are Willis Richardson and Randolph Edmonds.

Mr. Richardson deserves the credit of being a pioneer. Born in Wilmington, North Carolina, in 1889, he attended school in Washington and then entered the Government service as a clerk. In November, 1919, he indicated the line of his chief interest by a paper in the *Crisis* entitled "The Hope of a Negro Drama." His first play to be presented on the stage, *The Deacon's Awakening,* was given in St. Paul, Minnesota, in 1921. Two years later came *The Chip Woman's Fortune,* to which reference has been made in connection with the Ethiopian Art Players; and *Mortgaged* was presented by the Howard Players in 1923. Two years later *The Broken Banjo* was awarded the Amy Spingarn Prize in a contest conducted by the *Crisis,* and in 1926 the same prize was awarded to a three-act piece, *Bootblack Lover. The Broken Banjo* may be considered representative of these early productions. In one act the play tells the story of a Negro woman, her banjo-loving husband, and her good-for-nothing brother and cousin who constantly loiter about the home. The husband objects to the constant feeding of the brother and cousin; in his absence from the house one day his banjo is broken; and later the two relatives give him up to the police as implicated in a murder, after swearing not to do so. A knife and an ax play a part in the action, and there are suggestions not always followed up, as when Emma wants to know how her husband is spending his money. With all of the shortcomings, however, it can be seen that the author is endeavoring to come to grips with life. Quite as much may be said of *Compromise,* tragic story of the relations of a white and a Negro family. In 1930 Mr. Richardson compiled *Plays and Pageants from the Life of the*

Negro, and five years later he and May Miller were the chief authors of *Negro History in Thirteen Plays.* These books were designed to bring together such short dramatic pieces as could be used by members of clubs or by young people in school, but the first impression one has on reading them is a sense of unreality. One of Mr. Richardson's plays, *The Black Horseman,* goes back to Numidia in the year 20 B.C., while *The King's Dilemma* is set in "the future" and the place is "the last kingdom of the world." *The House of Sham* is set in the present century but has a moralizing air. Also distant is Maud Cuney Hare's *Antar of Araby.* Miss Miller's little comedy, *Riding the Goat,* comes closer home, being set in Baltimore and using a theme suggested by Negro lodges; but her *Graven Images* goes back to the Egypt of 1490 B.C. *Ti Yette,* by John Matheus, takes place in New Orleans in 1855. A Creole quadroon has leanings toward a white lover, while her brother, Racine, would rather kill her than see her compromised. Racine himself is proud of his African heritage but has a self-conscious air and uses stilted language, as when he says to Ti Yette, "How can I eat when my own sister bites me with mortal poison?" The second book, *Negro History in Thirteen Plays,* is much like the first. Of Mr. Richardson's five contributions only one is concerned with the Negro in the United States, and that is the one dealing with the episode of Crispus Attucks before the Revolutionary War.

Perhaps more promising than these productions is the work of Randolph Edmonds. This writer was born in Lawrenceville, Virginia, in 1900, and, after attending the St. Paul's School there, was graduated from Oberlin in 1926 and in 1932 received the Master's degree at Columbia. In the course of his struggle for an education he saw much of life in sawmills, railroad camps, and factories, and his attention was directed by Paul Green's *Lonesome Road* to the drama of Negro peasant life. Mr. Edmonds became professor of English and director of dramatics at Morgan College in Baltimore, in which capacity he became also the founder and the first president of the Negro Intercollegiate Dramatic Association, but in 1935 went to the recently organized Dillard University in New Orleans. In 1930 he published *Shades and Shadows*, six stories in fanciful vein cast in dramatic form, influence coming from such authors as Maeterlinck and William Sharp. Not yet had he found his true bent, but he did so with *Six Plays for a Negro Theatre* (1934), a little book that must henceforth have high place in any study of the Negro drama. Said the author: "I am fully aware of the fact that there are many Negroes who do not like dialect plays. It has long been my opinion, however, that it is not the crude expressions of the peasant characters that contribue to this dislike, but rather the repelling atmosphere and the 'psychology of the inferior' that somehow creep into the peasant plays of even the most unbiased authors of other racial groups. . . . In these plays I have made an attempt to meet most of the usual objections raised against the dialect dramas with a combination of four elements that I explained somewhat at length in an article in one of our leading newspapers. They are worthwhile themes, sharply drawn conflict, positive characters, and a melodramatic plot." About the sharply drawn conflict and the positive characters there can be no doubt, but perhaps it is the melodramatic plot that Mr. Edmonds will want to watch. *Breeders,* for instance, the story of a young slave girl who is about to be forced into a union against her will, is especially violent in its action. The author shows to best advantage in *Bad Man*, a one-act play in which the Negroes working at a sawmill are accused of the murder of an old white man. When the mob forms, Thea Dugger, who all his life has been "a bad man, driftin' from one camp tuh another, shootin' and cuttin' and fightin'," becomes the hero, giving his life to save his friends. If Mr. Edmonds will refine his art and place less reliance on sensational effects, he will undoubtedly go far in his chosen field.

The Negro Intercollegiate Dramatic Association was organized in March, 1930, in Baltimore by representatives of Howard University, Hampton Institute, Morgan College, Virginia Union University, and the Virginia State College. The aim was to encourage the study of the drama and especially to use the college organizations as laboratories for the production of plays and the study of Negro folk material. Each year there is a tournament of one-act plays with one of the five institutions acting as host. In the first tournament, held at Morgan College in 1931, Hampton Institute was the winner with Paul Green's *The No 'Count Boy*. In the second and fourth tournaments Morgan College was the winner with two of the plays by Mr. Edmonds, *Bad Man* and *Nat Turner*.

We may now consider the careers of four of the performers on the professional stage who have been most conspicuous.

CHARLES GILPIN

Charles Gilpin (*c.* 1872-1930) was born in Richmond, Virginia, the son of hard-working parents, and his years in school were limited. When twelve years of age he went to work in a printing-office and thereafter did anything that came to hand, meanwhile dreaming of success on the stage. While still a young man he began his career as a variety performer in Richmond; in 1903 he was one of the Gilmore Canadian Jubilee Singers; in 1905 he was with Williams and Walker; the next season with Gus Hill's *Smart Set*; and then, from 1907 to 1909, with the Pekin Stock Company of Chicago. Eleven of forty candidates at the Pekin were finally selected for serious effort in the drama, and there was a month of success in New Orleans; but the play had to give way for a minstrel show, and soon the company was disbanded. Then followed for Gilpin ten years of hope deferred and bitter disappointment; but he held to his vision, worked for a while with the Anita Bush Players at the Lincoln Theatre in New York, then led in organizing the Lafayette Players. In 1919 came a chance to play William Custis, the old Negro in John Drinkwater's *Abraham Lincoln*. The part was not a great one, but it at least offered a chance, and led to an engagement for the title role in *The Emperor Jones*.

Gilpin's acting at the Provincetown Playhouse on the opening night, November 3, 1920, made stage history not only for the Negro but for the country. The drama is little more than a long-drawn-out monologue, but so thrilling was the individual performance of the star that it was soon necessary to take the production from the little house in which it was presented to an uptown theatre, and there it ran for months. For once the critics were agreed. Alexander Woollcott said of the producers in the *New York Times*: "They have acquired an actor, one who has it in him to invoke the pity and the terror and the indescribable foreboding which are part of the secret of *The Emperor Jones*." Kenneth MacGowan wrote in the *Globe*: "Gilpin's is a sustained and splendid piece of acting. The moment when he raises his naked body against the moonlit sky, beyond the edge of the jungle, and prays, is such a dark lyric of the flesh, such a cry of the primitive being, as I have never seen in the theatre." In the *Tribune* Heywood Broun said of the actor: "He sustains the succession of scenes in monologue not only because his voice is one of a gorgeous natural quality, but because he knows just what to do with it. All the notes are there and he has also an extraordinary facility for being in the right place at the right time."

At the close of the season Gilpin received the vote of the Drama League as one of the ten persons who had contributed most to the theatre in the course of the year, and he was also awarded the Spingarn Medal. While such honors came to him, those who knew him best will always think of his career as one representing the difficulties faced by the serious Negro artist. After years of striving and waiting—such years as sometimes defeat even a strong man—he triumphed, with a brief day of success and applause. Even then came the question, "What next?" There was no to-morrow; never again came such an opportunity. Yet he had done his work. A torch-bearer, he not only helped to organize the companies that were to play a part in the new day, but at one bound bridged the chasm between popular comedy and the legitimate drama.

RICHARD B. HARRISON

Richard Berry Harrison (1864-1935) was born in London, Ontario, Canada, the son of fugitive slaves.

Years before, his father had swum through the icy waters of the Ohio on a stormy night as he made his way to freedom. The son sold newspapers and while still in his youth left home for Detroit, where he was befriended by Edward Weitzel, drama editor of the *Free Press*. He studied and in 1891 began to appear professionally as a reader. For a brief period he was associated with Paul Laurence Dunbar, and he gave all the old favorites, especially scenes from *Julius Cæsar* and *Damon and Pythias,* meanwhile dreaming that some day he would play Shylock in a real theatre. Then came tours of the Southern states and Canada, appearances on Chautauqua and Lyceum circuits, and readings in tents, churches, and schools. Harrison was already advanced in middle life when he began to work at the Agricultural and Technical College in Greensboro, North Carolina, where he remained seven years. He was under contract to a concert bureau and was working in the churches in New York early in 1930 when the casting agent of a new production looked him up and offered him the leading role.

The play was *The Green Pastures.* As he read the script Harrison naturally had some doubts. Some friends in the ministry with whom he talked over the matter made no point against the moral tone of the work but said that they could see little to recommend it as drama. One or two others assured him that only good could come from the production. Still he hesitated. Twice he returned the script, and twice he was asked to keep it anyway. At last came the day when a final answer had to be given, and suddenly, hardly knowing what he was doing, he consented to serve.

The rest is stage history. The play thrilled New York as that city had not been thrilled in years. In addition to its dramatic appeal it seemed to make for good feeling. Dr. Edward A. Steiner said, "On Broadway I went to see a show, and I saw God." Franklin P. Adams, of the New York *World*, said, "It stirred and moved me more than any play I can remember to have seen."

Tributes to the chief performer were in number beyond all estimate. The morning of his seventieth birthday found him in Norfolk, at the beginning of a Southern tour. There awaited him messages from the presidents of fourteen colleges or universities and the governors of seven states. Perhaps no greeting touched him more than that which he received on his return to his birthplace, London in Ontario. In the delegation was the Mayor, who said: "I have come to welcome you home. These gentlemen with me are the Aldermen of the city. Others who are here are business men and some of your old associates with whom you went to school and battled in your younger days. We have come to escort you to the London hotel, where we shall have dinner, and then to a reception at the church where you were baptized."

So far so good; yet it would not be fair if mention were not made of the fact that the touring of *The Green Pastures* company brought sharply forward two of the chief grievances of the Negro in connection with the theatre. In the capital city of Washington, when the play came to the National Theatre, members of the race of the actors themselves were not permitted to attend, except at one segregated showing at the close. Traveling conditions also left much to be desired. Giving all possible consideration to questions of expediency, many still felt that the popular aggregation lost a great opportunity when it failed to take a positive stand for justice.

Meanwhile, after its first three months of showing, the play was awarded the Pulitzer Prize. The next year Harrison himself received the Spingarn Medal. He had played "de Lawd" for five years without missing a performance, 1,657 times, when he was stricken in New York just before the matinee on Saturday, March 2, 1935. Twelve days later he died. "Carry on," he had said to his understudy; "the world needs this play." It was his to give men a new vision, covering frailty with charity and harmonizing all with the spirit of the divine.

ROSE MCCLENDON

Rosalie Scott (1884-1936), who became the wife of Dr. Henry P. McClendon and was known on the stage as Rose McClendon, was born in New York, attended there the Twenty-eighth Street Public School and the Hunter Normal School, and later continued her studies under private teachers. Soon after her school days were ended she began to write plays for Sunday School exercises and other events at the St. Mark's Methodist Episcopal Church. Realizing the need of the training of young people in dramatics, she sought to prepare herself for the work by enrolling for a year in Sargent's Dramatic School. The director, seeing her ability, insisted that she stay longer, and she remained three years.

In the autumn of 1919 Mrs. McClendon was asked by Butler Davenport to take a part in the play *Justice*, which he had written after a visit to the South. In 1923 she appeared on Broadway in *Roseanne*. Her next venture was in *Deep River* in 1926, and now the critics were enthusiastic about the flashes in her performance, one likening her to Eleanora Duse. At the close of the year she appeared as Goldie, the wife, in *In Abraham's Bosom*. The play won the Pulitzer Prize and she herself received from the *Morning Telegraph* an award for one of the year's best pieces of work on the stage.

From 1927 until 1930 Mrs. McClendon played the part of Serena in *Porgy*, touring both the United States and Europe. Then came parts in *The House of Connolly*, *Never No More*, *Black Souls*, *Brain Sweat*, *Roll Sweet Chariot*, and *Panic*, though it is doubtful if she ever had a role that did her talent justice. Her last appearance was in *Mulatto*, from which she retired in December, 1935, on account of illness. In the spring of that year she had led in organizing the Negro People's Theatre, which after a summer of successful effort was incorporated in the Federal Theatre Project, of which she became director.

The quality of the work that made this artist distinguished was to be seen in one of the earlier productions in which she appeared, *Deep River*. The story is one of Creole New Orleans in 1835. In the scene of the quadroon ball, in the part of an elderly matron, the actress had to come very slowly down a winding staircase and then walk through a court before passing off the stage. The feat was an ultimate test of dignity and poise, but so skillfully was it performed that each night it won prolonged applause. Alexander Woollcott said in the *World*: "When *Deep River* was having its trial night in Philadelphia Ethel Barrymore slipped in to snatch what moments she could of it. 'Stay till the last act if you can,' Arthur Hopkins whispered to her, 'and watch Rose McClendon come down those stairs. She can teach some of our most hoity-toity actresses distinction.' It was Miss Barrymore who hunted *him* up after the performance to say, 'She can teach them *all* distinction.' "

PAUL ROBESON

Paul Robeson has had the benefit of unusual education; at the same time he is largely self-taught, and

PAUL ROBESON

one is glad that this is so, for his gifts are such as would suffer by excessive cultivation. He was born in Princeton, New Jersey, in 1898, and was favorably situated even in his early years. At Rutgers, where he attended college, his career was one of extraordinary success. His scholarship won election to Phi Beta Kappa; he took the freshman prize in oratory, the sophomore and junior prizes in extemporaneous speaking, and was a member of both the Glee Club and the debating team. In sports he became a four-letter man by reason of distinction in football, baseball, basketball, and track work, and was selected by Walter Camp as an "All-American" end. In 1919 he was graduated, being a speaker at commencement, and in 1923 became also a Bachelor of Laws at Columbia.

Already, however, Mr. Robeson's interest was in the theatre, and, after passing his bar examination, he turned from the court room to the stage. Just a few months after leaving Columbia he had his first important part, that in O'Neill's *All God's Chillun Got Wings*, and thus was at the center of the controversy that raged about the presenting of the play. Soon also he was on the concert stage or in popular shows as a singer, his remarkable voice being especially adapted to songs of heart interest; and no one who has ever heard him can forget his rendering of "Water Boy" or of "Ol' Man River" in *Show Boat*. A little later than Gilpin he took the leading part in *The Emperor*

Jones, and in 1930 a score of encores greeted his London debut as Othello. Since then he has appeared in concert and in various moving pictures; and to-day he is at home in Russia or France hardly less than in England or the United States.

In his travels Mr. Robeson has been alert to the interests of those with whom he sojourned and to anything that might assist in the enrichment of his art. "I find," he says, "that the handicraft of certain periods of the Chinese and African cultures is almost identical, and that the Negro is more like the Russian in temperament and character." About matters beyond the stage he also has positive opinions. To one interviewer he said: "I believe there is no such thing in England and America as *co-operation* from the NAACP point of view. Our freedom is going to cost so many lives that we mustn't talk about the Scottsboro case as one of sacrifice. When we talk of freedom we don't discuss lives. Before the Negro is free there will be many Scottsboros. The Communist emphasis in that case is right." It thus appears that Mr. Robeson's thinking is as independent as his singing is superb.

XI

MUSIC IN RECENT YEARS

H. LAWRENCE FREEMAN—CLARENCE CAMERON WHITE—NATHANIEL DETT—WILLIAM GRANT STILL—WILLIAM L. DAWSON—ROLAND HAYES—JULIUS BLEDSOE—MARIAN ANDERSON

THE history of Negro music in the United States in the twentieth century is in general that of the recognition of this music as a whole, of success on the international scale on the part of two or three singers, of a beginning in the composition of works in large form, and of such developments in recent years as might give concern for the welfare of the serious musician. The advance of the radio and the talking picture has affected all workers in the field, and for the Negro there has been special difficulty. It is not surprising accordingly that there have risen comparatively few musicians of the rank of those whose reputations were established two or three decades ago.

Great impetus came from three visits of Samuel Coleridge-Taylor in the early years of the century. On the first of these, in November, 1903, he was guest conductor for the Coleridge-Taylor Society in Washington, organized in 1902 by John T. Layton; and the performance of the *Hiawatha* trilogy in Convention Hall brought together one of the most distinguished audiences in the musical history of the capital. Societies more than ever before were now organized in different parts of the country; young people were encouraged; and the standard was greatly elevated. A little later Mme. E. Azalia Hackley, a woman of fine presence and unusual enthusiasm, turned from the concert stage to the giving of what she called folk festivals in different centers, especially in the South; and she too was an inspiration to many. In New York Daisy Tapley, a mezzo-soprano, led in giving a series of educational concerts; and Maud Cuney Hare, of Boston, a capable pianist and lecturer, traveled much, emphasizing demonstrations of Creole music. Meanwhile the Washington Conservatory of Music was founded by Harriet Gibbs Marshall. Outstanding among the organizations in the Middle West was the Choral Study Club, of Chicago, organized in 1900 largely through the effort of Pedro T. Tinsley. Where there was so much incentive and so much talent, naturally there was aspiration that looked toward grand opera. Theodore Drury, of New York, especially had the vision, and he organized a company that, with many handicaps, gave annually for three or four years at the Lexington Opera House a performance of *Aida*, *Carmen*, or *Faust*. Prominent among the vocalists of the period

Photograph by A. N. Scurlock

ROLAND HAYES

was Sidney Woodward, possessor of a clear and singularly beautiful voice, who studied in Boston, meanwhile singing in churches there, and later became a teacher in Jacksonville. All earlier effort crystallized in 1919 in the organization of the National Association of Negro Musicians, the purpose of which was "to discover and foster talent, to mold taste, to promote fellowship, and to advocate racial expression."

COMPOSERS: H. LAWRENCE FREEMAN, CLARENCE CAMERON WHITE, NATHANIEL DETT, WILLIAM GRANT STILL, WILLIAM L. DAWSON, AND OTHERS

A pioneer and an earnest worker in the early years of the century was Gerald Tyler, a graduate of the Oberlin Conservatory of Music who became assistant director of public school music in St. Louis, and who, with all of his duties, wrote numerous songs, among them "Dirge for a Soldier," "Syrian Lullaby," and "Ships that Pass in the Night." The music of the Negro and of the world suffered signal loss in the early death of Edmund T. Jenkins, of Charleston, South Carolina. While still a student at Morehouse College in Atlanta, this young man was called upon to make a trip to London with the Jenkins Orphan Band, organized by his father. He remained to enter the Royal Academy. Already able to play on half a dozen instruments, he was soon awarded a scholarship. In one year, 1916-17, he was awarded a silver medal for excellence on the clarinet, a bronze medal for his work on the piano, and, against brilliant competition, a second prize for his original work in composition. The year also witnessed the production of his "Prélude Réligieuse" at one of the orchestral concerts of the Academy. In 1925, in the *Opportunity* contest, he won first prize with his "African War Dance," designed for a full orchestra, also second prize with his "Sonata in A Minor" for the violoncello. He died in Paris in 1926 after an operation when just slightly more than thirty years of age.

A man who has worked long and hard but to whom full recognition has come only in recent years is H. Lawrence Freeman, now of New York. This composer has had wide experience as the director of church choirs and choral societies, and in the composing of operas was a pioneer. Born in Cleveland, Ohio, in 1875, when not more than seven years of age he could "pick out songs and all kinds of melodies by ear." When he was ten he organized a boys' quartet, and himself arranged the music, sang soprano, played the piano, and generally acted as director. When he was seventeen years of age and living in Denver, a friend had tickets for the performance of the Emma Juch Grand Opera Company, which opened the new Broadway Theatre with *Tannhäuser*. To the youth the music was a revelation, and for months thereafter almost daily he was composing new songs. Later he studied with Johann Beck, founder of the

Cleveland Symphony Orchestra. Mr. Freeman now has to his credit not less than fourteen operatic works, prominent titles being *Voodoo, Vendetta,* and *The Octoroon. Voodoo,* in three acts, is set in Louisiana. Lolo, Queen of the Snake on a plantation near New Orleans, is in love with Mando, a young swain of Creole extraction, who in turn is in love with Cleota. After vainly endeavoring to separate the pair, Lolo swears vengeance with the words "Voodoo! Voodoo!" and at a revelry of the Negroes on the plantation openly avows her hatred, crushing under her heel a charm which Mando has secured from Fojo, the witch doctor. In a wild scene of incantation and witchcraft Cleota is brought forth to be sacrificed to the god of Snake; but a shot is heard and the snake, sorely wounded, disappears in the foliage. Mando endeavors to restore Cleota to consciousness, but is in despair until Chloe, Lolo's own mother, appears and counteracts the evil her daughter has wrought. After Chloe departs, however, Lolo, who has been hiding behind a tree, again throws a spell over Cleota. Mando now sees her, snatches his rifle, and kills her before she has accomplished her purpose. This opera was presented at the Fifty-second Street Theatre in New York on September 10 and 11, 1928, with a Negro cast and with the composer as conductor, being dubbed by the *World* a "lusty infant" in the field. Through it and other works of Mr. Freeman passion surges tumultuously. Some of his effects are massive but he is always in firm control of his rhythms. At a concert in Steinway Hall in New York in March, 1930, excerpts from nine of his operas were given, and *Voodoo* has since been purchased by the Paramount film company. In 1929 the composer received from the Harmon Foundation a first award with gold medal.

Clarence Cameron White, born in 1880 at Clarksville, Tennessee, after study in the public schools of Washington and at Howard, spent five years in the Conservatory of Music at Oberlin, where he played first violin in the orchestra. He continued his studies in England, where he was associated with Coleridge-Taylor, then for some years conducted a studio in Boston, for six years taught at the West Virginia State College, and later at Hampton. He has composed numerous pieces for the violin, these including his *Bandanna Sketches*, also arranged for orchestra and band; and a suite, *From the Cotton Fields*. In 1928, with his colleague, John F. Matheus, Mr. White made a visit to Hayti for the purpose of studying folk-lore and collecting musical material. Two years later he was awarded a fellowship by the Rosenwald Foundation, and one result of his study was the opera *Ouanga,* based on the life of the Haytian liberator, Dessalines, the libretto being by Mr. Matheus. In 1927 he received a first award and a gold medal from the Harmon Foundation.

R. Nathaniel Dett was born of musical parents in Drummondsville, Ontario, Canada, in 1882, but at the time of the World's Fair in Chicago moved with the family to the American side of Niagara Falls. When he was still a boy his playing of the piano gave evidence of a sympathetic touch and power in improvisation. By the time he was fourteen he was able to give a recital featuring selections from Beethoven, Chopin, and McDowell, and some of his own little pieces. In 1908 he received the degree of Bachelor of Music at Oberlin, and later was honored with the degree of Doctor of Music by Howard (1924) and Oberlin (1926). Studying at Harvard in 1920-21, he won the Bowdoin essay prize with his paper, "The Emancipation of Negro Music," also the Francis Bott prize in composition. After teaching at two other institutions, Mr. Dett in 1913 entered upon his period of service at Hampton, where he remained until 1931. He conducted the Hampton Institute Choir on its tours in the United States, Canada, and Europe, winning the plaudits of many distinguished audiences. He has composed several suites for the piano, chiefly *Magnolia*, *Enchantment*, and *In the Bottoms;* his "Danse Juba" became very popular; and he excels in the writing of anthems. *The Chariot Jubilee*, a superb production, was written at the request of the Syracuse University chorus and its conductor.

Within very recent years there has been marked attention to the symphony. In 1931 the *Afro-American Symphony* of William Grant Still was performed by the Rochester Symphony Orchestra, later being heard in Berlin, Stuttgart, and Leipzig. The composer was born of educated parents in Mississippi in 1895. After attending Wilberforce and Oberlin he went to the New England Conservatory in Boston and later studied in New York. For a while he gave his time to arrangements for musical comedy companies, but soon turned away from all such effort to devote himself mainly to works in large form. Not many of his compositions have as yet appeared in print but several have won the favor of very critical audiences, and in general Mr. Still is a man from whom much may be expected in the future. In 1934 he received a Guggenheim Fellowship. He has been referred to as one "who uses Negro music as the basis of his composition in modern vein." On June 15, 1933, the *Symphony in E Minor* of Florence B. Price, a graduate of the New England Conservatory, was included on a program of the Chicago Symphony Orchestra at the Century of Progress Exposition. The work was one largely based on Negro themes. The next year the composer was invited to appear as soloist in her "Concerto in D Minor," for piano and orchestra, at the Chicago Musical College. Mrs. Price has written, among other things, numerous songs and pieces for the piano, a sonata, a passacaglia, and a fugue for the organ, and two symphonic poems; and much of her work has appeared over the imprint of the foremost publishers of music in the country. On

July 3, 1933, a music drama, *Tom-Tom,* by Shirley Graham, was given its first performance in the municipal stadium in Cleveland. The author had studied at Oberlin, Howard, the Institute of Musical Art in New York, and in Paris, and for three years served as director of music at Morgan College in Baltimore. The production of her work was spectacular, with a full orchestra, five hundred singers and dancers, and with Jules Bledsoe in the leading role.

Prominent in all such effort was the performance, in November, 1934, of the *Negro Folk Symphony* of William Levi Dawson by the Philadelphia Orchestra under the direction of Dr. Leopold Stokowski. The composer of this work was graduated at Tuskegee in 1921. Making his way to Kansas, he studied for a year at Washburn College in Topeka, in 1925 was graduated with first honors at the Horner Institute of Fine Arts in Kansas City, Missouri, and then studied in Chicago, receiving in 1927 the degree of Master of Music at the American Conservatory. He was given the first chair in the trombone section of the Civic Orchestra of Chicago after a competitive examination in which he proved himself able to read music written in the alto clef. In both 1930 and 1931 Mr. Dawson took first prize in the Wanamaker Music Contest, and in the former year the second prize also. In 1931 he went to Tuskegee to organize and direct the School of Music, and two years later his group of one hundred singers was on the program on the opening night of Radio City Music Hall. Meanwhile he had consigned his symphony to Dr. Stokowski. He has said of it that "the central theme is melancholy, a sort of wail, a type of hymn, related to jazz in its rhythm." The new work was received with the greatest enthusiasm, and the successful production was repeated a week later at Carnegie Hall in New York. Olin Downes, writing in the *Times*, said of the host of people who attended: "The end of the concert saw a majority of them remaining to applaud long and lustily and to call Mr. Dawson several times back to the stage. Some will attribute this acclaim to the audience's impulse to honor a gifted artist of the Negro race for a signal achievement. In this they would be partly right, but if they estimated the symphony by any such measurement they would be signally wrong." A little more than three months later the Birmingham Civic Symphony Orchestra closed its season with a brilliant performance of the symphony directed by Dorsey Whittingham.

Another musician who has now been prominent for some years is Carl R. Diton, originally of Philadelphia and more recently of New York. Mr. Diton received his training largely at the University of Pennsylvania and studied for a year in Munich. For several years he taught at Paine, Wiley, and Talladega in the South, but, feeling the need of being nearer the great musical centers, returned at length to

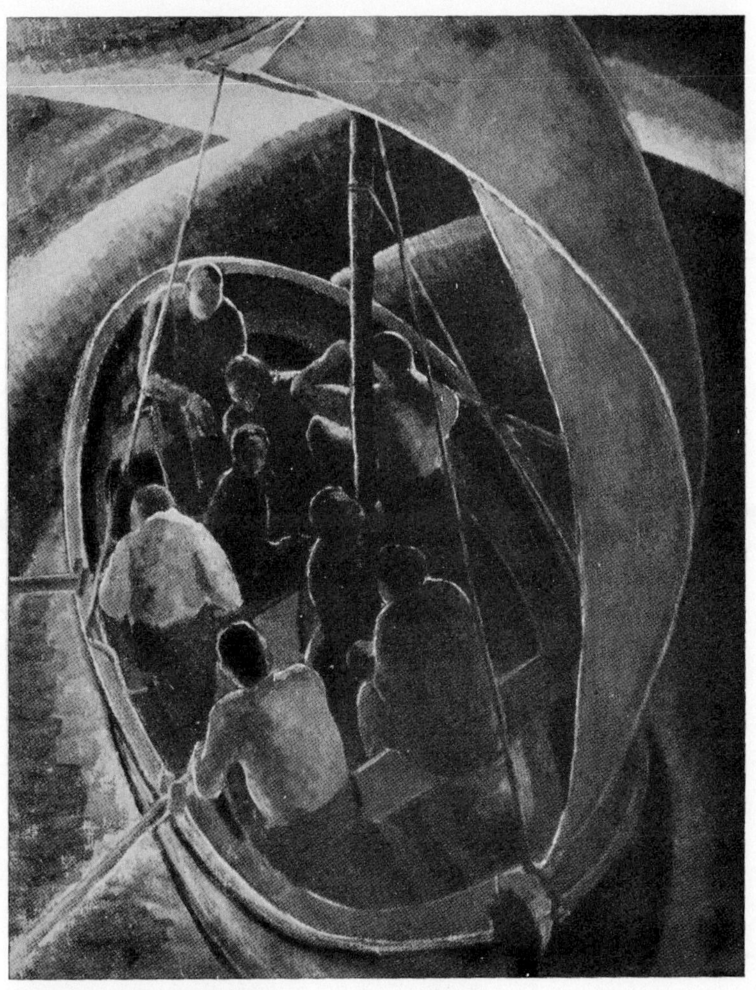

Photograph by James Latimer Allen
By Courtesy of Harmon Foundation

ROLL, JORDAN, ROLL
by Malvin Gray Johnson

the East. He has done much work in the transcribing of Negro spirituals and several of his songs have been published by Schirmer. In 1929 he received from the Harmon Foundation a second award and a bronze medal, and the next year was graduated from the vocal department of the Juilliard School of Music.

Camille L. Nickerson (Mus. M., Oberlin, 1932), a member of the faculty of the School of Music at Howard, in 1936 became president of the National Association of Negro Musicians. Aside from being a skillful performer on the organ, she has worked much with Creole and Negro folk songs.

Somewhat apart from the musicians who have emphasized an academic background are those who have become known in the amusement field. Prominent among them is "Duke" (Edward Kennedy) Ellington. There are many who feel that jazz should have no place at all in a consideration of serious music, because its appeal is not the highest and because it raises question of musical value. On the other hand it is contended that the jazz performer could not create his deliberate effects without some degree of musicianship. Mr. Ellington has surpassed others in his field primarily by reason of an original note in his compositions. An extended article on his work by Chester Rosenberg appeared in the *Crisis* for February, 1936.

SINGERS: ROLAND HAYES, JULES BLEDSOE, MARIAN ANDERSON, AND OTHERS

Immediately after the war there rose to his greatest heights a singer, a tenor, whose career is unique even in the crowded annals of the stage.

Roland Hayes was born in 1887 in an humble home near Curryville, Georgia, fifty miles from Chattanooga. His father died when he was twelve years old and three years later his mother moved to Chattanooga. There the gifted boy found a job in a factory that made paper weights. He had to unload pig iron, charge the cupolas with fuel, and carry ladles brimming with melted ore. Sometimes the flakes of liquid metal would fall and burn his feet. For such service he was paid eighty cents a day. Later he became a core maker in the factory. Meanwhile he sang in a little church choir, and at seventeen met Arthur Calhoun, a young man who had studied at Oberlin and who was teaching in Chattanooga. Then came the first of the great spiritual experiences of the future singer. Calhoun took him one night to the home of a white man in the city who was interested in music. The boy sang, and before the evening was over his host played for him records of Caruso, Sembrich, and other artists. "That night," he said later, "I was born again. It was as if a bell had been struck, that rang in my heart. And it has never ceased to ring there."

Before long came an opportunity to work with the Fisk Singers, who were making a special trip to Boston, and soon the young man became a pupil of Arthur Hubbard. He took his mother to Boston, and after a while came the first of many appearances in Symphony Hall. Then came another great experience, a second rebirth. One night in California a man said to him that there was something in his singing that was not in that of white artists, and asked him what it was. "What did I know of myself, of my people?" he asked when alone with himself. "Here we are in America. We were lifted out of our old environment and set down here—aliens in body and in soul. Shreds and tatters of our ancient qualities still cling to us even now; but what was the original fabric like?" He wanted to go to Africa, perhaps to learn the secret of it all. The world, however, was unsettled after the war, and he lingered in England. There the Negro was not popular at the moment; but the way was cleared, and on May 31, 1920, Roland Hayes gave the first of many recitals in London. He appeared before the King and Queen, and received a special token from the sovereign. In New York he has filled Carnegie Hall again and again, singing amid the greatest enthusiasm. Under the Boston Symphony management he has toured Europe and America, making all audiences wonder at the spell cast by his voice. Said the *Pravda* of Moscow after one of his concerts: "Out of every song with its deeply musical mood was born a feeling of wonder reaching such a high point in technique that we can speak of it only with the highest praise. The voice of Hayes does not belong to the strong or brilliant type; his voice is rather soft-hued for a tenor, perhaps not even vivid for his highest notes. He is typically the lyric singer, lacking the strongly pathetic tones but capable at the same time of causing his hearers to experience just what he feels. Everything coarse or rude and affected is entirely strange to his artistic nature. The thoughtful and sweet Schubert or the mighty Brahms, the indisputably good Italian arias, the sad humor of the Negro hymns, he gives them all in such a way that every moment one forgets about the artist as interpreter who comes between the audience and the song."

Of the other men who are now before the public, we have already spoken of Paul Robeson in connection with the stage. Whatever this gifted individual touches seems to succeed. His singing voice is not only round, smooth, and manly, but has the quality of extraordinary appeal. Julius (better known as Jules) Bledsoe, born in Waco, Texas, in 1899, studied at Bishop College and Virginia Union, and first thought of pursuing the profession of medicine. In order to study to that end he enrolled at Columbia, but was soon persuaded by friends to give serious attention to music. A baritone, he especially excels in noble or dignified parts. His dramatic ability led to his being offered the leading role of *In Abraham's Bosom,* in which he played opposite Rose McClendon; and his singing of the theme solo, "Ol' Man River," in *Show Boat* for two years brought great popularity. In 1932 he sang the role of Amonasro in Verdi's *Aida* in a performance by a summer grand opera company at the Municipal Stadium in Cleveland, receiving an ovation. Later he appeared in various cities in Europe in Gruenberg's opera based on *The Emperor Jones,* and in 1933 was engaged by the New Chicago Opera Company to sing with Caterina Jarboro in *Aida.* R. Todd Duncan, who is on the faculty of the School of Music at Howard, has a fine baritone voice and a deep sense of musical values. In the winter of 1935-36 he was on leave of absence from his work taking the leading role in the folk opera *Porgy and Bess.* One must also note the Hall Johnson Choir, which within recent years has filled engagements at Town Hall in New York, appeared in the Lewisohn Stadium Concert series, and otherwise been very successful.

Of the women there have been several within recent years whose ability commanded attention. Especially in the second decade of the century Mme. Anita Patti Brown, a product of the Chicago conservatories, delighted many audiences by the sympathetic quality of her singing. She appeared not only in the United States, but in the West Indies, South America, and England as well. In the same period Mme. Mayme Calloway Byron, of Chicago, returned from war-torn Europe after appearances with the Philharmonic Orchestra in Munich and Dresden, and other successes, but in the disturbed conditions in her home country never quite received the tokens of public favor that she deserved. Mme. Florence Cole Talbert, born in Detroit, received much of her early training at the University of California, and later entered the Chicago Musical College. At her graduation in 1916 she was awarded the diamond medal. Since then she has appeared much in concert, her repertoire including many operatic selections. Mme. Evanti (Lillian Evans), of Washington, a coloratura soprano, after early training and experience at home, went to Italy to study further for the opera. She made her debut at Nice in *Lakme* and about 1930 appeared in several other Italian cities. Since then she has won wide favor by reason of the culture of her presence and the finish of her work. Caterina Jarboro (Catherine Yarborough), of Wilmington, North Carolina, and New York, was for some time with popular shows, but in 1926 left for serious study in France and Italy. In May, 1930, she made her debut as Aida at the Puccini Theatre in Milan, and in the summer of 1933, working with the Chicago Opera Company at the Hippodrome in New York, created a sensation by her brilliant singing in the part. Abbie Mitchell, one of whose early teachers was Harry T. Burleigh and who while still very young became the wife of Will Marion Cook, has had a remarkable career, one disclosing indomitable perseverance. Beginning as a singer and actress in musical comedy, she experienced at length almost a complete breakdown as a result of the strain of such work, then retired to prepare herself for the concert stage. In Paris one of her teachers was Jean de Reszke. When she reappeared she was a finished and cultured soprano, with a singularly pure and limpid tone, and since has won high praise from the music critics in leading cities. A young artist of superb endowment, just now at the threshold of her career, is Louise Burge, a contralto, for some years a student at Howard and more recently at the Juilliard School of Music. Perhaps the best description of Miss Burge's voice is that given by a little child, who said, "It sounds like an organ." One must also note Dorothy Mainor, who has been associated with the Westminster Choir; Ethyl Wise, from the Howard School of Music and now of Nashville; and Anne Wiggins Brown and Ruby Elzy, of the professional stage.

Marian Anderson is now one of the outstanding singers of the world. She first won notable success in her home city, Philadelphia, as soloist with the Philharmonic Symphony Orchestra. Later came a concert in Town Hall in New York. Her reputation was further enhanced in 1925 when she won over three hundred competitors in a contest conducted by the New York Philharmonic Orchestra, the prize being an appearance as soloist at one of the concerts in the Lewisohn open-air series. Since then Miss Anderson has sung in most of the large cities of Europe, winning special favor in music-loving Sweden and Austria. A series of concerts that she gave after returning to the country late in 1935 was in the nature of a triumphal progress. The *New York Times* said of her voice after a recital: "It is a contralto of stunning range and volume managed with suppleness and grace. It is a voice that lends itself to the entire emotional gamut, responsive to delicate nuance and able to swell out with opulence and sonority."

PIANISTS, ORGANISTS, AND VIOLINISTS

Foremost among concert pianists within recent years has been Hazel Harrison, originally of Chicago, recently a teacher at Tuskegee, and now of Howard University. This artist went to Germany for prolonged periods of study; she worked especially with Busoni, and now exhibits complete command of her chosen instrument. Her programs give prominence to Bach and Liszt and regularly give an impression of masterly achievement. To hear her rendition of "St. Franciscus Walking on the Waves" is to have an experience one can never forget.

Raymond Augustus Lawson conducts in Hartford one of the leading studios in New England. His technique is highly developed; he has more than once been a soloist at the concerts of the Hartford Philharmonic Orchestra and has appeared on other notable occasions. He has also had the pleasure of seeing different ones of his students pass on to important places in the musical life of the country. Roy W. Tibbs studied first at Fisk and Oberlin (Mus. B., 1912; A.M., 1916), has since spent longer or shorter periods in study abroad, and is now a professor at Howard University. In April, 1934, he appeared as soloist with the Washington Symphony Orchestra directed by Hans Kindler. He is also giving increasing attention to the organ. Melville Charlton studied at the College of the City of New York, won a scholarship at the National Conservatory of Music, and in 1915, at the age of thirty-two, had advanced so far in his profession as to become an associate of the American Guild of Organists. For some years he served as organist at St. Philip's Episcopal Church in New York, resigning to accept a similar position at the Religious School of Temple Emanu-El. He has also done work as a composer and in 1930 received from Howard University the degree of Doctor of Music.

To-day there are many capable violinists, but certainly one of the most brilliant is Louia Vaughn Jones, who since 1930 has been teaching at Howard University. After completing his high school work in his home city, Cleveland, Ohio, Mr. Jones entered the New England Conservatory, graduating in 1918. In the course of the war he served as a band leader; returning, he did post-graduate work at the Conservatory; and then was abroad again, mainly in France, for seven years. His playing is now such as seldom fails to thrill or inspire an audience.

Among the musicians who are beginning or are just well started on their careers are, among the pianists, William Allen (Mus. M., Oberlin), now of Fisk University, and Warner Lawson, of Hartford, Connecticut, capable son of a distinguished father; among the organists, Orrin Suthern, of Cleveland and Tuskegee, and Carlette Thomas, of New York, an associate of the American Guild of Organists; and, among the violinists, Gertrude Martin, of New York, Bernard Mason (Mus. M., Oberlin), recently of Greensboro, North Carolina, and Everett Lee, of Cleveland, Ohio.

Several teachers at different institutions have worked earnestly for the cause of music. Prominent among them are Miss Lulu Vere Childers, who as dean of the School of Music and director of the choir has held aloft the standard at Howard; Kemper Harreld, also a concert violinist, who recently celebrated the completion of twenty-five years of service at Morehouse College; and Frederick D. Hall, formerly at Clark in Atlanta, who has recently returned from two years of study abroad to take up his duties at the new Dillard University in New Orleans.

XII

THE NEW TEMPER IN PAINTING AND SCULPTURE

ARCHIBALD J. MOTLEY, JR.—AARON DOUGLAS—RICHMOND BARTHÉ

IN NO field of Negro endeavor has development been more rapid within recent years than in that of the fine arts. Except for the work of two or three well known figures, little that could command attention was done before the World War. Since 1920, however, scores of young people have been active, and several have now gone beyond the realm of promise to that of assured and even notable achievement.

Not only has the development been swift; one might also note a change of emphasis. Formerly there was effort along traditional or conventional lines. We had in the main, as Dr. Alain Locke has said, Negro artists but not Negro art. With the new day came freedom and more attention to racial subjects. A tendency toward self-expression followed in the wake of the war, and this was manifested in art as in literature and life in general. As early as 1921 the 135th Street Branch of the New York Public Library included in its activities an exhibition of the work of Negro painters and sculptors.

The new temper found a special source of inspiration. In 1925 the Harmon Foundation of New York, organized by William E. Harmon, decided to take as a part of its effort the recognition of individual achievement. Creative work by the Negro was chosen as an experiment, and art was one of nine fields selected. The result exceeded all expectation. Where it was thought that six or eight artists might take part in the first competition, not less than nineteen entered. A catalogue issued by the Foundation in 1935 gives sketches of a hundred and nine, with brief mention of several more; and there have been numerous exhibitions.

The colleges have also helped in the advance. At one institution or another are earnest spirits in the vanguard of what seems like a great awakening. At Howard University the director, in many ways a pioneer, is Professor James V. Herring; and associated with him are Lois Mailou Jones, James A. Porter, and James Lesesne Wells, all of whom have exhibited frequently. To Atlanta University went in 1931 Hale A. Woodruff, who is especially interested in murals and was one of the first to receive a Harmon award. Three years later to the same institution went Nancy Elizabeth Prophet, a graduate of the Rhode Island School of Design who continued her studies in Paris, and whose sculpture has been exhibited widely both in the United States and abroad. At the Cheyney State Teachers College is Laura Wheeler Waring, who, since studying at the Pennsylvania Academy of Fine Arts, has been abroad for more than one period and in 1927 received the Harmon gold award in the Fine Arts. Elton Clay Fax, who received his degree at Syracuse and completed four murals for the Dunbar Junior High School in Baltimore, is now at Claflin University; and Allan Freelon, who was graduated at the University of Pennsylvania and for four years held a scholarship at the Pennsylvania Museum School of Art, is an assistant director of art in the public schools of Philadelphia. One must note also such a well organized institution as the studio in New York founded and directed by Augusta Savage. In this in 1935 there were as many as forty-six active students.

There is not one of these workers who does not deserve far more detailed mention than has been given. In greater degree than some others Miss Prophet strikes the moral note, seeking to make of art an influence in the lives of those with whom she works. "It is my earnest desire," she has said, "to mean something to those whom I touch, in a moral way, and from the point of view of character building." Mr. Woodruff is perhaps at his best in his landscapes; his color is always well adjusted to the mood of nature with which he deals. Laura Wheeler Waring is not to be claimed for any modern or extreme school; she has illustrated books for some of the leading publishers in the country. Miss Jones has specialized in water colors and Mr. Wells in woodcuts. Mr. Porter painted a mural for the Twelfth Street Branch of the Young Men's Christian Association in Washington, and more recently has been at work on a series portraying Negro life in Washington and New York. His "Roof-Tops" marked an important change in his work. Formerly he had faced the problem of increasing the intensity of color and of keeping a sense of reality at the same time. Now he paints natural objects without any decrease in the gamut of color. Mr. Freelon is a member of the Gloucester Society of Artists and North Shore Artists Association. He has exhibited often at Wanamaker's and elsewhere, has lectured at Bryn Mawr and Swarthmore, and sold several paintings and aquatints. His "Gloucester Harbor" is a superb piece of work.

With all that has been accomplished much remains to be done. The Negro people of the country are not yet art-minded. The result is that the artist is not encouraged in a practical way nearly as much as he deserves. This may partly account for the fact that not more of those in the field have risen to the heights. One of the most capable men, Mr. Aaron Douglas, has recently said: "In all the fifteen million Negroes there are not more than a dozen painters and less than a half dozen sculptors of outstanding attainment." A moot question in this connection is that of the influence of native African art on the American Negro painter or sculptor of to-day. This may easily be overemphasized; any influence has for the most part been indirect. In Cleveland, for instance, are several artists, not identified with the Negro race, who, like some men in Paris, have received inspiration from African primitives. Among them are Paul B. Travis, Viktor Schreckengost, and Clarence H. Carter. In 1927 Mr. Travis went to Africa and made his way up from Cape Town through Rhodesia and Uganda to Cairo, studying native workmanship as he advanced. The result in his painting was a richer and a more vigorous tone than he had ever exhibited before. His "Still Life—East Africa" shows a fruitstand with mountains for a background, all being characterized by breadth of treatment, strong clear color, and much attention to detail. "Pygmy Hunters in Congo Forest," also aflame with color, shows striking figures worked into a tapestry of foliage and flowers of the jungle. When the young Negro artist sees a prominent worker succeeding with material and technique so unconventional, he too may be led to attempt something of the same sort; but the influence may be said to be not so much African as what is regarded as modern. To assert then, as is sometimes asserted, that American Negro painting and sculpture of to-day find their real roots in Africa, is perhaps to claim just a little too much.

If now we remember that several of the teachers

who may not be mentioned further are also moving forward in a creative way, we may proceed to note at least a few of the artists whose contributions have been most distinctive. At once we find a cleavage between those who are in line with tradition and those who may be said to work in modernistic vein. Prominent in the first group would be the late Edwin A. Harleston, William McKnight Farrow, Laura Wheeler Waring, and Palmer C. Hayden. Mr. Harleston, whose home was in Charleston, South Carolina, after graduating at the old Atlanta University spent seven years at the School of the Museum of Fine Arts in Boston. He excelled in portrait work and just before his death in 1931 was associated with Aaron Douglas in executing the murals in the Library of Fisk University. Mr. Farrow, born in Ohio in 1885, studied for eight years at the Art Institute of Chicago and is now superintendent of the printing shop of the Institute, having also served as assistant to the curator of temporary exhibitions. As early as 1915 he took first honors in figure and still life at the Lincoln Exposition and since then has been represented in numerous exhibits. Mr. Hayden excels in the treatment of marine subjects and in 1926 received the Harmon gold award. Somewhat more difficult to place is Albert Alexander Smith, who in more recent years has lived in France and whose highly distinctive work is represented by "Dancing Time," "Generations," and "Bilbas—Spain"; and Clarence Lawson, who was gradu-

Photograph by DeWitt Ward

THE BLACKBERRY WOMAN
by Richmond Barthé

ated at the Art Institute in Chicago in 1935 with a firm grasp of form and of the history of art, is just at the beginning of his career. Outstanding among the modernists are Archibald J. Motley, Jr., Aaron Douglas, and Richmond Barthé.

PAINTERS: ARCHIBALD J. MOTLEY, JR., AARON DOUGLAS, AND OTHERS

Archibald J. Motley, Jr., was born in New Orleans and studied at the Art Institute of Chicago and abroad, meanwhile often working as a day laborer to keep himself going. In 1928 he gave at the New Galleries in New York the first one-man show by any Negro artist since that of Tanner. Practically all of the paintings exhibited were sold to collectors and just a few months later Mr. Motley received the Harmon gold award. Among his first pictures to attract attention were "Octoroon Girl," "The Picnic at the Grove," and "Mending Socks." In 1935, under the auspices of the Illinois Emergency Relief Commission, he completed a mural for the Nichols School, Evanston, Illinois; and fourteen pictures done under Federal auspices were placed in public buildings in Chicago. In that city Mr. Motley has been represented in the Art Institute exhibitions every year since 1921; his "Blues" and "A Surprise in Store" were at the Century of Progress Exposition; he had pictures in the exhibition of Chicago artists at the Whitney Museum in New York in 1933, also in that of American artists in Toledo the next year; and he has taken the Eisendrath Prize of the American-Scandinavian Foundation in Stockholm.

Aaron Douglas, a graduate of the University of Nebraska, studied art in New York and Paris, then taught for two years in Kansas City. He has contributed drawings and designs to various magazines and illustrated several books, among them *God's Trombones,* by James W. Johnson, and *Black Magic,* by Paul Morand. He made the mural decorations for the Fisk University Library, Bennett College, the Sherman Hotel in Chicago, the 135th Street Branch of the Young Men's Christian Association in New York, the 135th Street Branch of the Public Library of New York, and the Hall of Negro Life at the Texas Centennial Exposition in Dallas. Representative of his strongest work are the four murals at the 135th Street Branch Library—"Jungle Dancers," "Visions of Liberty," "Songs of the Towers," and "Idyl of the Deep South." All are in the ultra-modern temper and in general the painter may be regarded as a pioneer in the so-called African style. The mural at Bennett College shows the Negro facing freedom at the close of the Civil War. Harriet Tubman, representative of strong womanhood, stands on a dismounted cannon breaking the shackles of ignorance, while before her are a worker and a mother leading their children into new paths of culture. In the autumn of 1936 Mr. Douglas gave an exhibition of his work at the University of Nebraska.

Malvin Gray Johnson (1896-1934), originally of North Carolina, went to New York while still a boy and studied at the National Academy of Design. He worked at commercial art for a living, but enjoyed painting the rural South and was an interpreter of the Negro spiritual. His "Swing Low, Sweet Chariot" won the Otto H. Kahn prize at the Harmon exhibit in 1928. "Meditation" shows a woman with rounded shoulders and heavy features but deeply expressive eyes leaning slightly forward with her head resting on her left hand. Some of the very last work that Mr. Johnson did is of remarkable vitality.

William H. Johnson, born in South Carolina in 1902, studied at the National Academy of Design and the Cape Cod School of Art, largely supporting himself meanwhile by work as a stevedore. In 1929 he received the Harmon gold award. His work is also in the ultramodern style, representative pictures being "Landscape," in which the influence of cubism is manifest, "Landscape with Sun Setting," "Sonny," and the striking "Self-Portrait." Within recent years the painter has spent most of his time in France and Denmark.

Two young men, Charles Alston, who was originally of Charleston, South Carolina, and Henry Bannarn, who came from Oklahoma to New York by way of Minneapolis, have co-operated in a Negro school and art center. Mr. Alston received the Master's degree at Columbia. He has completed two murals for the Harlem Hospital, and done illustrations for *Judge, Collier's,* the *American Magazine,* and the *New Yorker,* as well as designed book jackets for various publishers. Withal he has very definite ideas about what he attempts "When you paint Negroes who look like Greek gods," he says, "you're just faking." Mr. Bannarn is sculptor as well as painter. Among his most distinctive productions are some bleak, wind-swept landscapes. One of those taught by these men is Sara Murrell, a capable young woman who has already received a commission for a mural of brightly colored jungle animals for the children's ward of the Cumberland Hospital in New York.

Those who have been mentioned are only representative of scores of young Negro painters now at work. The African note is strong in the wood-cuts of James Lesesne Wells. One of the men who will bear watching is Samuel Albert Countee, who has recently made his way from Texas to study in Boston but who has already taken part in several exhibits. Outstanding among the cartoonists is E. Simms Campbell, who was born in St. Louis in 1906 and studied at the Art Institute of Chicago, where he won many prizes. Mr. Campbell has drawn illustrations for *Esquire, Judge,* and the *New Yorker,* and in 1936 took the Hearst prize of a thousand dollars open to all Americans for a cartoon on the subject of the greedy profiteer.

SCULPTORS: RICHMOND BARTHÉ AND OTHERS

Richmond Barthé, who was born in Mississippi in 1901 of Negro, French, and Indian parentage, studied for four years at the Art Institute of Chicago, and still another year in New York. The interest of a Catholic priest first led him to study painting, but later he turned to sculpture, and now works chiefly on Negro subjects. He sold "Blackberry Woman," "Comedian," and "African Dancer" to the Whitney Museum in New York, "Deviled Crab Man" to the University of Wisconsin, busts of Paul Laurence Dunbar and Booker T. Washington to the Armstrong High School, Richmond, Virginia, and "Toussaint L'Ouverture" and "Henry O. Tanner" to the Lake County Children's Home, Gary, Illinois. Mr. Barthé exhibited at the Century of Progress Exposition in Chicago and the Texas Centennial in Dallas, and otherwise has had wide recognition. Very recently he has been at work on two forty-foot panels for the Federal Government. These are to be in relief, in stone, and are to be used for the retaining walls of an amphitheatre on the Harlem River Housing Project. The subjects were suggested by the scenes of the dance and the Exodus in *The Green Pastures*.

Sargent Johnson, born in Boston in 1888, was early left an orphan. He began to model in clay while living with his grandparents in Virginia, but it was not until after his marriage that he was able to attend the California School of Fine Arts. There he learned to work in several media but proved to be most interested in sculpture. His work now shows unusual technical excellence, is clean and simple, without unnecessary detail, and strong in conception and execution. "Pearl," the statue of a child in blue-green porcelain and bronze, is a good example of his artistry; and of the bust "Chester" there have been several copies, at least one now being in Europe. In 1929 Mr. Johnson won the Harmon bronze award in the Fine Arts, and he has otherwise taken several prizes. In 1934 he was elected to the Council Board of the San Francisco Art Association.

In any consideration of Negro sculptors of to-day one must keep in mind Nancy Elizabeth Prophet and Augusta Savage, who have been mentioned among the teachers now at work. Leslie Garland Bolling, of Richmond, Virginia, who was largely self-taught, gave an exhibit of his wood sculpture at the Richmond Academy of Arts in January, 1935. Among the twenty-five pieces shown were "The Boxer," "The Shot Putter," and portraits of the Reverend Dr. W. T. Johnson and Bishop W. Sampson Brooks; but perhaps most captivating of all were "Aunt Monday" (washing) and "Sister Tuesday" (ironing).

ARCHITECTS

Architecture is still a comparatively new profession for Negroes. The architect differs from the engineer in that his emphasis is upon the æsthetic designing of buildings. He might naturally be expected to be a graduate of a recognized university or school of architecture. It is necessary accordingly to distinguish between those who are loosely termed architects and those who have satisfied the formal requirements for registry in a given district. If such standards are applied, the number of those to be considered will be greatly reduced. Even so, there are at least a few men who have not only approached their work scientifically but who have also had large commissions.

Paul R. Williams, of Los Angeles, after studying at the University of Southern California and the Institute of Design, became a certified architect in 1915. He has drawn plans for several fraternity and sorority houses in Los Angeles, for the residences of Corinne Griffith, Lon Chaney, and a number of other wealthy or well-known people, and competed in open competition with marked distinction. Hilyard R. Robinson (M.S. in Arch., Columbia, 1931), head of the department of Architecture at Howard University, has studied and traveled extensively abroad and been successful in several national and commercial competitions. Recently he has been architect for a Federal housing project to cost over a million dollars. Vertner W. Tandy, of New York City, studied at Tuskegee and Cornell, and has designed, among other things, the house originally built for Madam C. J. Walker on the Hudson River. Albert I. Cassell, of Washington, who studied at Cornell, has had opportunity more than others for the execution of an extensive program of construction using Federal funds. Within recent years he has given himself largely to designs for buildings at Howard University. These are in the Georgian style and include, among other things, three dormitories for women and a large recitation building (Frederick Douglass Memorial Hall), a power plant, a Chemistry building costing $623,000, and finally a Library building to cost $1,106,000.

BIBLIOGRAPHY

THE following bibliography is highly eclectic in method. It endeavors to keep constantly in mind the immediate subject of the present volume. Books that are mainly experimental or commercial, or that belong primarily to the province of history or sociology, are for the most part omitted. Nor does the list include general works of fiction that happen to use the Negro as a theme. There are three parts. The first includes only representative works by Negro authors. The second, somewhat more miscellaneous, gives the titles of books critical, biographical, or interpretative, several of which are not by Negroes. The third lists a number of the more important magazine articles.

I

Representative Works by Negro Authors

Baxter, J. Harvey L.

That Which Concerneth Me: Sonnets and Poems. The Magic City Press, Roanoke, Va., 1934.

Sonnets for the Ethiopians, and Other Poems. The Magic City Press, Roanoke, Va., 1936.

Bontemps, Arna

God Sends Sunday (novel). Harcourt, Brace & Co., New York, 1931.

Black Thunder (novel). The Macmillan Company, New York, 1936.

Braithwaite, William Stanley

Lyrics of Life and Love. H. B. Turner & Co., Boston, 1904.

The House of Falling Leaves (poems). J. W. Luce & Co., Boston, 1908.

Brown, Sterling

Southern Road (poems). Harcourt, Brace & Co., New York, 1932.

Brown, William Wells

Narrative of William W. Brown. Boston, 1847.

Three Years in Europe. London, 1852. Enlarged as *The American Fugitive in Europe: Sketches of Places and People Abroad; with a Memoir by the Author.* Boston and New York, 1855.

Clotel, or The President's Daughter, "a narrative of slave life in the United States." London, 1853.

Clotelle, "a tale of the Southern states," Boston, 1864, 1867.

The Escape, or A Leap for Freedom (drama in five acts). Boston, 1858.

The Rising Son, or The Antecedents and Advancement of the Colored Race. Boston, 1874.

Chesnutt, Charles Waddell

Frederick Douglass: A Biography. Small, Maynard & Co., Boston, 1899.

The Conjure Woman (stories). Houghton Mifflin Co., Boston, 1899; new edition, 1927.

The Wife of his Youth, and Other Stories of the Color-Line. Houghton Mifflin Co., Boston, 1899.

The House Behind the Cedars (novel). Houghton Mifflin Co., Boston, 1901.

The Marrow of Tradition (novel). Houghton Mifflin Co., Boston, 1901.

The Colonel's Dream (novel). Doubleday, Page & Co., New York, 1905.

Corrothers, James D.

The Black Cat Club (humorous sketches). Funk & Wagnalls Co., New York, 1902.

Cotter, Joseph S., Jr.

The Band of Gideon, and Other Lyrics. The Cornhill Co., Boston, 1918.

Cowdery, Mae V.

We Lift our Voices, and Other Poems. Alpress, Philadelphia, 1936.

Crummell, Alexander

The Future of Africa. New York, 1862.

The Greatness of Christ, and Other Sermons. New York, 1882.

Africa and America (addresses). Springfield, Mass., 1891.

Cullen, Countee

Color (poems). Harper & Bros., New York, 1925.

Copper Sun (poems). Harper & Bros., New York, 1927.

The Ballad of the Brown Girl, an old ballad retold, with illustrations and decorations by Charles Cullen. Harper & Bros., New York, 1927.

Caroling Dusk, an Anthology of Verse by Negro Poets (edited), decorations by Aaron Douglas. Harper & Bros., New York, 1927.

The Black Christ, and Other Poems, with decorations by Charles Cullen. Harper & Bros., New York, 1929.

The Medea (of Euripides) *and Some Poems.* Harper & Bros., New York, 1935.

Davis, D. Webster

'Weh Down Souf, and Other Poems. The Helman-Taylor Co., Cleveland, 1897.

Davis, Frank Marshall

Black Man's Verse. The Black Cat Press, Chicago, 1935.

Douglass, Frederick

Narrative of the Life of Frederick Douglass. Boston, 1845.

My Bondage and My Freedom. New York, 1855.

Life and Times of Frederick Douglass. Hartford, 1881.

DuBois, William Edward Burghardt

The Souls of Black Folk: Essays and Sketches. A. C. McClurg & Co., Chicago, 1903.

The Quest of the Silver Fleece (novel). A. C. McClurg & Co., Chicago, 1911.

Darkwater: Voices from Within the Veil. Harcourt, Brace & Co., New York, 1920.

The Gift of Black Folk. The Stratford Co., Boston, 1924.

Dark Princess (novel). Harcourt, Brace & Co., New York, 1928.

Black Reconstruction. Harcourt, Brace & Co., New York, 1935.

Dunbar, Paul Laurence

Oak and Ivy (poems). Dayton, Ohio, 1893.

Majors and Minors (poems). Toledo, Ohio, 1895.

Uncle Eph's Christmas, a one-act musical sketch. Washington, 1900.

Life and Works, edited by Lida Keck Wiggins. J. L. Nichols & Co. Naperville, Ill., 1907.

The following were all issued by Dodd, Mead & Co., New York, the poet's authorized publisher.

Poems:

Lyrics of Lowly Life, 1896.
Lyrics of the Hearthside, 1899.
Lyrics of Love and Laughter, 1903.
Lyrics of Sunshine and Shadow, 1905.
Complete Poems, 1913.

Specially Illustrated Volumes of Poems:

Poems of Cabin and Field, 1899.
Candle-Lightin' Time, 1901.
When Malindy Sings, 1903.
Li'l' Gal, 1904.
Howdy, Honey, Howdy, 1905.
Joggin' Erlong, 1906.
Speakin' o' Christmas, 1914.

Novels:

The Uncalled, 1898.
The Love of Landry, 1900.
The Fanatics, 1901.
The Sport of the Gods, 1902.

Stories and Sketches:

Folks from Dixie, 1898.
The Strength of Gideon, and Other Stories, 1900.
The Old Plantation Days, 1903.
The Heart of Happy Hollow, 1904.

Dunbar, Alice Ruth Moore (Mrs. Nelson)
The Goodness of St. Rocque, and Other Stories. Dodd, Mead & Co. New York, 1899.

Edmonds, Randolph
Shades and Shadows. Meador Publishing Co., Boston, 1930.

Six Plays for a Negro Theatre. Walter H. Baker Co., Boston, 1934.

Fauset, Jessie
There is Confusion (novel). Boni & Liveright, New York, 1924.
Plum Bun (novel). E. Mathews & Marrot, Ltd., London, 1928; Frederick A. Stokes Co., New York, 1929.
The Chinaberry Tree (novel). Frederick A. Stokes Co., New York, 1931.
Comedy: American Style (novel). Frederick A. Stokes Co., New York, 1933.

Fisher, Rudolph
The Walls of Jericho (novel). Alfred A. Knopf, Inc., New York, 1928.
The Conjure-Man Dies: A Mystery Tale of Dark Harlem. Covici, Friede, New York, 1932.

Grimké, Angelina W.
Rachel (a play in three acts). The Cornhill Co., Boston, 1920.

Harper, Frances Ellen Watkins
Poems on Miscellaneous Subjects. Boston, 1854, 1856; also Merrihew & Son, Philadelphia, 1857, 1866 (second series), 1871.
Sketches of Southern Life (mainly poems). Philadelphia, 1896.
Poems. Philadelphia, 1895, 1900.
Idylls of the Bible (chiefly "Moses, a Story of the Nile"). Philadelphia, 1901.
Iola Leroy (novel). Philadelphia, 1892.

Henderson, George Wylie
Ollie Miss (novel). Frederick A. Stokes Co., New York, 1935.

Hill, Leslie Pinckney

The Wings of Oppression (poems). The Stratford Co., Boston, 1921.

Toussaint L'Ouverture (poem). Christopher Publishing House, Boston, 1928.

Horton, George Moses

The Hope of Liberty (poems). Raleigh, N. C., 1929. (Note also *Poems by a Slave*, bound with *Poems of Phillis Wheatley*, Boston, 1838.)

Naked Genius (poems). Raleigh, N. C., 1865.

Hughes, Langston

The Weary Blues (poems). Alfred A. Knopf, Inc., New York, 1926.

Fine Clothes to the Jew (poems). Alfred A. Knopf, Inc., New York, 1927.

Not Without Laughter (novel). Alfred A. Knopf, Inc., New York, 1930.

Dear Lovely Death (poems privately printed at the Troutbeck Press one hundred copies for private distribution only). Amenia, N. Y., 1931.

The Dream Keeper and Other Poems, with illustrations by Helen Sewell. Alfred A. Knopf, Inc., New York, 1932.

Scottsboro Limited (four poems and a play), with illustrations by Prentiss Taylor. The Golden Stair Press, New York, 1932.

The Ways of White Folks (stories). Alfred A. Knopf, Inc., New York, 1934.

Hurston, Zora Neale

Jonah's Gourd Vine (novel). J. B. Lippincott Co., Philadelphia, 1934.

Mules and Men (mainly stories). J. B. Lippincott Co., Philadelphia, 1935.

Johnson, Georgia Douglas

The Heart of a Woman, and Other Poems. The Cornhill Co., Boston, 1917.

Bronze: A Book of Verse. B. J. Brimmer Co., Boston, 1921.

An Autumn Love Cycle. Harold Vinal, Ltd., New York, 1928.

Johnson, Fenton

A Little Dreaming (poems). Peterson Linotyping Co., Chicago, 1913.

Visions of the Dusk (poems). Trachlenburg Co., New York, 1915.

Songs of the Soil. Trachlenburg Co., New York, 1916.

Johnson, James Weldon

Autobiography of an Ex-Colored Man (published anonymously). Sherman, French & Co., Boston, 1912. New edition, with name on title-page and Introduction by Carl Van Vechten, Alfred A. Knopf, Inc., New York, 1927.

Fifty Years, and Other Poems, with Introduction by Brander Matthews. The Cornhill Co., Boston, 1917. New edition, The Viking Press, New York, 1928.

The Book of American Negro Poetry (edited). Harcourt, Brace & Co., New York, 1922; revised edition, 1931.

God's Trombones: Seven Negro Sermons in Verse. The Viking Press, New York, 1927.

The Book of American Negro Spirituals (edited with Introduction). The Viking Press, New York, 1926.

The Second Book of American Negro Spirituals (edited with Introduction). The Viking Press, New York, 1927.

Black Manhattan. Alfred A. Knopf, Inc., New York, 1930.

St. Peter Relates an Incident of the Resurrection Day (poem). The Viking Press, New York, 1930.

Along this Way (autobiography). The Viking Press, New York, 1933.

Larsen, Nella (Mrs. Imes)

Quicksand (novel). Alfred A. Knopf, Inc., New York, 1928.

Passing (novel). Alfred A. Knopf, Inc., New York, 1929.

Lynn, Eve (Evelyn C. Reynolds)

No Alabaster Box (poems). Alpress, Philadelphia, 1936.

McKay, Claude

Harlem Shadows (poems), with an Introduction by Max Eastman. Harcourt, Brace & Co., New York, 1922.

Home to Harlem (novel). Harper & Bros., New York, 1928.

Banjo, "a story without a plot." Harper & Bros., New York, 1929.

Gingertown (stories). Harper & Bros., New York, 1932.

Banana Bottom (novel). Harper & Bros., New York, 1933.

A Long Way from Home (experiences and impressions). Lee Furman, Inc., New York, 1937.

Payne, Daniel Alexander

The Pleasures and Other Miscellaneous Poems. Baltimore, 1850.

Recollections of Seventy Years. Nashville, Tenn., 1888.

Richardson, Willis

Plays and Pageants from the Life of the Negro. The Associated Publishers, Washington, 1930.

(With May Miller) *Negro History in Thirteen Plays.* The Associated Publishers, Washington, 1935.

Stanford, Theodore Anthony

Dark Harvest (poems). Bureau on Negro Affairs, 1519 Lombard St., Philadelphia, 1936.

Walker, David

Walker's Appeal, in Four Articles. Boston, 1829.

Walrond, Eric

Tropic Death (stories and sketches). Boni & Liveright, New York, 1926.

Washington, Booker T.

Up from Slavery: An Autobiography. Doubleday, Page & Co., New York, 1901.

Selected Speeches, edited by E. Davidson Washington. Doubleday, Doran & Co., Inc., Garden City, N. Y., 1932.

Wheatley, Phillis

Poem on the Death of the Reverend George Whitefield. Boston, 1770.

Poems on Various Subjects, Religious and Moral. London, 1773.

Elegy Sacred to the Memory of Dr. Samuel Cooper. Boston, 1784.

Liberty and Peace. Boston, 1784.

Letters, edited by Charles Deane. Boston, 1864.

White, Walter F.

The Fire in the Flint (novel). Alfred A. Knopf, Inc., 1924.

Flight (novel). Alfred A. Knopf, Inc., New York, 1926.

Rope and Faggot. Alfred A. Knopf, Inc., New York, 1929.

Whitfield, James M.

America, and Other Poems, 1853.

Whitman, Albery A.

Not a Man and Yet a Man (poems). Springfield, Ohio, 1877.

Twasinta's Seminoles, or The Rape of Florida (poem). St. Louis, 1884.

Drifted Leaves. St. Louis, 1890. (This condenses and combines two former works, with some additions.)

An Idyl of the South (epic poem in two parts). New York, 1901.

Williams, George W.

History of the Negro Race in America from 1619 to 1880. G. P. Putnam's Sons, New York, 1883.

A History of the Negro Troops in the War of the Rebellion. Harper & Bros., New York, 1888.

II

Other Books (including Collections), Mainly Critical or Biographical, Not Necessarily by Negroes

Brawley, Benjamin

Early Negro American Writers (selections with biographical and critical introductions). The University of North Carolina Press, Chapel Hill, 1935.

Paul Laurence Dunbar, Poet of his People. The University of North Carolina Press, Chapel Hill, 1936.

Cromwell, John W.: *The Negro in American History.* The American Negro Academy, Washington, 1914.

Dett, R. Nathaniel: *Religious Folk-Songs of the Negro.* G. Schirmer, New York, 1925.

Ford, Nick Aaron: *The Contemporary Negro Novel.* Meador Publishing Co., Boston, 1936.

Griffiths, Julia
Autographs for Freedom. Rochester, 1853.
Autographs for Freedom. Rochester, 1854.

Guillaume, Paul, and Munro, Thomas: *Primitive Negro Sculpture.* Barnes Foundation Press, Merion, Penn., 1925.

Hare, Maud Cuney: *Negro Musicians and their Music.* The Associated Publishers, Washington, 1936.

Hatcher, William E.: *John Jasper.* Fleming H. Revell Co., New York, 1908.

Johnson, Charles S. (editor): *Ebony and Topaz: A Collectanea.* National Urban League, New York, 1927.

Kerlin, Robert J.: *Negro Poets and their Poems.* The Associated Publishers, Washington, 1922.

Krehbiel, Henry E.: *Afro-American Folk-Songs.* G. Schirmer, New York, 1914.

Locke, Alain (editor)
Four Negro Poets. Simon and Schuster, New York, 1926.
The New Negro. A. C. Boni, New York, 1925.
(With Montgomery Gregory) *Plays of Negro Life.* Harper & Bros., New York, 1927.
The Negro and His Music and *Negro Art: Past and Present,* in Bronze Booklets. Associates in Negro Folk Education, Washington, 1937.

Loggins, Vernon: *The Negro Author: His Development in*

America. Columbia University Press, New York, 1931.

Odum, Howard W., and Johnson, Guy B. (editors)
The Negro and his Songs. The University of North Carolina Press, Chapel Hill, 1925.
Negro Workaday Songs. The University of North Carolina Press, Chapel Hill, 1926.

Ovington, Mary White: *Portraits in Color.* The Viking Press, New York, 1927.

Pike, G. D.: *The Jubilee Singers.* Lee & Shepard, Boston, 1873.

Sayers, W. C. Berwick: *Samuel Coleridge-Taylor, Musician: His Life and Letters.* Cassell & Co., London and New York, 1915.

Scarborough, Dorothy: *On the Trail of Negro Folk Songs.* Harvard University Press, Cambridge, 1925.

Schomburg, Arthur A.: *A Bibliographical Checklist of American Negro Poetry.* New York, 1916.

Talley, Thomas W.: *Negro Folk Rhymes.* The Macmillan Company. New York, 1922.

White, Newman Ivey, and Jackson, Walter Clinton (editors): *An Anthology of Verse by American Negroes.* Duke University Press, Durham, N. C.

III

Select List of Magazine Articles

(The arrangement is chronological, and articles of unusual scholarship or interest are marked *.)

* *Negro Spirituals,* by Thomas Wentworth Higginson. *Atlantic,* Vol. 19, p. 685 (June, 1867).

* *The Negro on the Stage,* by Laurence Hutton. *Harper's,* Vol. 79, p. 131 (June, 1889).

Mr. Charles W. Chesnutt's Stories, by W. D. Howells. *Atlantic,* Vol. 85, p. 70 (May, 1900).

Paul Laurence Dunbar, by Mary Church Terrell. *Voice of the Negro,* April, 1906.

Meta Warrick, Sculptor of Horrors, by William Francis O'Donnell. *World To-day,* Vol. 13, p. 1139 (November, 1907). See also *Current Literature,* Vol. 44, p. 55 (January, 1908).

* *The Story of an Artist's Life,* by Henry O. Tanner. *World's Work,* Vol. 18, pp. 11661, 11769 (June and July, 1909).

Indian and Negro in Music. Literary Digest, Vol. 44, p. 1346 (June 29, 1912).

* *The Negro's Contribution to the Music of America,* by Natalie Curtis. *Craftsman,* Vol. 23, p. 660 (March, 1913).

The Soul of the Black (on Herbert Ward's bronzes). *Independent,* Vol. 74, p. 994 (May 1, 1913).

A Poet Painter of Palestine (H. O. Tanner), by Clara T. MacChesney. *International Studio,* July, 1913.

Beginnings of a Negro Drama. Literary Digest, Vol. 48, p. 1114 (May 9, 1914).

George Moses Horton: Slave Poet, by Stephen B. Weeks. *Southern Workman,* Vol. 43, p. 571 (October, 1914).

The Negro in the Southern Short Story, by H. E. Rollins. *Sewanee Review,* Vol. 24, p. 42 (January, 1916).

* *H. T. Burleigh: Composer by Divine Right. Musical America,* Vol. 23, No. 26 (April 29, 1916).

The Emancipation of Negro Music, by R. Nathaniel Dett. *Southern Workman*, Vol. 47, p. 172 (April, 1918).

Some Contemporary Poets of the Negro Race, by William Stanley Braithwaite. *Crisis*, Vol. 17, p. 275 (April, 1919).

Racial Traits in the Negro Song, by N. I. White. *Sewanee Review*, July, 1920.

Our Debt to Negro Sculpture. *Literary Digest*, July 17, 1920.

Negro Sculpture, by C. Bell. *Living Age*, September 25, 1920.

* *Hindu Stories in American Negro Folk-lore*, by W. Norman Brown. *Asia*, Vol. 21, p. 703 (August, 1921).

* *Some Notes on Coleridge-Taylor*, by Herbert Antcliffe. *Musical Quarterly*, Vol. 8, p. 180 (April, 1922).

The Negro in Drama, by Rollin Lynde Harte. *Crisis*, June, 1922.

The Negro in American Literature, by Benjamin Brawley. *Bookman*, October, 1922.

Negroes as Actors in Serious Plays, by Esther Fulks Scott. *Opportunity*, April, 1923.

A Group of Negro Artists, by Francis C. Holbrook. *Opportunity*, July, 1923.

William Edouard Scott, Painter, by Francis C. Holbrook. *Southern Workman*, February, 1924.

* *Arts and Crafts of the Negro*. *International Studio*, March, 1924.

Stories in Sculpture, by Madeline G. Allison. *Opportunity*, March, 1924.

A Note on African Art, by Alain Locke. *Opportunity*, May, 1924.

* *The Musical Genius of the American Negro,* by Clarence Cameron White. *Étude,* May, 1924.

Allan Randall Freelan, Artist-Teacher, by Francis C. Holbrook. *Southern Workman,* May, 1924.

The Negro in Literature, by William Stanley Braithwaite. *Crisis,* September, 1924.

Who Invented Jazz? by Robert Haven Schauffler. *Collier's Weekly,* January 3, 1925.

Biographical Sketch of Archibald H. Grimké, by Angelina Grimké. *Opportunity,* February, 1925.

Ira Aldridge, by Charles S. Johnson. *Opportunity,* March, 1925.

William M. Farrow: Artist and Craftsman, by Francis C. *Holbrook. Southern Workman,* March, 1925.

Negro Art and America, by Albert C. Barnes. *Survey,* March 1, 1925. Reprinted in Locke's *The New Negro.*

Art of the Ancestors, by Alain Locke. *Survey,* March 1, 1925.

To Certain of Our Philistines, by Alain Locke. *Opportunity,* May, 1925.

A World-Famous Singer whose Parents were Slaves (on Roland Hayes), by Mary B. Mullett. *American Magazine,* June, 1925.

Roland Hayes, by Sterling Brown. *Opportunity,* June, 1925.

Opportunity, November, 1925. The whole number is devoted to an important series of articles and reviews based on works in the field of music.

More of the Negro in Art (well illustrated), by Alain Locke. *Opportunty,* December, 1925.

Where Jazz Comes From, by Earl Chapin May. *Popular Mechanics*, Vol. 45, p. 97 (January, 1926).

The Triumph of Ancient Negro Art, by Paul Guillaume; *Negro Art, Past and Present*, by Albert C. Barnes; *Primitive Negro Sculpture*, by Thomas Munro, and *The Negro Spirituals and American Art*, by Lawrence Buermeyer—all in *Opportunity*, May, 1926.

The Significance of "Lulu Belle," by Hubert H. Harrison. *Opportunity*, July, 1926.

Negro-Art Hokum, by George S. Schuyler. *Nation*, Vol. 122, p. 662 (June 16, 1926).

The Negro Artist and the Racial Mountain, by Langston Hughes. *Nation*, Vol. 122, p. 692 (June 23, 1926).

The Drama of Negro Life, by Alain Locke. *Theatre Arts Monthly*, October, 1926.

Primitive Negro Sculpture (on Blondiau African Collection), by Stark Young. *New Republic*, Vol. 50, p. 17 (February 23, 1927).

Art Lessons from the Congo (on Blondiau Collection), by Alain Locke. *Survey*, Vol. 57, p. 587 (February 1, 1927).

Good and Bad Negro Art (on Blondiau Collection), by Thomas Munro. *Nation*, Vol. 124, p. 242 (March 2, 1927).

The New Negro as Revealed in his Poetry, by Charlotte E. Taussig. *Opportunity*, April, 1927.

The Negro Literary Renaissance, by Benjamin Brawley. *Southern Workman*, April, 1927.

African Plastic in Contemporary Art, by Harry Alan Potamkin. *Opportunity*, May, 1927.

The Vogue of the Negro Spiritual, by A. M. Chirgwin. *Edinburgh Review,* Vol. 247, p. 57 (January, 1928).

Archibald J. Motley, Jr. Opportunity, April, 1928.

Beauty Instead of Ashes, by Alain Locke. *Nation,* Vol. 126, p. 432 (April 18, 1928).

Primitive Negro Sculpture and its Influence on Modern Civilization, by Albert C. Barnes. *Opportunity,* May, 1928.

Negro Poets and their Poetry, by Wallace Thurman. *Bookman,* Vol. 67, p. 555 (July, 1928).

The Negro's Contribution to American Art and Literature, by Alain Locke. *Annals of American Academy of Political Science,* Vol. 140, p. 234 (November, 1928).

Richmond Barthé: Sculptor, by William H. A. Moore. *Opportunity,* 1928.

The Dilemma of the Negro Author, by James Weldon Johnson. *American Mercury,* Vol. 15, p. 477 (December, 1928).

1928: A Retrospective Review, by Alain Locke. *Opportunity,* January, 1929.

Negro Authors Must Eat, by George W. Jacobs. *Nation,* Vol. 128, p. 710 (June 12, 1929).

The Negro as Writer, by John Chamberlain. *Bookman,* Vol. 70, p. 603 (February, 1930).

A Decade of Negro Literature, by Robert T. Kerlin. *Southern Workman,* May, 1930.

Elizabeth Prophet: Sculptress, by Countee Cullen. *Opportunity,* 1930.

Some Reflections on the Negro in American Drama, by Randolph Edmonds. *Opportunity,* October, 1930.

This Year of Grace (on outstanding books of the year in

Negro literature), by Alain Locke. *Opportunity*, February, 1931.

Black Truth and Black Beauty (a retrospective review of the literarture of the Negro for 1932), by Alain Locke. *Opportunity*, January, 1933.

The First Negro Symphony. Literary Digest, March 4, 1933 (helpful, though the symphony discussed was not strictly the first).

Negro Character as Seen by White Authors, by Sterling Brown. *Journal of Negro Education*, April, 1933.

The Promise of Negro Literature, by Benjamin Brawley. *Journal of Negro History*, January, 1934.

Negro Art on Review at the National Museum, Washington, by James A. Porter. *American Magazine of Art*, Vol. 27, p. 33 (January, 1934).

From Bell Stand to Throne Room (autobiography), by R. Nathaniel Dett. *Étude*, February, 1934.

Toward a Critique of Negro Music, by Alain Locke. *Opportunity*, November and December, 1934.

The Eleventh Hour of Nordicism (retrospective review of the literature of the Negro for 1934), by Alain Locke. *Opportunity*, January, 1935.

* *Jes Like a Natchel Man* (on Richard B. Harrison). *Christian Herald*, March, 1935. (In spite of the title, this is a detailed and carefully written account of the career of the actor.)

The Magic of African Negro Art (on exhibition at Museum of Modern Art in New York). *Literary Digest*, March 30, 1935.

African Negro Art Exhibition at the Museum of Modern Art. Theatre Arts Monthly, Vol. 19, p. 305 (April, 1935).

African Art: Classic Style (on same subject as last two articles), by Alain Locke. *American Magazine of Art,* Vol. 28, p. 270 (May, 1935).

Ira Aldridge, by Cyril Bruyn Andrews. *Crisis,* October, 1935.

Hollywood Presents Us, by Cecil D. Halliburton. *Opportunity,* October, 1935.

Deep River: Deeper Sea (review of the literature of the Negro for 1935), by Alain Locke. *Opportunity,* January and February, 1936.

**Versatile Interests of the Early Negro Artist: A Neglected Chaper of American Art History,* by James A. Porter. *Art in America,* Vol. 24, No. 1, p. 16 (January, 1936).

The Negro in American Culture, by Aaron Douglas, in *First American Artists Congress, 1936,* New York City, 1936.

Creative Negroes. Literary Digest, August 1, 1936.

Spirituals to Symphonies, by Shirley Graham. *Étude,* November, 1936.

Anyone interested in Negro painters and sculptors of recent years will want to be sure to consult the catalogues and other pamphlets of the Harmon Foundation, 140 Nassau St., New York City, among which are the following:

Negro Artists: An Illustrated Review of Their Achievements.

Exhibition of the Work of Negro Artists, 1931.

Exhibition of Productions by Negro Artists, 1933.

INDEX